JEFFERSON'S CHILDREN

EDUCATION AND THE PROMISE OF AMERICAN CULTURE

LEON BOTSTEIN

DOUBLEDAY
NEW YORK LONDON TORONTO SYDNEY AUCKLAND

PUBLISHED BY DOUBLEDAY
a division of Bantam Doubleday Dell Publishing Group, Inc.
1540 Broadway, New York, New York 10036

DOUBLEDAY and the portrayal of an anchor with a dolphin
are trademarks of Doubleday, a division of
Bantam Doubleday Dell Publishing Group, Inc.

Book design by Fearn Cutler

Library of Congress Cataloging-in-Publication Data

Botstein, Leon.
Jefferson's children: education and the promise of American
culture / Leon Botstein. — 1st ed.
p.   cm.
1. Education—Aims and objectives—United States.
2. Educational anthropology—United States.   3. Educational
sociology—United States.   4. Politics and education—United
States.   5. High schools—United States.   6. Education,
Higher—Aims and objectives—United States.   I. Title.
LA210.B65   1997
370'.0973—dc21   97-3839
CIP

ISBN 0-385-47568-3
Copyright © 1997 by Leon Botstein
All Rights Reserved
Printed in the United States of America
October 1997
First Edition
1   3   5   7   9   10   8   6   4   2

CONTENTS

ACKNOWLEDGMENTS

The views put forward here are my own. However, for better or for worse, what is redeeming in them comes from the work of others.

The first debt (and perhaps apology) I owe is to my teachers. I grew up in a home in which the teachers of my parents were nearly mythic figures. Like my parents, I have been the beneficiary of the confidence of distinguished and eminent elders. I wish to remember Christian W. Mackauer and Gerhard Meyer of the University of Chicago as exemplars of great teaching, and Hannah Arendt, Judith Shklar, David Landes, Roman Totenberg, and Harold Farberman as individuals of ambition, eminence, and distinction who took the time and care so that I could learn from them.

I wish to thank my colleagues, particularly Dimitri Papadimitriou, Stuart Levine, Mark Loftin, and Susan Gillespie, and my students at Bard College. I could never repay the debt of gratitude I owe Bard and its community, past and present, where I have lived and worked for over twenty-two years, including those friends at Simon's Rock in Great Barrington, especially Elizabeth Blodgett Hall, U Ba Win, Bernard Rodgers, Robert Strassler, Emily Fisher, and Murray Liebowitz.

Several individuals deserve credit, including Bill Thomas, my editor, who managed to overcome my reluctance to write this book; Ben

Martin, who worked for a summer as a research assistant and vindicated my faith in the quality of the undergraduate education at the University of Chicago today; Barbara Haskell, who read the entire text and made crucial suggestions; Peter Aldrich, Mary Backlund, David Botstein, Paul Connolly, Richard Fisher, Jack Honey, Leon Levy, Martin Peretz, George Soros, Susan Weber Soros, Charles P. Stevenson Jr., Karen Wilcox, Richard Wilson, and Irene Zedlacher, with whom over many years many ideas were debated; Dorothy Miller and Amie McEvoy, my long-suffering colleagues in my office, who helped produce the manuscript; and Lynne Meloccaro, who made excellent editorial suggestions throughout the entire manuscript. All of these individuals helped indirectly and directly with the development of the ideas and the text. Last but not least, I wish to thank my friend David E. Schwab II, the Chairman of the Board of Bard College, who has heard everything in this book more than once, has stood by me unreservedly, and has explored tirelessly with me the issues of education.

This book (and most everything else I do) bears the hallmarks of the family in which I grew up, in which I was the youngest. The engagement my grandparents, my father, my mother, and my siblings all had with ideas, with service to others, and with work has left its imprint. My parents and grandparents taught me what it means to survive all manner of loss, pain, distress, and anguish with as little despair, rancor, or bitterness as possible. This gratitude for being in the world, despite all difficulties, has stayed with me. It has made it possible for me to pass on a tradition of the love of learning and work to Sarah, Abigail, Clara, and Max.

L.B.

INTRODUCTION

This is a book of opinion. It seeks to take its place in the tradition of reasoned polemics. It was not written in anticipation of agreement. Rather, it seeks to forge some connection between the daily lives of the reader and the matter of education. In this way perhaps the book can contribute to what so far has been a pedestrian, if not moribund, public debate about education and culture. Therefore, this book was not written exclusively for educators and other specialists but for a wide range of readers. It is my view that at this time a book directed at the general reader regarding culture and education would be more beneficial than one directed at the professional community, which in recent years has been inundated by reports, scholarly tracts, and unnecessarily hostile exchanges.

Many of the issues raised routinely among educators are presented in this volume, but with the intent of bringing the public into the debate rather than leaving the questions to be addressed exclusively by experts. Frequently, books are written primarily for the satisfaction of a targeted audience, those whom the author knows ahead of time only want their beliefs confirmed. I hope this small volume will cause readers of all persuasions to think about issues of learning, education, and culture in helpful ways. Above all, the reader should note that this is not another report on the state of education. It is not an exposé based on extensive empirical research. The public-policy recommendations do not seek to benefit from a daunting external display of science and scholarship. There are no footnotes.

The ideas in this volume are the result of three decades of engagement with learning, teaching, and the arts in America. Each of these decades has held its unique surprises. From the vantage point of the late 1960s and early 1970s, five quite remarkable aspects characteristic of the late 1990s provide the context for the consideration of the relationship between education and society, which is the subject of these pages:

1. The striking revival of religion in American life, particularly among young people, professionals and intellectuals far from the heartland of evangelical Protestantism, is startling even though it might have been foreseen. After all, many young political radicals of the late 1960s turned in the early 1970s to gurus and alternatives to Western spirituality. But that fact does not explain the renewed vitality in Christianity, Judaism, and Islam throughout the population, even among today's university faculty and students, many of whom are children of the student generation of the 1960s. One ought to hesitate comparing the 1960s in America to the 1790s in Europe, but in both contexts, after the collapse of facile expectations about the prospects for utopian change as a consequence of radical political action, revived spirituality and religious fervor eventually came into the forefront.

2. The demise of rationalist and secular attitudes in public life and the resurgence of religion may strike us as unexpected, but one could hardly have anticipated the collapse of communism and the phoenix-like revival of simplistic notions of free competition and the beneficial consequences of less government and unregulated reliance on the marketplace. An unvarnished laissez-faire attitude has once again permeated the way we think about society and culture. Any confidence in the ability of government to intervene constructively, even in education and culture (consider, for example, the demise of public support for those art forms that are not commercially viable by the standards of

large Hollywood enterprises in film, television, and music), has disappeared.

It is as if we believe that all social and cultural needs can now be met by private initiatives. Indeed, the accumulation of wealth in America by individuals since 1970 has been staggering. But equally extreme has been the growth of inequality—the distance between rich and poor. However, there has not been a concomitant growth in philanthropy, except in that increasingly powerful element of America's life, organized religion. And even if more of the very rich should begin to give, the patterns, habits, and rituals of private philanthropy do not inspire confidence in terms of the capacity of the private sector to take care of what needs taking care of on behalf of the public good.

3. Faith in private enterprise and the free market has traditionally been associated with the cult of the individual. One might expect, therefore, that we are living in an age of renewed individualism. But the opposite is the case. No doubt our culture seems fixated on star personalities, even in business. However, our obsession with individualism is restricted to a narrow category of fame and wealth. By comparison with thirty years ago, we all are somewhat more inclined to answer the question "Who am I?" with statements that identify ourselves as part of a subgroup, most often an ethnic group. Willingly, we embrace standardized group labels once considered a burden or an embarrassment.

Ironically, much of today's highly prized ethnicity has little historical authenticity. Ethnicity as it is now defined does not mirror the degree of historical continuity that it implies. The actual linkages and commonalities between American Jews today and European Jews a century ago (not to speak of Jews further back in time) are more highly attenuated than the various contemporary rhetorics of Jewish identity suggest. The same could be argued with respect to the connections between African Americans today and the slave population of a century and a half ago. Lateral influences in time and arranged along generational lines, between and among groups, may be more powerful than any tradition handed down from one generation to the next. In other words, there are fewer differences between concurrent subgroups than there are between descendants and ancestors in the same subgroup. Nevertheless, pseudo-historical constructions help to sustain the plausibility and popularity of each person's effort to define him- or herself in the world as part of some group. This is because much of the revival of ethnicity is the result of one of the main themes of this book: the prestige of nostalgia and a pervasive pessimism in our culture with respect to the present and the future.

Since the late 1960s, issues of identity have risen to the center of the educational debate in America. It is curious that we assume that issues of identity are initially fixed at birth but that nevertheless young people have to be guided to develop allegiances. The myth of individuality, defined as freedom from a group stereotype, has been either discredited or abandoned. A person's singularity and what he or she makes of life have encountered difficulty in remaining immune from a variety of rigid categorizations. Furthermore, we seem uncomfortable with the notion that people possess varied and overlapping identities. Identity may be fluid and not consistent. The image of what it means to be Black, Jewish, Italian, or Catholic is far too static to be helpful. Yet we use such simplified labels in order to understand the person next to us.

Hannah Arendt in *The Human Condition* identified natality as a concept intimately connected to action and particularly to one's political engagement in the world. What natality meant was coming to terms with the facts of one's birth, particularly place and parentage. But that insight regarding our need to address the immutable facts of our coming into the world did not imply that there was some uniform outcome for each individual. Being an American, a woman, a homosexual, having parents of a certain faith, or being a citizen of a region or neighborhood does not translate into certain fixed commonalities.

Ideally, education provides the individual with help in constructing meaning in life. That process ought not be reduced to choosing labels off a metaphorical shelf. Rather, it should invite the act of creating oneself out of the myriad possibilities and experiences of life. Identity as we now define it is a fiction of a kind, which then becomes a barrier to recognizing differences among and between peoples, even when they are considered to be in the same group. We also fail to account for instability and change in the various partial identities we have, particularly when we consider ourselves in terms of the work we do in the world.

This brings us to the question of prejudice and the difficulties we encounter in confronting individuals we consider basically different from ourselves. One of the dangers of an otherwise noble and sensible liberal piety is that prejudice by definition is bad. Prejudice, which is tantamount to espousing a view for which there is no demonstrable evidence and which may be in contrast to an objective fact, can be relatively harmless. One may have a view of something one doesn't know anything about. However, one needs to be prepared to abandon that view in the face of knowledge and experience. The possession of prejudices is not nearly as dangerous as the inability to abandon them.

In fact, having prejudices, which can be considered hypothetical but categorical judgments, is not only inevitable but may even be desirable if acknowledged. First we must redefine what we mean by prejudice. Prejudice is part of a necessary habit of making judgments and discriminating between and among things in the world. Prejudice can be, after all, just a form of the expression of taste. Much of what we regard to be an individual's personality is often little more than the unique amalgamation of prejudices about value and meaning in ordinary life. We are led to believe in a quite moralistic way that all prejudices lead directly to hatred. This is too reductive. For example, the anti-Semite who relishes membership in a truly private club that does not admit Jews is, we are told, on a continuum that leads to genocide. This, indeed, may not be true. The crucial distinction is between private prejudice, to which we all are subject and where expression is protected by freedom, and the misappropriation of such private views as the basis for public action and policy. It may be possible for an individual who doesn't want to associate with Jews, doesn't want members of the family to marry Jews, and feels uncomfortable with Jews to be committed to an overarching concept of politics and citizenship, which protects all people no matter how different they may appear: to the guarantee of civil rights and freedoms for all. Individuals may be prejudiced in the sense that they do not want to be around people whom they consider undesirable, even though such dislikes may be based on falsehoods. Those same individuals can and should insist that human rights are a central set of guiding principles that ensures for all people equal protections, opportunities, benefits, and freedoms, including the right to hold and express personal prejudices. It may be reasonable to assume that among the "righteous Gentiles" honored for saving Jews during the Holocaust, there were some who were anti-Semitic, privately speaking, but who were politically opposed to all forms of oppression and political discrimination. Therefore, they were willing to risk their lives, not because they were philo-Semitic, held some version of vague humanism, or were neutral in their attitudes. This circumstance should only deepen our admiration for their courage and idealism. Perhaps if we allow people to express their prejudices in benign ways that do not intrude on public policy, we might reduce the likelihood of a connection between personal prejudice and political hatred that results in violence and destruction. A healthy tolerance of private prejudices may be the necessary safety valve of a free and diverse society. Facing prejudice and controlling it, as opposed to repressing it or denying it, may be the essential precondition for genuine acceptance, openness, tolerance, and cooperation in the political arena.

The point of education is therefore to encourage young people to distinguish between personal prejudice and political obligations. Personal prejudice cannot be the basis for laws or procedures in society. One of the reasons that we teach civilizations and cultures other than our own and insist that young people read fiction and nonfiction that comes out of a global context is that we want to teach our children to be able to imagine the strange and the unfamiliar and the different with empathy. Empathy can help us to realize that all prejudice, if it extends beyond reasonable limits, visibly contradicts hard facts. It is amazing that a racist has no difficulty accepting a blood transfusion or an organ transplant donated from the group that he or she vilifies. The moment all racists and haters of others enter a hospital, they place the pseudointellectual foundations of racism, whatever they may be, at the door and submit to the human universality of applied science.

Fanatics who are paranoid or believe in a conspiracy theory, as well as the devoutly religious who believe in a metaphysical realm, God, or a future cosmic event, have the advantage of holding beliefs based on fundamental unverifiability. Evidence against a conspiracy can be construed, for example, as a further sign of the conspiracy. The Second Coming of Christ cannot be denied as "wrong." But claims about so-called racial difference such as the role of skin color, particularly when they are alleged to override commonality, are all assertions that are undone not only by complex facts and information—for example, biology—but by everyday experience. Education can be a bulwark against hatred if it allows the individual to recognize and value the sameness in humanity over surface difference.

Education must provide the younger generation with the tools to be self-critical about what is knowable and what is not knowable and the basic distinctions between truth and fiction. Education also helps the individual reconfigure experience in ways that lead to changed conclusions. One of the first steps of education should be the disassembling of today's popular and lazy language of identity politics, which grotesquely simplifies daily life and distorts the attempt to understand historical change. That simplification obscures what needs to be done, particularly in eliminating the economic and social barriers faced by those segments of society against whom the political abuse of the privilege of personal prejudice has been most egregious. Above all, in education the open expression of ignorance in the form of prejudice in the classroom must be encouraged as a first step in undermining false-hoods.

This is imperative because far too often we rely on negative contrasts (consider, for example, what it means to be "white") in order to establish group solidarity (the "I'm not like them" syndrome). As a consequence, all group characteristics, both negative and positive, do not seem transferable between groups, leading to a totally false picture of the way inheritance and genetics work. It is as if being born into an ethnic group and being part of one are dominant determining factors in who one is and what one thinks, overriding everything else.

This tendency is most destructive in the way we use the nefarious concept "race" (a pseudo-scientific category that ought to be discarded) and the way we consider gender. White America trivializes those who are not white by making each minority individual stand as some sort of representative of color. How often do we hear claims by individuals who invoke "the woman's perspective" as if gender were a constant variable whose character and influence are uniform? In the end, science may be our only hope in that it will further illuminate the nature of difference. The DNA analysis of the remains of Philistines, Israelites, and Canaanites uncovered through archaeology may turn out to show that one group is indistinguishable genetically from the next. Yet owing to cultural distinctions, they were segregated in history, myth, and burial.

Despite our romance with ethnicity, as Americans we are not less united or more "fragmented" (that favorite phrase of doomsayers) than at previous moments in our past. Rather, what has vanished with the demise of the popularity of the melting-pot metaphor for the nation is the confidence that we might be able to construct positive models of citizenship in a democracy that stress what we hold in common and the possibilities that remain for being considered just an individual with multiple, shifting, and overlapping connections with others.

4. The lure of subgroup identities in terms of religion and ethnicity has run parallel to the domination by negative issues in local and national politics. The issue of crime—too frequently a thin camouflage for tensions about race and poverty—was already central to the politics of the 1970s. But since that time we have added a war on drugs, a dangerous fear of immigration, and a staggering enthusiasm for building prisons and incarcerating people.

Even the most attractive and nearly nonpartisan political issue of our time, concern for the environment, is cast negatively. We do not talk about innovative ways to improve the environment but instead have assumed that human ingenuity and progress threaten an inheritance in nature that we must protect. We want to prevent industry from doing harm, and we wish to clean up the disasters of the past. Noble as these sentiments are, they remain deeply skeptical at heart about science and technology. We have given up on our cities as places of beauty. We rarely talk about the city as a human achievement and as a constructive modern environmental creation. We glorify the wilderness and celebrate a concept of nature that excludes or delimits the activity of human beings. Our sense of unspoiled nature is dependent, after all, on the fact that most of us live in cities or in suburbs. This, too, reflects a profound and disturbing ambivalence in the nation about society and progress.

Insofar as most of our political concerns are framed in terms of protecting ourselves against evils, we have lost any creditable way of talking about positive initiatives that might be taken on behalf of ourselves. It is no accident that the expenditures on prisons accelerate in California at the rate investment in education declines. American citizens, despite their cynicism about government, are willing to invest in using force to lock up criminals and to seal the border, even though these efforts are staggeringly expensive and far less effective than advertised. We seem to show little reluctance to spend $25,000 a year on each prisoner. Yet we resist spending $5,000 a year on a pupil in school. We are even willing to contemplate censorship by government (for example, pornography) and the restriction of freedoms and rights, particularly with respect to sex and birth (for example, abortion), and illness and death (for example, assisted suicide). Despite our mistrust of government and our embrace of the free market, we are enthusiastic about using the power of law and the state to use force to insulate and protect us, often from ourselves, by limiting freedom of action.

There is little constructive discussion on anything that might shift the focus from control to prevention. We do not discuss how to manage and encourage immigration—an inevitable fact of life and a continuing key to America's greatness. There is no serious and open discussion concerning some other means than unenforceable prohibition to control drugs. And where is the public will to try to prevent crime as opposed to punishing criminals? All we can imagine is the reinstitution of the death penalty. Americans seem to have lost all capacity to think positively and creatively about improving the world in which we live. When it comes to education, all we can muster is lip service and rhetoric. Given the emphasis on things we do not like—crime, aliens, and drugs—any effort to seriously consider learning, the arts, and culture as important parts of our public and civic life seems doomed.

Americans seem fascinated by murder, violence, and abuse, all deviant and destructive aspects of life. We put no stock in trying to generate the will among our citizens to use their imaginations and human skills in ways that might improve the quality of a normal life. We seem unable to counterbalance the overwhelming sense of rage, hate, envy, and fear that prevails in our public life. Since most elections and political careers are determined by manipulating the short-term reactions of the public, little long-range thinking or courageous articulation of alternatives is heard, except for the simple, radical, and alluring claims that by dismantling government (with the sole exception of the government's police role), everything will improve spontaneously. But it has not and will not.

5. This brings us to the last surprising circumstance of the 1990s, which concerns the place the American university holds in the public arena. There are more students in universities and colleges than there were three decades ago. There is a greater link between university science and social science and government and industry. But at the same time, most of what is taught and learned, particularly in the humanities, despite the publicity it may receive, seems to make little real difference in the way we act. No doubt many university professionals are influential in the formation of taste and fads, even in the way the television and print media talk about culture, values, and politics. That

is precisely the problem. The role of the university as an influential place of critique, of new ideas, and of constructive challenge quite autonomous of everything around it is not as strong as one might have expected. The vacuum, in terms of the discussion of what we might do together as a nation on behalf of present and future citizens, has been tacitly and explicitly sustained by the university.

The university properly needs to be an affirmative component of the way things are. But it could be more challenging of the status quo. The one arena in which it functions somewhat in this way is in science, where novelty and discrediting or outdistancing the past are highly prized. But the university ought to be more courageous and independent. This is a matter of concern, since the community of thoughtful and active citizens with myriad interests who are not officially connected to a university but yet products of its schooling—the independent, nonexpert, well-educated public—is an endangered one. Therefore, in public policy we are more dependent on (and defer to) certified university-based expertise. As citizens we are less likely to dissent, even when fundamental values, not expertise, are at issue. Uncritical deference to expertise has helped to stifle dissent and debate even within the university.

The power of credentialed expertise, particularly in education, is considerable. It is invoked as a crucial defense against being held liable in the courts by individuals or pilloried by a legislature or the press. The most extreme case of this was the contretemps about the official accusation of sexual harassment of a seven-year-old in a public school in New York State, which led to his being sent home. Here was a case in which common sense was lost amidst a sea of official bureaucratic rhetoric and sophisticated, jargon-laden claims about pedagogy and psychology.

It is for this reason that this book, if only to strike a contrast, seeks to be direct. It does not ask the reader to defer to the authority of the writer, but it does ask the reader to question not only the writer but the arguments and issues at hand. The passivity of many able and decent citizens in thinking and acting when faced with the possibilities offered by a democracy cannot be a good sign. This book seeks to jolt some of those individuals into action. As electoral politics become ever more a function of money and more distant from the everyday lives of citizens, new ways must be found to reinvent democratic debate and participation.

CHAPTER I

THE PARADOXICAL POLITICS OF NOSTALGIA

I. NOSTALGIA AND HISTORY

"My first observation . . . is that it is impossible for the arts and sciences to arise, at first, among any people unless that people enjoy the blessing of a free government." This statement, from the *Essays* of the Scottish philosopher David Hume, makes what today seems like an obvious point. When he wrote it in the eighteenth century, political freedom was still an aspiration, not a reality. Rhetorical and philosophical advocacy on behalf of freedom sought to highlight the benefits freedom would bring. Foremost among those benefits was progress in science, culture, and education.

Since the ideal of scholarly truth, the experimental method of science, and uncensored expression in the arts are intimately bound up with freedom of thought and freedom of movement, a democracy seems an indispensable and logical precondition for the development of a culture of quality. A great civilization—one in which the arts and sciences flourish and are widely shared and supported—should emerge as a central achievement of political freedom.

When reading Hume today, we might feel some sense of wonder at his having to express his conviction so deliberately. Perhaps that wonder derives precisely from the fact that the freedom he had in mind is now considered so integral a component of modern American society.

At the end of this century, a greater number of us, in terms of race, gender, and social class, experience more political freedom (in the sense of having a voice in our government through the right to vote) than we did fifty or a hundred years ago.

The paradox we face today is that we have become so accustomed to the privileges of freedom and have taken them so for granted that we now use freedom against itself. Instead of taking seriously Hume's quite characteristic eighteenth-century view of the consequences of freedom, we have abandoned the obligation to use our freedom to nurture education and culture. Even worse, we have fallen into the trap of turning Hume's observation upside down; we hold the achievement of "the blessing of a free government"—modern democracy—responsible for our own failure to deliver to ourselves and our children a culture of quality and high standards.

Therefore, what was obvious to Hume's generation two centuries ago seems both naive and implausible as we conveniently wallow in an apparently analytically rigorous cultural pessimism. We have exchanged the eighteenth-century optimism we associated with the founding fathers regarding the promises held by freedom for an antidemocratic posture that became popular at the turn of the nineteenth century. We often lazily associate this posture with a distorted and selective enthusiasm for the writings of Friedrich Nietzsche. In this view, freedom in modern democracy has led to a deleterious emphasis on egalitarianism. Equality in turn has become construed as the enemy of excellence and therefore of exactingly high standards in education and culture.

However, there is no evidence that excellence and equality are incompatible, particularly in a democracy. In the first place, the condition of culture and education today is not nearly as debased as has been so commonly and conveniently asserted. Furthermore, we as a society have chosen not to test Hume's proposition seriously. We have not shown the will to realize the opportunities and benefits for the "arts and sciences" inherent in contemporary democracy.

It is only in the second half of the twentieth century that "the blessing of a free government" has been widely shared. Freedom on a

large scale—and consequently a greater degree of political equality—
are novelties, historically speaking, even in America. And yet we remain content not to encourage and develop a culture worthy of the
freedoms most of us now enjoy. Those segments of society that have
reaped the fruits of freedom for more than one generation are reluctant
to do what is really required to extend the benefits of education effectively to others. Those who only recently have become enfranchised
remain suspicious of the standards of excellence and ideals of culture
inherited from a past from which they considered themselves excluded.
They level the charge of elitism and are wary that a discriminatory and
biased set of cultural values will be imposed on them.

The truth of Hume's observation was vindicated by early modern
history. The eighteenth and nineteenth centuries saw unparalleled
progress in science, art, and technology, prompted by a massive expansion of educational, scientific, and artistic institutions, which in turn
were established by populations whose increasing wealth and power
demanded more political power and freedom. Conversely, if the benefits of social and political power—particularly the right to be educated—reside only in the hands of a few, then how can a society hope
to produce the continuous advancements and innovations that sustain
the arts and sciences?

During the second half of this century, America has made phenome-
nal progress in the extension of basic democratic rights. Civil rights
legislation directed against racial discrimination, the women's movement (which worked to realize the potential inherent in the extension
of suffrage to women), and the one-person, one-vote principle established by the Supreme Court under Chief Justice Earl Warren were
pivotal landmarks in achieving a broader realization of precisely what
Hume termed "free government." The fact that fewer than half of
those with the right to vote exercise that right indicates how banal our
democratic rights have become in our society; self-determination, a
fundamental freedom denied to so many for centuries, is now so thoroughly taken for granted that we feel we can ignore it and the potential
it holds for progress in the future. Today's passivity and pessimism

notwithstanding, American society, despite the substantial problems it faces in realizing the economic and social benefits of a free government, has achieved an astonishing victory in establishing and maintaining the basic elements of political freedom. Therefore, for the first time in history, we possess the preconditions and the means to ensure the growth and development of the arts, science, and education.

In light of these circumstances, the way in which we persistently choose to represent what is possible as a result of the "blessing" of democracy is a surprising, biting irony. Concurrent with the expansion of democracy since the mid-1960s, a pervasive sense of cultural deterioration has come to dominate our sense of the world in which we live. We believe we are members of a culture in decline. We fear for moral and cultural standards and values. And, to exacerbate this irony further, we express our sense of doom by invoking the image of a vanished but glorious past: a time before most of us had freedom to the extent that we enjoy today, when freedom was less prevalent and the use of arbitrary authority and power more common. We allege that the world in those bygone days was far more cultured and refined than it is today. A less democratic, fair, and free society seemed to have had a more stable system of values and maintained a greater premium on excellence.

Why is it that so many adult American citizens persistently believe that things were better yesterday than they are today? Why have so many in the younger generations adopted, in their tastes and judgments, their own form of cultural nostalgia that mirrors the pessimism of their elders? What is the cause of this recurrent and tenacious nostalgia?

There is little genuine optimism about the future because we have come to believe that, as the rhetoric of many recent aspirants to the presidency would have us think, our moral and cultural decline is the result of years of massive and almost insurmountable error and mismanagement. The start of this decline is usually dated somewhere in the 1960s, an era marked by a crucial struggle to extend democracy and come to terms with issues of race and gender inequality. Selective memory, willful distortion, and even downright falsehood combine to generate a pessimistic account of history. It infiltrates our conversations, our beliefs, and our popular culture. We talk about the "dumbing-down" of America as if individuals in the past had ever been smarter. We are certain that people are less literate and that standards of taste are crumbling rapidly. Vulgarity and violence generally seem to be on the rise, and in their wake we observe the ruins of community and family life. In light of this kind of fear and paranoia about the present, it is easy to forget that the past had any ills of its own.

This habit of selective nostalgia predominated at the November 1996 dedication I attended of the Eldridge Street Synagogue on the Lower East Side in New York City as a national landmark. Amid the sentimental remembrances, there was no mention of the poverty, disease, overcrowding, crime, discrimination, and disastrous working conditions of a century ago, but only of community (whose virtues were indeed considerable), Yiddish songs, grandmother's cooking, and tall stories. The Eldridge Street Synagogue is indeed a landmark, not because it reminds us of an idyllic past now vanished, but because it symbolizes the will and fortitude of America's immigrants, those who came to America a century ago with no evident prospects for themselves. Faced with hate, exploitation, and uncertainty, they struggled to escape the Lower East Side in order to find more secure and comfortable lives for themselves and their children. Yet when we recall the past, we degrade that achievement by sentimentalizing the conditions that our ancestors struggled so hard to overcome.

We believe that our pessimism about what is possible today is actually the courage to "face facts." Yet we are so deliberately selective in what we choose to call history that facts are often bent to fit our current preconceptions. Take, for example, the widespread belief that there has been grade inflation in schools and colleges. Within other arenas of human achievement, we do not question obvious improvements. We do not express disbelief, for instance, that athletic records can be broken by succeeding generations. We also accept that more dedicated amateurs and ordinary people display improved skills in sports and standards of fitness. In some cases, minimum standards in technical prowess, as in conservatories of music, seem to improve steadily. And we expect continuous advancements in the speed, smallness, efficiency, and power of computers and gadgets designed by scientists and engineers.

However, when it comes to something we consider a standard of morality and culture, such as our children's academic performance in school, or the art and literature produced today, we suspect that we are victims of deception. New art never seems as good as that of the past. When we see that grades are in fact getting better, the possibility does not occur to us that perhaps people are really doing better and that there may be cause for satisfaction and hope. Rather, we are more inclined to believe that today's standards are lower and that teachers are less rigorous and more poorly trained.

Our inclination to interpret reported evidence is highly tendentious. We are disinclined to read positive signs in the data that we get in reports on education, and we fail to take into account the conditions of schooling today that limit unambiguous signs of progress. If one chooses to look at the glass half-full as opposed to half-empty, perhaps the performance of Americans in school has been better than we have any right to expect. And we dismiss the rare cases of self-evident good news. However, when reports on education communicate bad news— which is more often the case—we see in the results confirmation of our sense of cultural deterioration.

A pervasive climate of cultural pessimism is not new; in fact, it appears to be a consistent companion of historical progress in modernity. During the eighteenth century, a debate raged between those who celebrated the ancients of classical civilization as the pinnacles of human achievement and those who defended the superiority of the moderns. Since the early nineteenth century, the rise of industry and the growth of cities—the radical transformation of the conditions of life—brought with it a fear of loss. Matthew Arnold's classic 1869 tract, *Culture and Anarchy*, is perhaps the most famous historical predecessor to our current way of thinking. Advancements in externals—the mode of industrial production, speed of transport, accuracy of measurement, standards of living, hygiene, and medicine—were understood as camouflaging hidden costs, primarily in the arena of values: morality, taste, learning, and judgment. In the nineteenth century, the preindustrial natural landscape, the rural village, and even the Middle Ages became objects of nostalgic glorification, with little regard for the enormous hardships and limitations that had been eradicated by historical change.

Today, few, if any, take the side of modernity. Confidence in our own time seems implausible. Pessimism has become the battle cry of hardheaded thinking, armed with apparent evidence and ironclad logic. Optimism has become the province of vagary, New Age dreaminess, naiveté, and lack of concreteness and knowledge. At best, if one is still willing to concede technical improvements (in computers, for example), one immediately associates these improvements with the toll they will take on standards of taste (for example, the quality of writing) and character (for example, the prevalence of such personality syndromes as attention deficit disorder).

The point to remember in all of this is that most of the complaining about the present and future has a tenuous basis in fact. No one alive today has firsthand experience of the late nineteenth century, and so we are dependent on written history, twice- or thrice-told oral reminiscences, and simplified popular interpretations that tell us more about today than yesterday. Despite our nostalgia for simpler times, the evidence clearly suggests that after the devastation of World War I, the 1920s—marked by corruption, gangsters, and union conflicts as well as jazz, speakeasies, and flappers—were hardly a violence-free decade of family values and good government. The 1930s witnessed, in addition to glamorous Hollywood musicals, the Great Depression and the rise of fascism. The 1940s brought us Auschwitz and the atomic bomb (which makes any nostalgia for World War II particularly dubious). In the 1950s, schoolchildren hid under desks and in the bomb shelters of the cold war, Little Rock was torn apart in the wake of efforts to end legal segregation between white and black, and McCarthy and the blacklist created a climate of fear that found little reflection in the vacuous representation of family life on television at the time. In the 1960s, social strife, generational conflict, and the Vietnam War marred the decade, which left us with the sedated, hedonistic lifestyle of the counterculture. The 1970s brought us the gas crisis, huge inflation, and the hostages in Iran, but these problems are somehow left out of our present fashionable nostalgia for that decade. The 1980s, the superficially prosperous age of Ronald Reagan, takeovers, and Wall Street arrogance, saw both an unprecedented widening of the gap between rich and poor and the final flight of American manufacturing overseas. Where, then, was the great age that America yearns for? Was it even earlier than this, perhaps in the nineteenth century, when there was no modern medicine and no antibiotics, when there was violence and poverty in the immigrant cities in the East, strife among Italians, Poles, Irish, and Jews, and a Jim Crow "Old South"? Or was it the eighteenth century, which never resembled anything that came out of Hollywood, when illiteracy and poverty dominated and life expectancy was half of what it is today?

Progress has not been inhibited by our many troubled attempts to realize our potential. It is well to remember that every age has had its problems as well as its triumphs, and history has always had its doomsayers, dismayed not at the prospect of what changes may bring, but at the prospect of change itself. We know that in terms of education and social freedom, more of us are better off now than our ancestors were in the first half of the century. And perhaps our perception that, in terms of culture and civility, we have had to pay a high price for material progress and comfort is really the loss of something we never actually had.

II. EDUCATION AND POLITICS

In America, education and politics have historically made bad bedfellows. Few issues are raised as often with so few positive results. In the first place, the tenure of most politicians is not long enough for them to be judged by what they might accomplish or fail to do in education.

Second, the current political rhetoric concerning education is mired in banalities. Politicians share with most of today's citizens who went to school an instinctive sense of expertise, regardless of whether they did well, poorly, or dropped out, marked by an almost inexhaustible supply of prescriptions based upon limited and selective remembrances.

At the same time, education is a favorite topic for officials running for election because, politically, it is high-yield and relatively low-risk. Education is about the young, who, by any reasonable comparison to ourselves, are innocent. Therefore, education is about the future, which, by definition, is a matter of conjecture. Education suggests hope while providing a convenient medium for faulting prior administrations. Since the early 1970s, America has even been more obsessed than usual with the state of education. Education has now become a primary symbol for despair in current society. Our public school system has repeatedly been declared a failure. Poor schools and low standards are held responsible for America's failure to compete in what we have come to accept as a global economy in which we do not dominate as much as we feel we deserve and as we did after World War II. During the mid-1980s, Americans focused on unflattering comparisons with high-school-age achievement in Japan and Germany. We know that the economy will be increasingly dependent on science and technology, and we have become properly concerned about maintaining our superiority in those fields. Therefore, we ask: are our high school students doing as well in science and mathematics as, for example, Japanese students? (During the cold war, we asked a similar question about students in the Soviet Union.)

Education now holds center stage in our political debates, less for itself than for what it does or does not do in terms of learning. It has become a metaphor for the condition of our culture and country. The supposed decline in educational standards has become the pivotal justification for our sense that in general we are living in an era of decline. Consequently, nostalgia succeeds because we are convinced that once upon a time our schools did better than they are doing now. The facts do not bear this assumption out. Even conservative experts such as

Robert Herrnstein and Charles Murray, the authors of the notorious *The Bell Curve,* found that "there is no evidence that the preparation of the average American youth is worse in the 1990s than it has ever been." The progressive educator Deborah Meier cited the work of Dale Wittington, who in 1991 compared the performance of American seventeen-year-olds from 1917 to 1987. He found that there was very little change in over half a century in the basic information possessed by that age group.

Our memories are indeed unreliable. Consider the complaints that have plagued American schools like a broken record throughout this century. In 1935, the American Council on Education issued its report "Secondary Education for Youth in Modern America," which declared that "existing institutions are quite unprepared" to deal with the requirements of modernity. The failure of schools constituted "a fundamental threat to the national welfare." A prominent educator, Harl L. Douglass, was convinced that American youth circa 1937, in comparison with the past, were being shortchanged by the nation's schools. The *Sputnik* crisis of 1957 and 1958 unleashed a massive public outcry about how poorly our schools were serving our interests. Arthur M. Schlesinger, Jr., in 1957 remarked that American schools had "become archaic, teachers downgraded socially and education neglected." And those who still yearn for the good old 1950s might be referred to the scathing assessments by Sterling A. Dow, Harvard's senior classical historian, who, writing in the *Journal of General Education* in 1951, expressed his horror at the inadequate preparation of entering college freshmen at Harvard.

It seems that in education as well as in other aspects of our culture, we yearn for a past that itself was dissatisfied. No one alive today can claim to have been part of a school system convinced of its own quality. One can easily argue the opposite case: that American schools have done pretty well considering how much more democratic they are in terms of who goes and who stays in school. David Tyack and Larry Cuban in their 1995 critique of school-reform efforts, *Tinkering Toward Utopia,* rightly point out that most arguments about progress or regression in our political discussions about education are myths. Having said that, it is important to realize that the dominant myth of the 1990s has been the conclusion that we must restore American schools to a level of quality and standards they have lost. If one demolishes the historical premise of this position—that there were higher standards and better schools in the past—then the entire politicized agenda of restoring American education—getting it back on track—is discredited, leaving an uncomfortable vacuum.

No doubt there have been changes. But those changes, in and of themselves, are causes for optimism, not pessimism. In 1960, only 41 percent of the population had completed more than four years of high school. In 1994, that figure rose to 91 percent. In 1960, only 7.7 percent of Americans had completed four years of college; in 1994, that number reached 22.2 percent. In the same period, the percentage of African Americans completing college has grown from 3 percent to over 12 percent. In 1955, 17 percent of the eighteen-to-twenty-four-year-old population was in school. Today, over 50 percent of the same population is in school.

Through the 1990s, America has sustained a high school graduation rate of over 75 percent of the seventeen-to-eighteen-year-old age group. The post–World War II era has nearly realized the promise that in this country access to education can be rendered democratic. Even if one were to believe that the schools used to be better, there is no denying that there are many more literate Americans than there once were and that we have a much better schooled citizenry than we used to. What is disappointing is that there seems to be an inverse correlation between the statistics, such as the number of diplomas we give out and the number of years spent in school, and the quality of democracy. Our more educated fellow citizens—the very adults who wallow in nostalgia for the schools and colleges they attended—seem less inclined to discuss political issues carefully, more tolerant of the sound bite, less interested in voting, more susceptible to clichés and spin doctors, and more pessimistic about government.

In terms of income and race, if we consider the much larger spectrum of students going to school and completing school, we might come to the conclusion that the oft-cited decline in SAT scores, for example, has turned out to be less steep than might have been predicted. The drop in SAT scores was about 10 percent in a period when access increased ten times that much. In fact, our schools may have handled the opening of their doors to the majority of our children, particularly in adolescence, much more successfully than we might have hoped. The public school may be among the most resilient, flexible, and consistently successful government institution in our modern history, even though to some that may not be saying much at all.

III. LIBERALS AND CONSERVATIVES

Consider yet another paradox. Bemoaning the state of education ought to fuel a desire for change. But when it comes to education, we are resistently conservative. No one quite believes that having been a patient makes one an authority on medicine. But having been to school—one's autobiographical experience as a pupil and student—has long sufficed as a basis for a respectable opinion about schooling. It seems good enough to be the sole basis of a general attitude, replete with Benjamin Franklin–like maxims about how we need to go back to basics and the high standards of the past. Many of us are quick to say that we know what worked and what did not, and who the good teachers were and who were not. If we think of ourselves as having been shortchanged by schools, we may become confident about what should have happened or what sorts of experiences did not happen enough. Some of us go so far as to resist change, as if to say, "Nobody did that for me, so why coddle the next generation." We revel in the fast pace of change in the world, except in terms of education. Insofar as education is, by definition, an act of cultural preservation, conservatism is warranted, but the resistance to change has gone too far. It has retarded the chances for improvement by glorifying a tradition that has never worked.

Few of us are critical enough of the stories we tell about our own schooling. Children are not always the most trustworthy of witnesses in the first place, and adults who recount their childhood experiences are even less so. When it comes to education, we have the particularly revealing habit of implicitly giving the patina of objective recollection to the way we tell our life stories. Each of us carries throughout our lives a sort of oral history of prejudices, pleasant occurrences, and resentments about the time we spent in school. We are reluctant to question our own memories and our embellished accounts of what happened when we were six, eight, eleven, or sixteen. Since we do not relinquish any of these easily, it is extremely difficult to change anyone's mind about education. In short, we all seem to know what good schools are, even though we have done little to produce them. The pervasive cultural pessimism that has overtaken the country has a dangerous ally in the resistance to thinking critically about our own school experiences.

The focus of much of the public debate about education and the ire of the citizenry seems to be the curriculum. Many of us are appalled that one or another subject that was once in the curriculum no longer seems to be taught or is now taught in an unrecognizable form. Geography, grammar, arithmetic, and spelling are perennial targets. Adults are angry that children are not learning the basics anymore. New subjects, methods, and materials are suspect. As a nation we yearn for the good old days of our own childhood, supposedly before all the daunting problems we face in our adulthood took over—crime, violence, loss of ethical standards, and economic competition from abroad. And we want our children's curriculum to mirror our own sanitized version of our past.

There is particular outrage at changes in the school curriculum that are the result of the passage of time in politics. Before 1954 and the case of *Brown v. Board of Education*, in a segregated society without civil rights for the descendants of slaves, and before the massive migration from Mexico, Puerto Rico, and Asia, we believed America did not have to worry about multiculturalism or bilingualism. Once again, history is falsified. A century ago there was much more polylingualism in our society and less ethnic and religious homogeneity. The hatred and segregation among European immigrant populations has been forgotten; it was ameliorated by intermarriage, economic progress, and assimilation. Political leaders in America during the 1890s were sure that America would collapse under the weight of unassimilatable immigrants from Italy and Eastern Europe. In 1900, there were more bilingual Americans as a percentage of the population than there are today. And there were more foreign-language newspapers and journals. Dwight David Eisenhower was born in Abilene, Kansas, a bilingual German-English community. Furthermore, linguistic theory and cultural history do not support the idea that human societies develop most productively when totally monolingual. What evidence do we actually have that learning only one language is advantageous or that polylingualism retards intellectual achievement *or* cultural identity? The current hysteria of proponents of "English only" movements notwithstanding, monolingualism seems to be our fate, since English, like Latin centuries ago, has become the dominant political, economic, and scholarly language of the world. This is the result of real politics—America's superpower role and cultural politics—and the dominance of American mass culture and scientific institutions.

It seems fashionable to focus on the dilemma that in today's schools unquestionably important historical figures, events, and even classic works of literature that were important to us and still seem current have become, with the passage of time, distant and irrelevant to new generations. For older Americans, World War II still carries the emotional power of a recent event. But for many years now, that war has been as unimportant to schoolchildren and young people as World War I was to the currently middle-aged segment of the population when it was in elementary school. Our inclination not to confront the passage of time can blind us to dramatic generational shifts in the way history is conceived. Consider the reaction in Germany to Daniel Goldhagen's controversial 1996 book, *Hitler's Willing Executioners*, which placed the blame for the Holocaust exclusively on pre-1945 German anti-Semitism, which he claimed reveled in the idea of extermination. The crowds of young Germans who came to hear him during his book tour were not dealing with their own past. For nearly fifty years there have been practically no Jews in Germany. The most prominent minority are Turks. Rather, the young embraced Goldhagen and his thesis more as a matter of contemporary theater. He offered a moment of entertainment that constituted an act of rebellion against the contemporary adult German establishment. The young exploited for their own purposes a quite distant piece of history, dimly connected, at best, with the generation of perpetrators, their grandparents.

When we wonder why a new generation never heard of something, we should remember that when we were children, adults also bemoaned the erosion of memory. In both the North and the South after 1865, several generations went to great lengths to keep the enmities, exploits, victories, and defeats of the Civil War alive. They, too, have faded, revived only by the occasional Hollywood blockbuster movie or television miniseries.

The reconstruction of history has always occurred. Our parents knew things and ascribed importance to personalities and events that we barely recognize. George Santayana, Pearl S. Buck, and Albert Schweitzer were once great names that appeared in school books. New heroes and heroines now appear, and, as any review of past history textbooks will show, our sense of our national past has shifted its focus regularly from one generation to the next. As time passes, a nearly unpredictable array of important items vanishes. Likewise, tastes change with respect to literature, art, and music. We often judge the schools according to the extent to which they preserve for the next generation the very same world we believe was presented to us as children. Only in science (and sometimes, as in biology and astronomy, not enough) do we tolerate change and progress. When we lament how little history young people know, we measure their knowledge exclusively in terms of European and American history. But for children born in the 1980s and 1990s, in comparison to someone coming of age in the 1940s, knowledge of Asia, the Middle East, Latin America, and Africa has become as important as knowledge of England and Germany was fifty years ago. Today's college students, for example, know much more about the non-Western world than their parents or grandparents did as college students.

The only competitors to education in terms of issues of public policy on which citizens share a comparable familiarity rooted in long-term personal experience might be the family and sex. Even though both are unlikely to be as much the province of direct taxation, government regulation, and bureaucratic legislation as education, family and sex have become less and less matters of private life and more ones of nearly obsessive political debate. Sex and the family are the only issues that sustain the public's attention without compulsion. Treating them as politics has filled the vacuum left by the erosive boredom and cynicism we feel toward the rest of our collective political life. In other words, a sense of ineptitude in dealing with or even debating such public issues as race, economic inequality, health, and international affairs causes us to impose all the weight of our anxiety about the world we live in onto discussing and regulating private life. Perhaps we feel we can resurrect a collective existence as community, state, or nation by centering our attention on the one experience we know we share in common: the domestic sphere and the search for intimacy.

Given our pessimism and lack of will to focus, in a candid way, on the need to have better schools, we at least should resist the few efforts that are made to gloss over the facts and make things look better than they really are. Consider the recalibration and redesign of the Scholastic Aptitude Test (SAT) administered by the College Board. In 1995, the scores went up, largely because the test was reconfigured. From now on, the scale for measuring SAT test results will also be "recentered." Absolutely nothing substantive has been achieved; rather than trying to design a more sensible test or at least make students score higher on the second-rate standardized tests, on which we still unfortunately depend, the Educational Testing Service (ETS), in a self-serving manner, changed the terms of measurement to suggest the appearance of progress.

Without lapsing into nostalgia, it can be said that there was one brief moment when education became successful as an American political issue, after *Sputnik*. The Russians seemed ahead of us in ways that threatened our sense of security. James Bryant Conant, the former president of Harvard, a chemist and a veteran of the brilliant collaboration between government and science that built the atom bomb, wrote a scathing book entitled *The American High School* in 1959. In the wake of *Sputnik* and the baby boom, new funds and reforms were put into place. Progress was made, only to be eroded in the late 1960s by the turmoil over the Vietnam War and the counterculture. The fate of this moment rings familiar. In the late 1930s, the progressive effort to reform and improve American schools was cut short by World War II. And now we face a political sensibility that lumps education together with welfare as an example of excessive and wasteful government intrusion, making a long-overdue contemporary equivalent of the Manhattan Project in education politically unthinkable.

America has never given the effort to improve education enough time. The deadly combination of nostalgia for yesterday and pessimism about today has caused us consistently to mishandle important opportunities. The result is that there is little confidence that anything can be done. The outpouring of negative prose and official hand-wringing about the standards, cost, and consequences of American education since the early 1980s seems to suggest that the post-*Sputnik* effort to improve the schools was a failure, when it actually introduced important results. But it was only a beginning, which explains why there has been no lasting improvement. One example of how the beginnings of progress were aborted is an objective that was at the heart of the *Sputnik* era: increasing the number and quality of American scientists and engineers. There was a growth during the 1960s in the number of Americans entering the fields of science and mathematics after college. However, the National Academy of Sciences has documented a decline since the early 1970s in the number of American-born graduate students in all fields of science. We are fast eroding a bastion of mid-twentieth-century American excellence: science and technology. That decline has been masked by an overall growth in the numbers of sci-

ence and mathematics graduate students in American universities
made up of foreign students.

The situation today is even further complicated by the growing
belief that the state monopoly on the delivery of schooling is wrong.
We no longer trust government even to deliver the mail, and we have
come to loathe large public bureaucracies. New justifications for this
sentiment have emerged in the wake of the 1960s. Groups concerned
with moral values and religion now castigate public education and have
come to regard government-run schools as instruments of moral decay.
Although we hear all too much about violence and weapons in schools
and too little about learning, our attention keeps returning to the desir-
ability of school prayer. It is as if a moment of silence or even overt
expressions of sectarian allegiance will cure ignorance, boredom, passivity, and illiteracy.

Our schoolteachers may be better paid, but they are not as respected as one would wish. Few Americans fervently hope that their
children grow up to become elementary and high school teachers. Professionals in education themselves are partly to blame. The teachers'
unions often act in an antiquated, trade-union manner, and there is too
much self-serving rhetoric about conditions of work and too little genuine idealism about the quality of education. From school administrators
we encounter too much jargon, and from state education officials too
many regulations and bureaucratic deterrents to individual initiatives.
Defensiveness dominates the response of educators.

Some of that defensiveness is justified. Citizens are much too impatient. They want cheap, magic solutions, and when they do not happen, they are angry. Better schools, they believe, should cost less.
Schools and teachers should succeed where parents and the community
fail. An adult population addicted to television and the movies wants its
children to read. Close to half of all American children watch up to five
hours of television a day. One might wish to see less interest-group
politics, less mistrust, and more generosity around the subject of education. As is already clear, a quick fix is unlikely; the ideals of schooling

cut against much of popular culture and values. It may take at least two decades for large-scale results to be evident. As a nation, perhaps we should adopt a perspective on school reform akin to Japan's traditional attitude toward economic development. We must look to the long run of decades rather than quarterly and annual reports. However, in a society concerned about crime, violence, immorality, and a loss of jobs and confidence about the nation, citizens are understandably unwilling to wait.

Education therefore remains the ideal rhetorical issue for politicians, since it is easy to castigate the current state of affairs without the expectation that one will do something about it. After all, children cannot vote. William Bennett, when he was secretary of education under Reagan, used his power and influence to get the federal government entirely off the hook. He argued that federal programs of compensatory education could not work and that it was, finally, not the public schools but the home that was responsible. Presidents Bush and Clinton, either explicitly or tacitly, continued to hide behind the presumed constitutional barrier to large-scale federal involvement. Inaction on the national level has become plausible. Even Clinton's second State of the Union Address, which highlighted education, asked for far too little. Education is left to languish as an object of domestic budget-cutting tinged with the brush of wasteful government spending.

But the public continues to vent its collective frustrations about what is happening to this country by pointing to how poor our schools are. Education for the next century must be both a national and a local issue. On the one hand, local school boards dominate the governance of schools. We are still mired in an antiquated system of funding based on an eighteenth-century measure of wealth: local real estate. On the other hand, even though localities influence the schools and each state controls its own educational policy, there turns out to be more uniformity in the schools than the American patchwork-quilt system of governance implies. Within states and between states, textbooks and standards are more alike than they are different. The reasons for this lie in the dramatic uniformity of our lives, whether that sameness is measured by the products we purchase, the entertainment we seek, or the things we all need to know and do such as reading and writing.

The local school board election and budget are, for many communities, the last vestiges of direct democracy where average citizens can see that their voices will still be heard. For those living in rural and suburban America, local school politics are a welcome relief from the sense of apathy and powerlessness that citizens feel with respect to statewide and national elections. Communities can set salaries, cut programs, and micromanage the schools in ways that demonstrate that they control how their tax dollars are spent. Children become the innocent victims of the failure of other forms of democracy to give the electorate a sense of tangible influence and power.

This points to one of the potential flaws in the now-popular charter school movement. It raises the possibility that the ambitions and prejudices of small groups of parents and citizens will be privileged over national and state standards. While the movement can lead and has led to productive innovations and has liberated teachers and pupils from the regressive hand of centralized control, the danger persists that curricula and attitudes can become insulated by small local groups from legitimate standards of skills and knowledge, thereby penalizing children. A common public school system with strong elements and standards shared across state and local boundaries is still a viable and necessary ideal of democracy.

In 1983, President Reagan released a report entitled *A Nation at Risk*, which, as it turned out, struck a raw nerve in our patriotism. Our schools were accused of fostering mediocrity at a time when the cold war was still going and America was frightened of global economic competition. Schools were held responsible for the decline in American economic competitiveness and in national self-confidence. A series of books, ranging from Diane Ravitch's 1983 history of education, *A Troubled Crusade,* to the late Allan Bloom's *The Closing of the American Mind,* published in 1987, helped to coalesce a widely shared explanation of what was wrong with American education and when and why it ran into trouble.

The 1960s became the pivotal decade in which this presumed corrosive evil of mediocrity took hold. Before then, it was alleged, there was an educational system that worked. Then came the liberal 1960s, whose progressive ideas undermined standards and challenged the social and political role of the school in generating shared American values. Part of the liberal agenda was opening up the schools to the disadvantaged at the expense of maintaining standards. Open enrollment and affirmative action on the university level became symbols for programs that permitted pupils to go from one grade to the next and even graduate without sufficient levels of achievement. It became plausible to argue that diversity and access had been achieved at the expense of merit.

The truth is that the liberals of the 1960s were not responsible for a decline in standards. A mix of factors, including the loss of education's virtual monopoly on women with professional ambitions as a source of first-rate teachers, combined to further reduce the chances in the 1970s that post–World War II American schools would become adequate. The unsavory truth remains that our schools were never as good as we might wish to imagine. The 1983 Reagan report had the virtue of focusing the nation's interest on education. It raised the question of whether the liberal agenda of equality and access could indeed be reconciled with a standard of excellence. The full extent of Hume's "blessing of a free government," in terms of education for most Americans, had been a reality for barely two decades.

Unfortunately, the politics of the 1980s only strengthened the political appropriation of the idea of excellence and high standards by the neoconservatives as an attack on liberals. Both sides failed to rescue the idea of quality from partisan politics. The liberals were more interested in issues of funding and content—spending more money and revising the history curriculum and finding ways, properly so, to represent minorities in textbooks—as opposed to matters of quality and choosing materials purely on the basis of which subjects and texts could best inspire high achievement. But by the 1990s, it became clear that no one, black or white, rich or poor, was satisfied.

IV. THE FAILURES OF OUR SCHOOLS

But this is only part of the story. Our malaise about education is not entirely misplaced. The schools may not have been better in the past. They may have served a much more restricted percentage of the population. What fuels all the criticism of our schools and makes the virulent scrutiny of school budgets and resentment at teachers' unions so plausible is the unquestionable and most salient fact of all: that our schools, while not that bad considering the circumstances they face, are *still not as good as they ought to be*. The problem with education is not about the past; it is all about the present and the future. The real failure in our politics of education has to do with our disinclination to harness the politics of possibility.

Imagine the bell-shaped curve, which is nothing more than a visual description of the distribution of population arranged along a single standard of measurement. One can create a bell-shaped curve for lots of things, such as how the population performs in terms of how fast individuals can run. Such a curve can be generated for all important uniform points of comparison, such as life expectancy, weight, and height. If one created bell-shaped curves that measured levels of literacy, general knowledge, and familiarity with mathematics at age eighteen, one would get an accurate picture of the distribution of the performance of high school graduates according to tests that measure such things on a standardized basis. Setting aside for a moment whether tests adequately measure learning, it seems clear that one cannot create any public policy designed to change the natural distribution of populations. There will always be an elite that does well. There will be a bulge in the middle and a trail-off at the low end of performance. What can change, however, is the range of standards on which the bell-shaped curve rests. If all Americans were to eat more, the distribution of population would shift upward on a scale of weight. The minimum weight, the average, the mean, and the upper ranges of weight will all change upward. The same is true for education. There is no evidence to show that we cannot push the total scale of educational performance higher, lifting all student performance, from the brightest to the weakest pupils.

Another way of thinking about this idea is to imagine a footrace. As we know from the Olympics, the speed at which one must run in order to win a gold medal has increased. The gold medalist from the Olympics fifty years ago might not even qualify in today's race. In fact, the slowest runner in today's race may have qualified for a medal one hundred years ago. The distribution of runners remains the same, but they run the same distance in shorter times. The task of education is to push the entire bell-shaped curve further toward a higher standard of educational performance. If one considers the bell-shaped curve a kind of snake, one can think of pulling at the head and pushing at the tail.

Getting grades, taking tests, and winning prizes in school are about competition and comparison. If one can get an A in reading at a certain level, then that means that a D or a failing grade is defined comparatively against the achiever who does the best. Any runner or competitive swimmer knows that he or she is running and swimming not only against the objective clock but against the potentially faster competitors. If we could find a way to improve the performance of our best students and lift the minimum performance of our weakest, we might stand a chance to raise the entire standard of all those in between. Too much of our educational policy has been directed in a static way against a mythical average student. Unlike good trainers and sports coaches, we have not pushed the performance of the entire team by targeting the best and the worst simultaneously.

It should come as no surprise, therefore, that even though our schools may never have been any better, the many bell-shaped curves that describe what our students learn today in school show dismal results. The entire scale of measurement is too low in terms of what could be achieved. The National Center for Educational Statistics of the Department of Education reported that during the 1990s only slightly more than one-third of all twelfth-grade students could be considered proficient readers. Fewer than one-third of our seventeen-year-olds can actually write a coherent paragraph about a simple topic such as what they did on their summer vacation. Nearly 90 percent of colleges must offer remedial instruction and tutoring. The tests that we give to determine the need for remediation are not that onerous. Therefore, it is disheartening to discover that as far as history is concerned, more than half of our twelfth graders fall below the standard of knowledge we would call basic. Only 1 percent attain "advanced achievement." For an idea of how simple these exams really are, consider that only 23 percent of high school seniors could correctly locate the Pyrenees, Japan, the Mediterranean Sea, or the Persian Gulf. A question involving the interpretation of a graph was answered correctly by only 9 percent of high school seniors.

A decade ago, in 1988 and 1989, only 7 percent of seventeen-year-olds were able to "understand the links between ideas, even when those links are not explicitly stated, and to make appropriate generalizations, even when the text lacks clear introductions or explanations." This is a fancy way of saying that very few of our seventeen-year-olds can think for themselves in a sustained, subtle, and systematic fashion that calls for the making of inferences. These statistics are even worse for the disadvantaged and the discriminated, students from poor families and African American and Hispanic students. Only 37 percent of New York State high school students completed a basic college preparatory curriculum. In the late 1980s, a flurry of publications hammered away at the fact that the level of basic math and science learning achieved by our seventeen-year-olds was frighteningly low.

From 1980 on, we have become accustomed to the neoconservative piety that throwing more money at the schools will not help. Furthermore, in the sustained wave of federal cutbacks starting in the early 1980s and new limits on property taxes and state aid, school budgets have had to adapt to fewer real dollars per pupil. The reasons schools work or do not work are no doubt complex; but we have to face the reality that for whatever reason, the performance of America's children could get much worse very quickly if we are not careful. The signs are already there. After a brief respite, the test scores of our most disadvantaged children, particularly among minorities, declined in the mid-1990s. In our cities the situation is catastrophic. The 1996 report on New York City schools shows that only 30 percent of third graders read at or above grade level. In the bottom 20 percent of the city's high schools, no more than 4 percent earned a Regents diploma, the certificate that indicates the achievement of an academic curriculum considered the minimum for going on to college.

We are accepting low standards of achievement as a status quo, when we should be continually pushing beyond them. Why isn't education today breaking records the way the Olympics are in sports? While money doesn't solve everything, there is little doubt that we have not invested sufficiently in schools. Yet it has become more convenient to accept the opposite point of view as standard and conventional wisdom, that the problem is purely a matter of mismanagement rather than money. An editorial in the *Investors Business Daily* in December 1996 brought out the now-familiar argument that the quality of our schools does not depend on how much we are spending. By comparison with other nations, America spends a good deal; it ranks sixth in the world in educational spending as part of the gross domestic product. We spend more than Germany, South Korea, or Japan on an elementary school child. Only Switzerland spends more. Yet American eighth graders ranked twenty-eighth out of forty-one countries in mathematics skills, well behind all four of these other countries.

The answer to this argument is quite simple. Everyone knows that the cost of something is dependent substantially on the context. The costs of building the same three-bedroom house on a rocky ledge in Montana are different from the costs incurred when building it in downtown Atlanta or on a level plot in North Carolina. Making shoes in New Hampshire costs more than making the same shoes in Brazil. The conditions this country presents for education—including the obstacles—simply demand more per-pupil expenditure in order to get the "same" result. Unlike the making of shoes, we cannot close the factory, so to speak, and have American children educated overseas. The diversity of America's population, the special traditions (and lack thereof) of life and culture, and, above all, the democratic structure of schooling, which does not segment children into ability tracks at age eleven or twelve, will result in higher costs. It should come as no surprise that it will cost more per pupil in this country to compensate for the cultural homogeneity of Germany and Japan. The best case for this argument is precisely the fact that Switzerland, a prosperous, xenophobic, but heterogeneous democracy (with its own cantonal variations of spoken German comparable to ebonics) that takes pride in the opportunities it gives its multilingual native-born citizens, must spend far more than Germany in order to achieve a competitive level of achievement for all its citizens.

If one still doubts that education needs more money in this country, consider the state of school facilities. We are facing a frighteningly out-of-date, dilapidated physical plant in our schools. In 1995, the General Accounting Office estimated that the nation required $112 billion of improvements to public school facilities. The situation in the inner cities in particular is desperate, since those physical plants are usually older and less well maintained. More than half of New York City's 1,050 school buildings are more than fifty years old. There is a slight boom in school enrollment facing us over the next ten years, which will only exacerbate the problem. Furthermore, class size is too large and remains an obstacle to better results. When there are more teachers who can pay attention to individual students, the results are better. This is really nothing but common sense.

v. The Motivation to Learn

Why aren't our schools better? The answer involves curriculum, teachers, buildings, and equipment. But one can also rephrase the question and ask why our children don't remember more of what is taught. Perhaps the problem doesn't rest solely with the buildings, the teachers, or the curriculum but with the attitudes of parents and children. Why study, why learn? Why remember after you have passed the test? Too often we talk about education only in terms of state-mandated standards and requirements. Perhaps we should focus on individual motivation and recollection. The failures of education—ranging from violence in school buildings to declining levels of achievement and lower SAT scores—are cited over and over as the yardsticks by which we measure the decline of America. Assuming that we would like things to get better, it is hard for education to succeed with those whom it must serve—our children—in such a doomsday atmosphere. The idea of progress and the rhetoric that asserts that a better future faces us have been crucial allies in the struggle to motivate the next generation. How can one expect children to sit attentively and dutifully behind desks, year in and year out, preparing to assume a responsible position in the world, only to discover that the world in which they live has already hit the proverbial iceberg and is sinking like the *Titanic*?

If there is any real decline, it has been a decline in hope. No generation of young people has been subjected to as much adult discouragement as today's schoolchildren and college students. Hopelessness and skepticism are nearly invincible foes for young people trying to find their place in the world, particularly our own, in which the fundamental clock of expectations has changed. Our expectations of children vis-à-vis school are still measured by a clock that ticks along in terms of years and decades, if not lifetimes and generations, a system that diminishes the relevance for the child of the day-to-day experience of being in school, since we expect children to sustain all by themselves a desire for long-term results.

School as we now conceptualize it was an invention of the late eighteenth century. During the next century, schooling for the general population flourished in Western Europe and America. In this century, the majority in the United States now has access to the full thirteen years of schooling that is considered a basic education. Yet this system of education retains a fundamental ratio that evolved over a century ago between time spent in school and adult life. A child is expected to invest thirteen years (and those with more promise, at least four more) on behalf of their adult lives and those of their children. Hard work in school finds its rewards slowly and at a distance.

Yet in today's world, adults measure their own lives in terms of much smaller units of time, consisting of moments, days, months, and quarters (particularly in regard to commerce and finance). We might consider years (the homes we live in) and perhaps decades (in personal relationships), but rarely do we think in terms of the lifetimes or generations that still dominate the time frame of effort and expectation we direct at the young in school. The young go to school in a world in which they do not have occasion to observe adults accepting the same delay between effort and result; few adults speak about their work or family or personal relationships within the extended framework of time that guides our organization of schooling.

Children observe how adults change where they live, where they work, with whom they live, what they own, and with whom they are friends with dizzying frequency. This reflects a norm of adult impatience: the expectation of quick and rapid gratification. The dissonance between the clock of school and the clock of adult life cannot possibly inspire children. Only among immigrant families, where parents are forced to think in terms of the achievement of stability, acceptance, and security, is the long-term clock that measures progress and success in terms of lifetimes and generations still a consistently dominant motivating factor among adults.

One of the more mundane reasons we romanticize the past and fail to recognize the challenges we face in motivating children is the rarity of adult contact with children. In 1970, 34 percent of the population was under eighteen; in 1990, that dropped to 26 percent. The demographer Harold Hodgkinson has observed that in America today one could easily spend a week without coming into prolonged contact with someone under eighteen. Only one-quarter of the population has a child in a public school. America has always tended to be more age-segregated than other cultures, but the declining percentage of those who are young worsens a bad situation. Our interest in the future and any real sense of what our children are doing and might do have become increasingly marginal. Far from being centered on our children, we have become insulated from the commonplace sense of hope that contact with children brings.

The problem may not be that we are teaching the wrong materials or getting too soft in our expectations. It may be that we are not successfully capturing the attention and imagination of young people. If curiosity is a natural state in children, then as they grow up and go to school they lose it. We seem to depress the love of learning or fail to nurture it. If, on the other hand, we believe that curiosity is learned, we haven't been very effective in stimulating it in schools. The apathy of parents and adults toward what children learn day to day (as opposed to the larger rhetorical political issues—budgets and school prayer, for example) is widespread. In its report on urban schools in 1988, the Carnegie Foundation found that in a New Orleans high school, for example, which required parents to pick up report cards, 70 percent of report cards remained unclaimed two months after the marking period. Furthermore, there is reason to believe that many Americans, despite what they say, are actually suspicious of more homework and tougher grading, as though that might harm their child.

Hypocrisy is one of the most daunting and pervasive aspects of democratic politics. We talk openly as if we want people to be more educated. At the same time, we fear intellectuals and are suspicious of experts. Our national heroes and heroines are not scholars, teachers, or scientists. When was the last time a famous movie star of either gender was cast as an experimental scientist or theoretician who did something good as opposed to unleashing some monstrous virus? Hypocrisy extends to other aspects of our political life, including issues of sexuality and drug use. An open discussion regarding the decriminalization of drugs, for example, seems impossible, not because the facts make debating a different set of policies toward drugs unreasonable. The prohibition on alcohol during the 1920s was overturned because, despite the law, drinking was something individuals could admit to or express desire for without being socially cast out. Drinking never lost its social luster or glamour. The largest sector of demand for drugs in this country comes from white middle-class America, not from urban minority populations or high school and college students. But few adults may be willing to admit to this fact. Silence and hypocrisy condemn the debate on how to eliminate a major blight on American life and contain the unquestionable damage that substance abuse does to society. Drug use and even addiction cannot be eliminated entirely. They can only be controlled, either by force and fear or by prevention and education. But the choice is never given us to debate rationally.

Likewise, we readily consume movies and videos that confuse sexuality with violence. We remain drawn to and fascinated by tales of desire and infidelity, and our society continues to sustain high divorce rates. Yet we turn on any public figure whose record isn't spotless. It is as if we do not wish to face our own ambivalence about those whose lives do not conform to our nostalgic ideal. If individuals succeed in some extraordinary way, we rush to make celebrities of them, but the process of glorification is merely a prelude to our greatest satisfaction, which occurs when they are knocked off the pedestal we ourselves have constructed. The very commonplace attributes or weaknesses of personal behavior, particularly concerning sexuality, become our most efficient weapon against those who excel. Hardly a year goes by without a revisionist biography that seeks to debunk as myth the achievements of a so-called great personage.

This pattern of hypocrisy in our public life wreaks its greatest toll on the young. It robs them of models to which they should aspire in two ways. First, it tarnishes the respect for great ambition and achievement and implicitly defines real excellence as an implausible ideal that should not be put forth as a standard. The young should be inspired by the extraordinary and atypical qualities—the aspirations and accomplishments—of great scientists, artists, politicians, entrepreneurs, civic leaders, and writers, rather than be deterred by their typical and totally understandable frailties. After all, exceptional qualities do not come in neat packages. One cannot expect Albert Einstein to have been unusual only in thinking about time and space.

Second, a false linkage between ambition and success on the one hand and disaster and failure on the other is created. It is all too reminiscent of, but less eloquent than, that offered by Greek tragedy that warned against pride. Pride and success were invitations to disaster. The personal behavior of Thomas Jefferson, Franklin Delano Roosevelt, and John F. Kennedy was no different from that of millions of ordinary men in the world. But their public careers were. We should inspire the young to achieve and enter public service without setting the unreasonable standard that high achievement will increase the prospect of pain and defeat as the result of commonplace weaknesses or must be or should be accompanied by some sort of hypocritical standard of saintly existence.

There is no inherent reason why our children cannot do better in school. They certainly have the time. Although this is a radical way of calculating, if one considers the total number of hours, only 9 percent of their year is actually spent *in* school. There is no reason that our schools cannot perform better. All the breast-beating and fulminating about education does not result in our finding ways to do what is necessary. At stake is not only the future of the American economy, jobs, and the quality of American democratic life. A century ago, a majority of Americans still lived on the land and worked the farm. Now a substantially larger population is fed with the labor of a very few agricultural workers. We are in the midst of a transformation equally dramatic in the area of manufacturing and industrial production. Education will be essential to how future generations create work and utilize the increasing portion of their longer lives in leisure. By the beginning of the next century, substantial progress toward better education could be made. The nation has the capacity to solve its educational problems.

Thomas Jefferson and his fellow drafters of the Declaration of Independence might have described these observations as self-evident truths. Their validity requires no expert testimony. They are matters of common sense and common experience. A school system—a mix of public and private institutions—that reaches all American citizens and teaches them to function in the modern world using written and spo-

ken language, mathematics, history, science, and the arts is clearly necessary and not beyond this nation's reach in practical, economic, and
technical terms.

The weakest part of America's educational system is located at the
juncture between adolescence and schooling. For all income classes,
races, and regions, the junior and senior high school years, from ages
twelve and thirteen to ages seventeen and eighteen, mark a time of
trouble. Adolescents rapidly lose interest in learning and become hope-
lessly distracted. Despite the energy, passion, courage, and curiosity
that come naturally to this age group, it is all too rarely that these
qualities are channeled into intellectual development. Our schools fail
to compete for the attention of our young people, who mature earlier
and are given adult freedom sooner than they did a century ago. The
traditional high school is an out-of-date strategy and system. In terms of
its curriculum, it remains in a useless middle ground that helps neither
fast nor slow learners.

Beyond the challenges posed by modern adolescence, we need to
be concerned about early childhood education, particularly among the
poor. An obvious priority for radical improvement is the schools in
America's largest cities, which are the most neglected and troubled.
Furthermore, our elementary schools need to find ways of encouraging
the so-called gifted and talented. We need alternatives to current expectations and standards for the very young. They, too, have been set
in a useless middle ground that helps neither fast nor slow learners.

American educators have become used to underestimating what
children can learn. Both they and the public have persistently confused
the speed of learning with the ability to learn. Therefore, we judge our
schools nearly exclusively by tests that measure speed of recall and not
the quality of thought. Standardized, timed, machine-graded tests are
poor measures of learning. Thinking carefully about a question is more
important than identifying the right answer. Knowing why one's answer was wrong is more useful than having arrived at the right solution
without comprehension. Pupils rarely get tests back quickly enough to
see not only what they got wrong but why. And testing should be used

as a key instrument of teaching. It has deteriorated into a device by which to assess how the overall system functions and to judge teacher performance. Multiple-choice tests are particularly egregious, since they do not allow for assessing partial or incomplete knowledge or approximate understanding. Not all wrong answers are the result of the same type or degree of ignorance.

Information divorced from any emotional or practical sense of why one wants or needs to know is hard to concentrate on, much less remember. Even though adults recognize this fact, our curriculum is driven by outdated expectations and conventions. We still teach arithmetic and geometry as mechanical tasks to children without communicating their power, utility, or beauty. As a result, children emerge from school without the ability to play with numbers, to estimate, approximate, and reason with quantities and shapes.

With the advent and distribution of electronic media, the opportunities to link ideas and facts to the desire for knowledge are now greater than ever before. However, in our schools that linkage has become bizarrely attenuated. The same children who flunk math understand baseball statistics. Children are capable of memorizing and recalling easily, yet because their desire to do so is not nurtured, that capacity remains largely unrealized. A child in the fifth grade can pass a test about the rivers and lakes of his or her own state, but the same pupil in high school does not understand the principles of geography or how to read a map. What is taught is not retained. Grammar, for example, is taught over several grades repeatedly but is simply not remembered. In judging our schools we ought to look as closely at the residues of schooling ten and twenty years after graduation in the habits of adults as at the year-end test scores at each grade level. For example, in its 1992 national report card, NAEP (the National Assessment of Educational Progress, a federal monitoring system) showed that compared to 1969–70, nine-year-olds tested better in science and mathematics in 1992, but the performance of seventeen-year-olds in the same areas had declined.

The NAEP report showed that since 1984 there has been no improvement among adolescents in proficiency levels in reading or writing. In 1992, only 43 percent of adolescent Americans could, according to the report, "understand, summarize, and explain relatively complicated information," and only 36 percent of pupils in the eleventh grade (as opposed to 39 percent in 1984) could "write complete responses" to test questions that contained "sufficient information." And this is after more than a decade of constant schooling. It should come as no surprise that NAEP also reported that reading for pleasure declines as pupils get older. Only 27 percent of seventeen-year-olds reported in 1992 that they read for pleasure. That number in 1984 was 31 percent, hardly a figure to brag about.

Despite the hand-wringing of pundits about America's decline, the alarmist rhetoric of politicians, and the verbiage of educators, we already know what is needed and what will work in schools. There are actually few genuine mysteries when it comes to education. For those in search of a quick technological fix, there is none, as educators already know. The same NAEP report that showed declines in the performance of adolescents revealed that over 80 percent of seventeen-year-olds reported using a computer. We still need what we have always needed: well-trained teachers who love learning and teaching in classrooms with few enough pupils so that real teaching can take place. Decreased bureaucracy, more caring, rigorous national expectations, less mindless testing, a longer school year, a more straightforward curriculum, better teaching materials and equipment, and clean and sound school buildings will carry us most of the way to the goal of excellence.

We have forced public schools to become overregulated on account of our fear of legal recriminations by a population more interested in finding fault and going to court than in what and how well their children learn. Ultimately, higher-quality education may or may not cost more than we spend on schools currently, but a system that works can be more efficient. A certain level of disorder can be creative and even helpful to learning, but sloppiness, waste, and patent inefficiency never are. America's taxpayers know that we are spending substantially on our schools. They are reluctant to spend more. But if the citizenry could be assured that the schools would work and operate with a minimum of waste, voters might be willing to pay the price, even if that price were higher.

Once again we come upon the paradox of today's politics. Imagine a map that lays out the spread of Lyme disease. Some regions are entirely free of it, and others are totally infested. If a map of educational disease were created, most of the country would be dark, with a few small islands of health. To make the point (which clearly has been made before) that theoretically we could educate our children and young adults properly does no good by itself. It smacks of the pulpit admonitions preachers make each week. Their moral prescriptions for what we ought to do may be right, but they rarely have much practical influence. In matters of personal conduct, we might desire to behave differently, but even when we know what is right, we fall short. Despite feelings of shame and guilt, it appears not to be in our nature to behave as well as we should even though we might like to behave better.

We may not have to be any kinder to our neighbor than we already are (even though that would be nice), but we can improve our schools. Humans are theoretically capable of learning much more than they do. Therefore, educating our children, the future citizens of America, requires an act of collective political will, just as we might combine forces to conquer a rampant disease. It is a matter of "bottom line" economic and social survival and self-interest. In contrast to matters of personal conduct, the nation can impose its collective will successfully in political action. Since 1939, America on occasion has managed to assemble resources from the public and private sectors to accomplish tasks more daunting than teaching children and adolescents. Winning World War II and creating the atom bomb in the Manhattan Project are examples; so, too, was the Marshall Plan. The postwar development of a national highway system and the transformation of the workplace through the spread of computers are two instances of how rapidly the nation can absorb and create change.

Given the state of our schools, it is ironic that the university system that was developed after 1945 in the United States is still the best in

the world. Now we must match that accomplishment in elementary
and secondary education. We must replicate for elementary and secondary schooling what was done for higher education after World War
II. The time is right. Skepticism notwithstanding, throughout the nation there is a sense of urgency similar to that which fueled the postwar
investment in higher education. After all, as a nation we have been
acutely aware for nearly two decades that we need better schools.

In the 1950s, the cold war and the fear of nuclear weapons made the
idea of supporting research in the sciences and social sciences both
sensible and politically viable. The problems facing the United States
now, at the end of this century, are no less compelling: economic and
technological competition from abroad and the fragility of the social
and intellectual foundations of American democracy. Despite the divisive fragmentation in terms of ethnicity, religion, and region in our
national politics, we all realize that the key to these problems is our
human capital—people—whose quality is contingent on motivation,
education, and training.

We face an opportunity for collective action that transcends partisan
politics. But the key difference between the war years after Pearl Harbor and the 1950s on the one hand and the 1990s on the other is that
then we were, as a nation, more optimistic, more fearless, perhaps less
complacent, and certainly less cynical.

VI. OVERCOMING SKEPTICISM

If the view that our school system was a victim of liberal social policy
intent on widening access at the expense of quality gained wide currency in the 1980s, the publication in 1995 of *The Bell Curve*, by Murray
and Herrnstein, and the debate it sparked marked its apogee. The
furor surrounding the book's controversial notions about race and intelligence masked the most repetitive and striking aspect of its overlong
text. The massive statistical apparatus in *The Bell Curve* is perhaps the
most convincing set of numbers showing how important education is to
our national future. The authors abused the appearance of scientific

argument to bolster a set of dubious claims about intelligence but at the same time gathered hard data about the failure of our school system.

Most of the debate about the book failed to focus on its only redeeming feature: the compelling correlations between levels of education and low income, crime, illegitimacy, and delinquency. It was clear that the health of contemporary society was dependent on education. For the next century, more than in the past, education will hold the key to the economic and cultural well-being of our country. The economy and the society in which we live require of its citizens knowledge and skills in an unprecedented manner. If we fail to offer a better system of education, we will face a highly stratified society characterized by violence and anger, a social specter of inequality reminiscent of the *ancien régime* before the French Revolution. Knowledge has truly become power.

The Bell Curve, however, was more than an indictment of the American school system. It mirrors the way we have come to think about education and schooling. The public assumes that intelligence can be defined. A simplified and facile construct of intelligence makes intelligence susceptible to exact measurement. The success of the book stems from the extent to which it gave already popular prejudices the appearance of fact. Like the public at large, the authors of the book assumed that since the mid-1960s there has been a sufficient effort at government intervention in education, particularly directed at the poor and disadvantaged. The results of those programs have been uneven; less has been accomplished than was promised. Now that there is an amassing of data covering a quarter of a century, the authors argue— along with conservatives throughout the nation, but with "facts" to back up their views—that it is clear that one cannot really improve the educational attainment of those who, by reasons of biology, do not have the capacity to learn as measured by tests.

If one were to believe *The Bell Curve*, intelligence is inherited and resistant to any environmental influence, no matter how nurturing. Groups such as Jews and blacks are not merely discrete entities in society; they appear to be biologically and racially distinct. According to the authors of *The Bell Curve*, statistics also legitimate grouping people together by measures of intelligence. The fact that those groups also fit together by indices of income and discrimination is dismissed as a mere correlation. Yet the very same sorts of correlations between tests and race are used to defend an argument of causation: that race and biology determine learning capacity. The authors axiomatically chose not to consider the parallels between income (as opposed to race) and test results as equally causal. The irony is that evidence in *The Bell Curve* offers more proof of the link between environment and education than between inheritance and education. And it showed, despite itself, how useless and unscientific the concept of race is.

The conclusion offered by *The Bell Curve* is that not everyone can learn equally well, and that no system of educational intervention will compensate for inheritance. Since intellectual inequality is, according to the authors, extreme and unfixable, the social consequences are disastrous. The few will dominate, and the many will be useless and become more discontent than they are now. Unfortunately, many citizens have embraced this conclusion with enthusiasm. It fits neatly with the proposition that government cannot and should not intervene in education, thereby keeping taxes low and abandoning the age-old idea that education was a constructive instrument of social mobility and offered a ladder on which the less advantaged could scramble upward.

The picture of the present and future that emerged from *The Bell Curve* is not pretty. The rebuttal to the authors must rest primarily in debunking its totally false facade of scientific certainty. We cannot define intelligence precisely enough to permit us to discuss the question of inheritance scientifically. We know too little about genetics and neurobiology. Therefore, we know too little to define the environmental factors and assess how they influence behavior. What we are able to measure and talk about is what the tests tell us, which is that too few of our citizens are learning the limited set of skills that can be tested. When authors like Murray and Herrnstein use the word *intelligence*, they hide the fact that we are far from possessing a clear and complete scientific definition of intelligence. Intelligence may turn out to be a nebulous amalgam of very different and disparate qualities.

The fact that educated Americans are willing to accept as fact unprovable propositions about intelligence, schooling, inheritance, and race that are actually guesswork and opinion only shows how dispirited we have become and how reluctant we are to tackle the problems of education. We would prefer to write the improvement of education for our children off as being conclusively beyond anyone's reach.

That America has never really tried to educate its citizens well, and certainly not those who are at the bottom of the social ladder, no longer seems to matter. What was begun in the 1960s under Kennedy and Johnson was merely a beginning that deteriorated. More was accomplished, particularly by Headstart, than has been popularly understood. The causes of the deterioration of the liberal initiatives of the 1960s include the exploitation of racial and economic disadvantage by ideologues and bureaucrats on the so-called left and intolerance and a cynical mixture of economic and political criticism and neglect from the so-called right.

At a time when the public is altogether disillusioned about government, the notion of improving public education through the public sector seems even more fanciful than it ever was. Ten years of polemics against American schools have resulted in the idea that perhaps government should get out of schooling and that the democratic dream of more and better schooling for all citizens is not merely impractical but impossible. The national call to arms in 1983 over the realization that our schools were mediocre has ended in a full-scale retreat justified by the belief that the war to improve education in our democracy is not the province of the federal government and not primarily a national issue. Even locally it is viewed as a possibly lost cause, unreasonable, and a waste of time and money. The commonplace view is that there are those who can learn and can profit from an education. They will find a way to do so, and nothing will help those who cannot.

It is truly ironic that both the confidence in education and the commitment to funding it have suffered among the most highly educated electorate in our history. Education was once seen as a privilege and opportunity by those who were denied access to it or could not afford it. Our illiterate and unschooled forebears had a much higher regard for education than do their descendants, who hold more high school and college diplomas than any previous generation. The adults who now seek to cut budgets and denigrate public schooling are its products.

One should not overestimate the power of evidence to convince anyone. A tiny bit of historical candor should suffice to puncture nostalgia. There was violence, immorality, corruption, ethnic conflict, prejudice, and vulgarity aplenty in our past, particularly in this century. There was even more pollution. Even if one cannot muster the same horror for the forgotten ills of the past as one can for the ones facing us now, there is little doubt that the seemingly terrible world we now live in is not the fault of our children. When we express horror at what goes on today, we seem to forget that we, the adults who went to school and college in greater numbers than any previous group of adults in American history, are responsible.

Adults make and buy the silly movies and vacuous journals and television shows. Adults manufacture and buy the automatic weapons. Adults break the laws. Adults fail to compete in the new worldwide economic system. And adults elect our leaders. Adults have no one to blame but themselves. If there really had been such a good school system in the past, the adult world would not leave so much to be desired.

The issue, therefore, is not how to reclaim virtue lost, but how to make the present and future better than the past. As far as education is concerned, the cultural pessimism that has become so popular and commonplace is the most difficult obstacle to overcome. The motivation of any child, whether four years of age or fourteen, is dependent on a sense of optimism around that child. No generation of American children has ever gone to school surrounded by adults—from parents to teachers—who as a group believed so overwhelmingly in the inevitability of decline.

The parents of my generation were convinced the world of their children would be better. One cannot expect a child to start school at five and work diligently for twelve and perhaps sixteen or more years surrounded by adults who have no patience to wait that long in their own lives or who think that things will be worse twelve or sixteen years later. Children are overwhelmed by adults in search of immediate rewards and impatient with the long view because adults do not trust the long term. In this climate of pessimism fueled by a longing for some mythical age gone by, how can one expect our children to sit still, learn, concentrate, compete, and be ambitious, much less be civic-minded and upright?

Without a belief in progress, for both the individual and society, there can be no expectation that the next generation will embrace learning and higher standards. If that is the case, then is there any reason to believe that progress is possible and realistic? Is faith in progress just another example of flaky wishful thinking, the sort of thing preachers say knowing full well no one takes what they say seriously since by definition they are dreamers?

The reason to be optimistic is that the presence of children alone is cause for hope. Some things might be getting worse, but some others get better. The progress we have made in technology and medicine is clear. There is more freedom in the world than ever before, and more literacy. Furthermore, if one takes a longer view, framed in terms of centuries, even if America is like the Roman Empire in the first century A.D., we still have hundreds of years to go, and in those hundreds of years there will be more opportunities to turn things around than we are probably entitled to.

One thing is certain: our children deserve more. We need to give them a better chance than we are giving them now. If we could do a better job in educating the next generation, we might see more progress than we see now. The time has come to suggest how we might make things better. College students are every bit as promising as they were in the past. Their capacity to write and think is much the same as it was twenty-five and fifty years ago. In some areas—technology, for example—they know more and can do more. Today's children and young people are in as good a position to outdistance their elders as any previous generation. The adult community now in charge has shown no evidence—whether in politics, culture, or economics—that the world it has helped to create cannot be improved upon. The final irony is that today's adults, who threaten to live well into their nineties and break the one-hundred-year age mark with increasing frequency, will be the primary beneficiaries of a dramatically improved system of education in America.

CHAPTER II

LANGUAGE AND HOPE

I. THE LANGUAGE OF PESSIMISM

A seemingly insignificant shift in the way we use words unmasks the meaning and consequence of our national embrace of an overriding pessimism, the primary obstacle facing any sustained progress in American education. When speaking, Americans regularly use the word *hopefully*, not as the adverb it is, but as a way of saying "I hope," as in "Hopefully things will turn out well." The traditional and theoretically correct use of *hopefully* can be found in such phrases as, "She ran hopefully toward the train station," or "He stood hopefully before the judge." *Hopefully* modifies a verb. It adds to its meaning by ascribing a state of hope to the actor as an action is being undertaken. If one were to substitute *breathlessly* for *hopefully* in these very same phrases, one could easily imagine how the word ought to be used. *Hopefully* is a way of indicating that one is doing something with hope in one's heart, so to speak.

Grammar and usage are never fixed. Language continuously evolves. It is both a symptom and a cause of historical and cultural change. When the notorious *Webster's Third New International Dictionary* was first published in 1961, critics seized on it because they thought the editors were condoning slang and incorrect usages, such as *ain't*. In fact, they were not. They were describing a nonstandard usage that had become so prevalent since the publication of Webster's 1934 second edition that they had to include it, if only to explain it, even if one does not like it. The editors were not passing judgment on style. Like the lexicographers of the *Oxford English Dictionary*, or the compilers of the standard lexicons of classical Greek and Latin, they were including words and defining their meanings by the way they are actually used. The difference between the *Oxford English Dictionary* and the lexicons of classical languages on the one hand and the standard dictionaries we use daily on the other is that an ordinary dictionary seems prescriptive and authoritative about usage and meaning without regard to the history of usage. That impression maintains an illusion about the static character of language over time. A dictionary and rules of usage help us to strike a balance between communicating precisely with our own contemporaries and with our literate past and also with future readers.

The most obvious evidence of change in our language can be found in vocabulary words. New inventions, the special character of English usage among migrating populations for whom English is not a native language, international trade, and politics all influence language. Not only are words created and items added, but old ones slowly vanish. Some words lose meanings, or change their meaning and assume new ones. The word *genius* is one example. Once, particularly in eighteenth-century philosophical argument, it denoted the peculiar essence of something. Now it is used to describe an exceptional individual. In American speech, colloquialisms that have distinct but distant historical origins, particularly Anglicisms such as one from the game of cricket ("that's a sticky wicket"), fade away. New expressions become commonplace in idiomatic speech. The adaptation of many Yiddish and Italian phrases into English is a case in point. Take, for example, the word *glitz*, which comes from the Yiddish adjective *Galizianer*. Among the Jews of Eastern Europe, there was a legendary divide between those who resided in Galicia (then part of Austria-Hungary) and those from Lithuania and northern Poland, who were called, also in Yiddish, "Litvaks." Those from Galicia were considered notoriously vulgar and tasteless, given to excessive displays of superficial brilliance. The word *glitz* is a contraction derived from its use in America in phrases first used on the Lower East Side of New York. Furthermore, the inflection of our speech and the timing and vocabulary of our humor have been profoundly influenced by immigrant languages. So, too, has standard American language been influenced by the linguistic contributions of African American culture.

Gradual alterations in the way we speak and write, therefore, reveal much about what and how we think. The controversy over *ain't* speaks volumes about a shift toward informality. It signaled the influence of a rebellion against upper-class convention and the embrace of working-class aesthetics in our self-presentation—shifts that occurred in society and mores after the end of World War II. Anxiety about the character and future of so-called standard English is therefore not merely an expression of aesthetic or literary taste, as the ebonics controversy has made painfully clear. We are unsettled if newcomers or those below us in education and social class do not meekly follow our lead. No doubt the balance between continuity and change necessarily tends toward continuity. Language changes slowly, and so it should, in order to retain and pass on a common linguistic foundation. Otherwise it would be even harder than it is today to learn from and argue with the past; we would be less able to preserve and renew our love of Shakespeare, Austen, Emerson, and Ellison. The virulent controversy over the revision of the Episcopal *Book of Common Prayer* in the late 1970s and early 1980s best exemplifies the quandary. The tradition of faith as experienced in language needed to be preserved while the access to prayer and doctrine for a new generation, whose language was different, needed to be opened up. Therefore, at stake in contemporary discussions about usage, expressed most visibly by William Safire of the *New York Times*, is not only a seemingly innocent enthusiasm for the integrity of language and high cultural standards. He and fellow neoconservatives are on the lookout in the way we use language for signs of something akin to (but far more serious than) a decline in manners—namely, a deterioration in the quality of our culture and a loss of respect for hallowed traditions.

Self-proclaimed protectors of the purity of language implicitly regard language as somehow having been fixed in a way that makes its grammar and proper usage normative and principled. The distinction between felicitous speech and awkwardness becomes more like the difference between right and wrong and good and bad. In the mid-twentieth century, a particular modernist aesthetic about language use came into vogue, represented by Strunk and White's *Elements of Style*. It was no mere coincidence that the norms of style were codified in the 1950s, at a high point in the social utility and economic prestige of the written word. That moment, in turn, was also a high-water mark in modern history of America's literary affinity with England. That definition of style preceded the widening of access to both the high school diploma and higher education. Ironically, it also coincided with the gradual demise of cultural Anglophilia as America spawned a contemporary culture less derivative of both England and continental Europe.

Even in as seemingly innocent a topic as language, one encounters a symptom of the paradoxical and unsolved challenge that has faced American education from the birth of the nation, first in theory and finally, in this century, in practice. Can the United States, in contrast with every other industrialized nation with which we might be compared, maintain an educational system that is equitable, fair, and democratic on the one hand, and excellent and competitive on the other, particularly when we have been, continue to be, and will remain a nation of immigrants, many of whom do not arrive with English as a first language? Can we create and fund a system of schooling whose minimum and maximum standards of literacy are as good as or better than those elsewhere, a system to which all Americans have access and the chance to achieve at the highest level, using a language that they share in common? To return to the evolution of the American language: Can we achieve the sort of excellence associated with aristocratic English culture in our own way, without imitating European models? Can we reconcile the real elements of American life—demographic changes and popular culture, for example—with traditional high standards of learning and thinking, using English in a sufficiently standard and differentiated manner so as to develop and maintain a great civilization?

Lurking in the background behind the anxiety expressed over the past several decades about the deterioration of language is the suspicion that during the very same historical period, from the 1960s on—in which more Americans completed more years of schooling than ever before—the standards and substance of culture have degenerated. Language and literacy have been the most frequently cited symptoms. The preservation of a high standard of literacy and the integrity of linguistic usage have been at the top of the agenda of those who fear cultural decline. The result of this emphasis on language among cultural pessimists has been a denial of language's inherent dynamic flexibility and adaptability. A romanticized view of traditional language use and proper style has been at the heart of cultural nostalgia. In turn, cultural nostalgia's most potent political antidote has been contemporary neoconservatism. Neoconservatism has two sides: one that talks about standards and quality and one that laments the decline of a specific intellectual and artistic heritage. By confusing the ideal of excellence with a particular realization of it—a style, a set of books, paintings, works of music—we limit ourselves and deny the possibilities for excellence in our own time. Neoconservatism is inherently doomed to inspire frustration and anger because it is motivated by an unachievable dream of cultural restoration. The past cannot be restored. Furthermore, since the past as we retell it is partly of our own invention, we are seeking to restore that which never existed.

Insofar as its sense of the future is contingent on an idealized past, conservatism, as a political ideology, runs the risk of always triggering disappointment. Ultimately, conservative political ideas fear the inevitable passage of time. This was the case a century ago when the writings of Max Nordau, the author of *Degeneration* (1892), were popular. Like today's conservatives, Nordau accused contemporary modern culture of leading society astray and called for a return to traditional middle-class bourgeois virtues and values. Intuitively, conservatism suspects that time is in a sense circular, and that change is merely an illusion of mortals—something like that cliché about "the more things change, the more they remain the same." Perhaps in some theological sense, in view of our mortality, we can accept the idea that the changes in our external realities, such as the means by which we travel and other technical and material developments, are ultimately superficial. However, political movements that self-consciously seek to stabilize, preserve, and uphold that which is regarded as traditional in the culture must not resist such changes but must co-opt them. Our conservatives, in contrast, sense that the passage of time is a constant threat. They are obsessed with decay, degeneration, and decadence, analogues of human aging and death. When one combines conservatism with either apocalyptic religious notions about redemption and the end of time as a liberation from worldly suffering or a rigid, sanctimonious moralism, then conservatism can become identified with the human struggle to delay damnation or the onset of doom. But even then, at its core, the task is grim and any positive results ephemeral. An assumption of human weakness, if not depravity, underscores conservatism.

The other extreme has its own pitfalls. Unrealistic optimism is frequently put forward in the form of utopian dreams. Utopianism, insofar as it is the polar opposite of nostalgia, possesses a dimension of destructive discouragement to the extent that utopian ideas construct a vision of human nature that seems implausible. Nonetheless, utopian political strategies, even when they become oppressive and dictatorial, as in the cases of communism and fascism, do disseminate visions of a better future. Faith in the possibilities of the Kingdom of God on earth can inspire resilience and optimism. But that optimism only gains credence insofar as it acknowledges the complexities of human psychology and action. Utopianism does damage in its lack of realism, which makes what *is* always fall short of what *can be*. Nothing is less appealing in the late twentieth century than a blind rhetorical assertion of the infinite possibilities of reason and progress without coming to terms with the current conditions for making improvements.

The most frequently disparaged word in contemporary political life—liberalism—has been caught in between conservatism and utopianism. That is its virtue. At its best, it circumvents questions about the ultimate logic of history and speculations about some sort of end point in human history. Although each of us, in our thoughts and actions, can be said to reveal some philosophical judgments about the meaning of time and history, most individuals avoid a conscious encounter with the longer-range question. We choose to remain eclectic and inconsistent in our views, usually avoiding extremes. But we retain a cautious belief in gradual improvement.

Any contemporary discussion of making things better in the future, particularly in education, literacy, and culture, must account for the peculiar and daunting legacy of the twentieth century. At the beginning of the twentieth century, many American and European intellectuals and artists rebelled against what they regarded as the legacy of the nineteenth. That legacy included a seemingly unbridled faith in modern industry and science. Late-nineteenth-century America was seen as a triumph of individualism and reason, a vindication of the possibility of progress in history in a context of freedom and competition. Critics of this late-nineteenth-century confidence and arrogance pointed to modern poverty, the slums of the cities, and the spiritual vacuum created by an overemphasis on material and commercial progress. Leo Tolstoy was perhaps the last century's most eloquent and well-known spiritual critic of modernity. Nevertheless, the generational rebellion led by artists and thinkers born during the last quarter of the nineteenth century, which gave birth to modernism, did not, despite a considerable philosophical skepticism, break free from an essential allegiance to the idea of progress in human history.

With the senseless slaughter that took place in the trenches of World War I, the twentieth century really came into its own. It was not only the barbarism of the war and its unexpected length that took its toll on the cultural pieties of Europe. Idealism itself, whether cloaked in the garb of patriotism or confidence in reason and progress, became untenable. Allegiance to the status quo became incompatible with the disillusionment that the war created. The 1920s were the era of radical experiments in the arts and in literature. Only those who turned to socialism and communism could maintain an attachment to the idea of progress. However, the unrelenting onslaught on the plausibility of progress unleashed by the events of 1914 was too sustained and too strong. First came the economic crises of the interwar period. Then came fascism and Nazism and the horrors of World War II and the Holocaust. The postwar period provided little respite. The communism that had evolved under Joseph Stalin and neo-Stalinism under Leonid Brezhnev revealed itself to be both cruel and corrupt. The atomic age ushered in its own forms of destruction and fear that humans would turn on themselves and the earth.

In the United States, the mid-twentieth century brought its own special disillusionments. The collapse of nonviolence in the 1960s, the political assassinations, the conflict over Vietnam, and the corruption witnessed in Watergate undermined any residual sense of trust and optimism. Since Watergate, no presidency has been free from mistrust and embarrassment with regard to its basic integrity. Despite the end of the cold war, Americans realize that a century of American economic dominance and political leadership has come to a close. At home, middle-class families know that real wages have stagnated during the past twenty years. The American dream has lost its economic underpinnings, despite recent and encouraging gains in domestic productivity.

A curious and terrifying aspect of these developments is that they defy and contradict any residual belief in progress. The individuals who designed, implemented, supported, and accepted—even tacitly and passively—the crimes and catastrophes of this century were literate and educated. The eighteenth-century English and American generations of David Hume and Thomas Jefferson—perhaps even the mid-nineteenth-century world of Emerson, George Eliot, Dickens, Disraeli, and Lincoln—assumed that ignorance, illiteracy, oppression, and poverty were essential causes of barbarism and violence. The spread of education would lead naturally—as part of social evolution—to superior ethical judgment and social justice. The paradox of the necessity of education for all at the end of the twentieth century is that literacy and learning per se are not sufficient to ensure moral and ethical progress. Education has become indispensable, but a better world will not emerge spontaneously from it, nor can a more humane world be constructed without it. The worst case is the one we face today: the illusion of sufficient education, which has generated an ill-deserved complacency.

Behind all modern schemes for public education, including Alexander and Wilhelm von Humboldt's work in Germany, Johann Heinrich Pestalozzi's reforms in Switzerland in the late eighteenth century, and the work of Horace Mann in nineteenth-century America, was a faith in the link between education and progress. The notion of progress was not limited to the material realm. A properly educated individual was viewed as being inherently more civilized. That individual could also grasp the interrelationship between freedom and reason and the necessity for treating one's fellow human beings well. Therefore, the educated individual was better prepared for democracy. With an education, citizens could not merely understand the logic and obligations of a world governed by written laws but participate in government, not as a result of the wealth and instruments of violence one commanded, but as a result of one's cultivated consciousness. No wonder John Stuart Mill made education the crucial requirement for enfranchisement in a democracy.

Before the twentieth century, education loomed large as the decisive social instrument of progress. Through it, a command of language could be cultivated. With literacy came the power of communication beyond the narrow confines of oral expression. In a world in which literate individuals had freedom (particularly freedom of movement) and access to political power, violence would no longer be the exclusive or primary means of dealing with one another. In a world in which material progress could be achieved, so that abject need would be alleviated, reason and compassion would triumph over the irrational.

However, any child in today's world knows that the horrors of this century are the work of the educated classes. The spectacle created by the hate and death in Bosnia and the passivity of the response by

Western democracies are like a final scene in the tragedy of the twentieth century. Among the victims, is any illusion left about a linkage between literacy and education and human progress? Since World War I, the written word, and now the spoken word, have become as much instruments of evil as good, spreading more propaganda, misinformation, disinformation, and senseless fear than clarity, truth, empathy, and tolerance. In previous eras in the Western world the image of the human instrument of violence was associated with tendentious characterizations of the "other." Europeans projected it onto the so-called uncivilized barbarians they sought to conquer: a Hun, Moor, Mongol, or Apache. The human instrument of violence in this century, however, has often turned out to be a well-dressed and -groomed, literate, and well-spoken individual who loves dogs and gardening. The ideal picture we have constructed of civility, which was realized by the well-mannered middle-class individual, has turned out to defy his well-cultivated appearance of harmlessness. He has turned out to be the ultimate barbarian. A survivor from the Warsaw Ghetto recounts how an SS officer, after rounding up women and children to be sent to Auschwitz, noticed a working piano (a rarity in the ghetto) and sat down to play Mozart, Beethoven, and Chopin beautifully. A staggeringly large community of German professors, doctors, lawyers, and artists—all respectable, well-educated people—participated actively in and went along with the slaughter of innocent human beings.

The fighters of the former Yugoslavia, whether Serb, Croat, or Bosnian, today are literate. They went to school. They ought to realize that what they are doing has no rational, positive, or logical purpose. Yet they believe in what language has taught them about national identity, ethnic differences, religious belief. Using the essential tool of intellectual enlightenment—language—they have manufactured a belief system that justifies hate and gives it meaning. Unfortunately, the articulation of that meaning demands that others die, suffer, flee, or submit.

The unique challenge facing the last generation born in this twentieth century—the children of those who will dominate the politics and culture of the first quarter of the next century—is how to respond to this paradoxical heritage. Since education has become a nearly universal social reality and not a dream, if it at all can help our society exit from the terrifying legacy of this century, then somehow the educational system we have created must be changed to achieve that end. But at the same time, the adult culture in which schools operate must emerge from its current phase of cultural pessimism. How can one restore a valid sense of optimism and progress? If one cannot, then it is unreasonable to expect that children will perform well in school, no matter how we choose what is taught and who teaches. The success of education in the nineteenth and twentieth centuries was predicated on a sense of progress. One generation of the less educated bequeathed better opportunity to the next. But now there appear to be few material, political, or ethical benefits ahead. We return once again to the challenge we face with our children presently in school. How can they and those who are about to enter be motivated to learn and do well?

We cannot ask children to be motivated and disciplined if we ourselves cannot come up with good reasons that we believe in for discipline and motivation. One feature of modern culture is that the easy answer of narrow self-interest—a motivation for learning and study based on a disregard for what happens to others or to one's community—will not work spontaneously. Every American child knows that among the richest and most envied individuals in society are athletes, rock stars, movie stars, and television personalities. Within popular culture there is little evident correlation between educational achievement and success, even though simply staying afloat (so to speak) economically within the spectrum of the middle class in the future will be more dependent on education than ever before. In the nineteenth century, narrow self-interest sufficed as a motivator for education. It was also expected that the mere accumulation of individuals pursuing their material self-interest would end up creating the best of all possible worlds. We no longer live with the illusion of a simple calculus of self-interest. And self-interest and education have been detached from one another in the popular imagination. A vacuum has emerged in which the pursuit of learning finds little encouragement.

II. LITERACY

Given the legacy of this century, it should come as little surprise that conservatism has become so attractive during the past decade and a half. Since contemporary neoconservatives locate the real decline in our civilization in the years after 1960, the image of a civilized world that is crumbling and of the ideal American culture of the past harbored by these neoconservatives, insofar as it has legitimate historical roots, is derived from qualities tied to the mid-twentieth century, the decades between 1920 and 1965. During these years, the older immigrant populations that had come to this country at the turn of the century became firmly acculturated, and significant immigration ceased. Only after 1965 did immigration resume. But the new immigration was different from the past, because it brought non-Europeans, particularly Mexicans and Asians, in large numbers. However, during the decades between the 1920s and the 1960s, for the first time in American history, the nation was insulated from a process of continual change from the outside in the form of large numbers of newcomers. The often painful process of social adjustment, gradual language acquisition, and cultural adaptation among immigrants, once a familiar aspect of our national landscape, disappeared. As older immigrants vanished through assimilation into the majority, we did not encounter a next wave. As older immigrants left their original neighborhoods, there were no replacements. The hiatus in immigration during the mid-century has led to many of today's unreasonable ideas and expectations regarding immigrants. These ideas are at odds with the history of immigration in America: that is, with our very own history.

These very same forty-five years between 1920 and 1965 represented both the apex and the early stages of decline in the prestige and importance of literacy. From the beginning of the spread of literacy in the late eighteenth century until the mid-1920s, writing assumed a preeminent position as the instrument of modern progress. Writing had become the crucial means of communication. Modernity—in the form of printing and distribution, the newspaper, and even the telegraph, up to the era of the silent moving picture—was dependent on the printed word. In business, politics, and private life, being literate, particularly with the ability to write, was crucial to success. As transportation improved and travel became more common in the second half of the nineteenth century, writing became ever more important as the exclusive form of communication over wide distances and flourished as documentation in travel literature and in the use of personal correspondence. An unusual but poignant example of the apogee of prestige accorded the written word in society is the scene in the 1925 silent film version of the Strauss-Hofmannsthal opera *Der Rosenkavalier*, created by Robert Wiene, the director of the legendary *Cabinet of Dr. Caligari*, in which a Habsburg Army regiment, set in the 1750s, gets letters from home. Even though far fewer than 5 percent of the army in 1750 (made up largely of conscripted serfs) would have been literate, mirroring the percentage of literacy in the total population, the scene shows every single soldier, regardless of rank, eagerly reading a letter from home.

The telephone and the automobile exerted more influence than we realize on the evolution of language and the role of the written word. One thinks of the 1959 film version of Laclos's *Dangerous Liaisons*, in which the letter-writing component of seduction was replaced by telephoning. The sound picture, the radio, the phonograph (and its successors), and television and video have compounded a revolution away from writing from the mid-1920s to today. Oral communication— speaking and listening—became more convenient and more important than writing and reading. It became possible to reach someone so easily that writing became unnecessary. The use of writing declined substantially in the decades after World War II. Before the advent of the home computer, the portable computer, the modem, and e-mail, we talked to people, whereas in the past we could only write to them. The writing we now do on e-mail is a new species of literacy, a mix of notated conversation and letter writing. Unlike old-fashioned forms of writing, it has the potential of being ephemeral and easily erased. It, too, may vanish with the continued progress of imaging technology.

Today, the important things in our private and political lives are communicated in person or by voice. Richard Nixon thought that his place in history would be secured by tape recordings of his conversations, not by the written records of the time or his subsequent memoirs. The telephone, not the dispatch, was the key instrument of critical power politics, as the 1962 missile crisis showed. We have gradually abandoned the idea that the written word has a prestige and permanence not accorded mere talking. And talking without taping has given us the flexibility of denying responsibility more readily.

The evolution of literacy and language in modern times has a useful parallel in the evolution of musical literacy since the end of the nineteenth century. That parallel contains a powerful cautionary tale. In order to hear music before the advent of the phonograph and radio, one could either listen to others or make music oneself. During the nineteenth century, one of the most rapidly growing consumer goods was the piano. It came in numerous shapes, sizes, and costs. Most individuals, in order to use it, had to be able to read music, and therefore sheet music became a thriving and successful business.

Before the massive growth in popularity of music in the nineteenth century, musical literacy was understood as the possession of an active command of the relationship between a notational system and sound. If one saw two notes, one was able to hear them in one's head and therefore sing the proper relationship, the right interval. If one had perfect pitch, so much the better, but that was hardly essential. Rather, it was the relationship between two sounds as indicated by the written notes. Likewise in rhythm, one could tap out the relationships and durations of the notes. Music was both read and written as an active and participatory experience.

The key point is that in order to "read" music in a meaningful way one had to be able to hear and process what one saw. Therefore, one necessarily had to be able to write down what one heard. The ability to transcribe sound, particularly distinct pitches, into written notation was assumed. One of the most frequently told stories about Mozart concerns his apparent ability to listen only once to a long, complex work and then write it down. What was remarkable was not the basic skill, but its extent. In the late eighteenth century, and well into the nineteenth, musically literate individuals could write down fragments—melodies, harmonic progressions, and rhythmic values—of what they heard. It is no wonder that in Mozart's day the voice and the string instrument, which had to be tuned and on which the notes had to be found without the frets of a guitar, were the building blocks of musical culture. The keyboard instruments of the day—the harpsichord and the fortepiano—had to be tuned constantly by the owner.

As the audience for music increased and the modern piano became the primary vehicle for music education and home entertainment, it became possible to eliminate the active part of reading music. One could learn by linking notes to fingerings. Musical literacy became more of a reproductive skill—the capacity to render something on the piano, which had all the notes tuned for the player. The piano became popular only when, like the car, it proved reliable over time. It stayed in tune for months, not for days. The driver of the car does not have to know how to fix it or how it works. The late-nineteenth-century piano—an industrially manufactured instrument replete with a metal frame and a rigid structure—was user-friendly.

Eventually, the active part of musical literacy—the discrimination between different notes and rhythms—vanished as a mass phenomenon. Musical literacy was redefined to denote the ability merely to read passively, to follow along as the music progressed. By the time the player piano, the radio, and the phonograph came into being, the need for even such passive skill disappeared. Today we have "re-created," with technology, an entirely aural musical culture, in which the written form—printed notation—is obsolete. The word "re-created" is used intentionally, since before the invention of notation, musical culture was a fully developed, wholly aural experience. Notation initially grew out of the need to preserve music, document it, communicate it literally out of earshot, and emancipate it from a specific time and place. Now that all those tasks can be accomplished by sound documents (for example, the CD), the old style of active musical literacy, which began to change and disappear in the nineteenth century, became superfluous. Genuine musical literacy was never easy to learn. The development of a mass audience determined the necessity for the simplification of written literacy in music and eventually its abandonment.

The analogy to ordinary literacy becomes clear. Educational statistics confirm the suspicion that we have become increasingly content to define literacy exclusively as the capacity to read, rather than the capacity to read *and* write. The passive ability to decode a sentence and describe its meaning now seems sufficient. Even our mode of testing asks the reader to locate the meaning and the right answer from a set of printed choices, rather than to write out a response from scratch. One key difference is that for the time being the computer has resurrected the need to command written notation. But the time is already arriving when much of the technology that is based on written commands and the transmission of text will become voice-activated. Pictures and sound will be required to create text. The need to be actively literate may be undermined by the very machine that has made it temporarily important again. The continuing dominance of visual media, the telephone, and the ease and low cost of travel, all of which encourage verbal and visual communication, will come to shape the character of the computer as well.

Although it is logical and obvious, it is somewhat ironic that print journalists have now emerged as key defenders of the written word. Television has forced the printed newspaper out of its monopoly on the transmission of news. But as the Viennese writer Karl Kraus, one of the greatest advocates of the power of language (he coined the saying that language is the mother of thought), pointed out, journalists have historically been experts in distorting language. The ruckus about yellow journalism and the inflated phrases of editorial pages advocating patriotism and hate during the twentieth century, particularly in the years surrounding World War I, the rise of European fascism, and the cold war, point to a legitimate suspicion regarding the way journalists use language. During the second half of this century, commercial advertising has made its own special contribution to a modern tradition of language manipulation. Advertising has had an enormous impact on the way we describe what we see, hear, eat, and smell and the way in which words influence how we buy and sell and fall in and out of love. Modern journalism and advertising vindicate the enduring power of language. They signal the centrality of the need to develop a critical literacy in our citizens, not an imitative one or a damaged one that makes us vulnerable and condemns us to passivity.

The fundamental importance of writing for education derives from the centrality of language to thought. Writing ensures the active command of language. Too often, however, the connection between language and thinking has been misunderstood, leading to traditional but misguided ideas about how writing should be taught. Many of us were taught to gather our thoughts, organize them, and then write them down. The truth is that writing is a process that generates thought. Only when we try to write something down do we discover what we really think. Writing is not the documentation of thought already formulated. The finished thought emerges most often from a reaction to drafts of that thought in writing. Therefore, revision is a crucial skill that needs to be taught.

Writing needs to be encouraged as a playful form of sketching and drafting. To return to the example of music: Beethoven did not formulate a completed piece in his head and then rush home to write it down. He carried a sketchbook and notated fragments of ideas. In response to those notated fragments, which he reheard in his head, he revised his written ideas and developed them further through the use of writing. The same process toward a finished product has been followed by painters and sculptors. From the early grades we need, therefore, to encourage children to experiment and to use writing not merely to document thought, but to create it. Once the motivation to write is developed and the habit of writing approached as a pleasure and an adventure and not a burden, then the basic rules of grammar and usage sufficient to ensure communication beyond the reach of personal contact will be learned and retained easily. No matter how advanced our technology may become, writing will remain central to thinking. The fact that writing has been and can be enjoyable and rewarding to all manner of human beings should be a source of optimism for educators and the public alike. Above all, the command of writing increases the likelihood that citizens will read and listen critically.

III. THE LANGUAGE OF OPTIMISM

Complaints about the way we speak and write ultimately carry some sort of criticism about the way we live. More often than not, there is a manifest political message. Although Safire's particular critique of language matches his conservative bent, his defense of certain patterns of usage reveals an interpretive insight that is indeed valid. The way we use language does tell us a great deal, even indirectly, about our views on political matters. Nowhere is this fact clearer than in the case of the use of the word *hopefully*. And in the case of *hopefully*, a concern about today's acceptance of a previously incorrect use is not misplaced.

To return to where we began: contemporary usage has given *hopefully* a new role. We say, "Hopefully, we will make a profit," or "Hopefully, Congress will pass that bill," or "Hopefully, the concert won't be too long," or "Hopefully, it will be a nice day and I will feel better." In all of these cases, what, in the past, ought to have been said is "I hope" instead of "hopefully." But even in this new use of *hopefully*, the speaker is communicating his or her state of mind—the expression of hope—with regard to some future occurrence.

The significance of the popularity of this use of the word *hopefully* is more than a matter of taste or lapse in good manners. Even the most educated among us have become accustomed to a circumlocution, a way of expressing hope without identifying ourselves either as the agent of that hope or as a responsible party capable of influencing or realizing the desired outcome. Insofar as grammar and common usage are reflections of the way we think and play the game of life with language, the change from "I hope" to "hopefully" is a sign of the disavowal of responsibility.

By saying "hopefully" instead of "I hope," we show that we don't want the hearer to identify us with the expression of hope. Perhaps we do not feel powerful enough or courageous enough to accept responsibility for what might or might not happen in the future. By saying "hopefully," we communicate the idea that someone else, or something other than ourselves, is capable of influencing the future. Doubt, a sense of powerlessness, and perhaps cowardice are sufficiently pervasive to make "I hope" either sound wrong or not convey what we really want to say.

Instead of "Hopefully, we will make a profit," if one said, "I hope we will make a profit," then the hearer might say, "If so, then what will you do to make that happen?" The traditionally correct grammar retains this sense of connection and accountability between the expression of hope and the individual expressing it. The traditional usage evokes a world in which individuals felt more capable of making a difference and more inclined to assume a role in the outcome of events. Even in cases where the expression of hope is about the weather—or some circumstance clearly out of our control—the correct usage lets people know clearly where one stands and what one wishes for. In a democratic society, becoming identified as the bearer of hope and expressing it are essential. But the new usage smacks of detachment and passivity.

The use of *hopefully* to which we have now become accustomed is a sign of the extent to which we have lost hope and live in a culture of pessimism. We no longer feel comfortable putting ourselves on the line. We talk about events in our lives and around them indiscriminately as if they are not in our control. We are not inclined to take responsibility. Most of all, we are increasingly disinclined to be found out as individuals who sustain hope as though we might be marked as fools or children.

Our current use of language suggests that we live in an age of greater hopelessness than in the past, when the usage that is now pervasive was understood as simply wrong. No doubt we would like things to get better, but we place more distance in our speech from that idea and its realization. We depersonalize hope and act, in speech, as if we ourselves are not in charge. The dramatic role industry and technology have played in the development of ourselves as individuals has exacerbated the plausibility of the new use of *hopefully*. We sense that our work is less dependent on us as individuals and less significant. We feel less in control in the face of technology that we do not command or understand and that yet seems to control our lives. The scale of government and society and the massive power of financial and commercial institutions dwarf us and leave us with little sense of our own capacity to assume responsibility.

The failure to assume personal responsibility, no matter how apparently reasonable, is a depressing and even dangerous way to think and act in a democratic culture that thrives on the free activity of individuals. Furthermore, it is devastating to the children of that culture. In an atmosphere of hopelessness, in which individuals are not inclined to express hope or to take on the responsibility to make things better, how do we expect children to behave and think? No other generation of children in the history of this country has suffered as much under the burden of such sustained adult hopelessness.

For a child starting in preschool at the age of three or four to be enthusiastic about going to school and learning requires that the child put a great deal of faith in the process of learning and schooling. On some level, the child must hope. For that child to sustain that attitude for twelve or more years, the surrounding culture must cultivate a parallel sense of hope. We ask children to spend at least twelve years working nearly every day for rewards that the adult population promises are out there for them. In our language (and in other ways as well) we signal a different, if not contradictory, message. If there is not an implicit sense of the possibility of progress for individuals and groups, then there is much less incentive for paying attention and doing well. Schooling and education by definition are about the future. If the future seems bleak and adults feel helpless and a vague sense of irrelevancy is linked to that which individuals try to do, then a child might be sensible to take a detached and cynical attitude toward the admonitions of adults that they sit still, be good, study hard, and the like. If adults do not believe all the rhetoric of values that seem to bolster the idea of hard work, excellence, and personal responsibility, then why should children? Subtle changes in usage reveal more than overt pronouncements of what seems right but what, deep down, is believed to be impossible.

Each previous generation of American schoolchildren has had some reinforcement about the possibilities awaiting them. But since the late 1960s, doubts about the prospects for progress have steadily eroded the atmosphere of tacit encouragement in which American schoolchildren have functioned. Even in the war years after 1941 and earlier during the Depression, those who were most deeply affected thought that over time things might be different.

The education of the next generation should offer one clear way out of this national paralysis. But without an environment of hope and optimism, nothing we do in the schools and for the schools will help. The reason for this rests in the influence that hopelessness has on our sense of time. It shortens our vision. If one doubts the prospects for the long term, then one concentrates on that which is immediately before one. Andy Warhol's notorious phrase about the fifteen minutes of fame afforded to everyone mirrors a sense of impermanence. The results of human activity seem more ephemeral not because of our adherence to a theology that underscores our mortality. Rather, we doubt the future, and therefore those projects that seek to help us elude mortality— creations of material and spiritual culture designed to last for generations such as institutions, works of art, buildings, and the like—seem more pointless than ever.

The shortening of the time frame that most people in America use to think about their lives has already been noted. On the institutional side, few of us are confident enough about the future to think in generational terms. Businesses are frequently founded and bought and sold many times within one generation. On the not-for-profit side, our lack of confidence in the culture has resulted in the few numbers of significant new institutions founded since 1960 in the arts, culture, and education. In the Northeast, the museums, libraries, orchestras, and opera companies are the very same institutions that were prominent at the end of World War II. Even in the West and Southwest, where a massive demographic change has occurred since 1960, the creation of new privately sponsored cultural institutions has not kept pace with the accumulation of wealth. In research and higher education, with the possible exceptions of Brandeis University and the Salk Institute in La Jolla, there has not been a single competitive, autonomous, major private institution of higher education and research founded in the post–World War II era, even though the resources have been available to do so.

Increasingly, we have turned to preserving the old—from landmark buildings to the landscape we identify as natural, because our conscience about eradicating the past has been awakened. But it has been awakened in part because we doubt ourselves and the future. The regret over the tearing down of Pennsylvania Station in New York City in the 1960s (or the horrendous destruction of old Bucharest by Ceauşescu to create his monstrous palace and boulevards) is justified because shortsighted greed and a lack of respect for the past dominated. But equally strong is the self-doubt that makes this generation unsure that what it creates is good or lasting or even deserves to last. Though it is unpopular to admit it, there is something rather appealing about the brash confidence of a culture that tears down the monuments bequeathed from the past because of an arrogance that the new will be better. That brashness is the moral equivalent of the natural ambition we seek to nurture in children. In today's climate of nostalgia for the past, neither Frank Lloyd Wright's Guggenheim Museum nor Marcel Breuer's Whitney Museum would have been permitted. The collapse of the aesthetic modernism of the mid-twentieth century during the 1970s and the eclectic appropriation in art, music, and architecture of past styles and mannerisms are mirrors of a society with its face turned backward without confidence in the future.

The work of many educators, including Theodore Sizer, Deborah Meier, and countless teachers and principals, and the enormous repository of knowledge about psychology and human development suggest that improvements in education can be made. An optimism about the future, which is natural to children, could be sustained and vindicated.

There is reason to believe that a better school system is a plausible political goal; a reasonable one and not fanciful or utopian.

Categorical denials that something can be done, particularly in politics and culture, cannot carry the prestige of scientific claims, and even scientific claims invite contradiction and replacement. The theories and propositions of science constantly await correction, criticism, and disproof. It is certainly our obligation to try to improve education and culture, a task for which there is no firm basis to consider it implausible. Since we are dealing with children and new generations, we can find reasons for hope. We then might voluntarily hear again that the way we use *hopefully* is wrong and philosophically out of tune, so to speak. If our children hear in our everyday language a willingness to take responsibility for the world they must grow up in by the way we express hope, then the crucial first step in improving our schools and making progress in our daily lives will have been taken.

A final note: The connection between hope and education is not arbitrary. The philosopher Ludwig Wittgenstein observed that hope is not an emotion. In the context of thinking about the differences between animals and humans, he came upon the notion that one really could not describe animals as having the capacity to hope, or express hope. Hope was different from an emotion such as anger or joy. Wittgenstein came to the conclusion that the possession of a language was a precondition for any reasonable capacity to hope. If one were to put that insight in a somewhat different form, one might be inclined to say that if we are to live with any degree of hope, we must first be able to talk and think. In other words, education is a precondition of hope. Without the command of language—and, by inference, thought, ideas, and knowledge—hope disappears or becomes meaningless. Yet, when everything else fails, we are subjected constantly by politicians, religious leaders, and pundits of all types to an appeal to mere "hope."

The consequence of this insight into the nature and meaning of hope is to place education even more into the center as a priority for this country. At stake are not only economic development, social cohesion and stability, and the health of our national consciousness and

political system. Our sense of individual self-worth and the sacred charter of life hang in the balance. Hope for ourselves, our children, and our
world is contingent on education. Survival depends on education, as
does freedom. The time has come to set pessimism aside and create an
educational system in this country adequate to enable future Americans to hope, and with that hope, to take responsibility for themselves
and the well-being of our society and culture.

CHAPTER III

REPLACING THE AMERICAN HIGH SCHOOL

I. EDUCATING AND ADOLESCENCE

The American high school is obsolete. It can no longer fulfill the expectations we legitimately place on it. It offers an inadequate solution to the problem of how best to motivate and educate American adolescents.

This was not always the case, but structures of education do not possess permanent, timeless validity. Unlike the laws of physics, social institutions are functions of history and of specific times and places. Nevertheless, educational arrangements such as the high school, even if they are creations of particular circumstances from the past, can adapt well. They should not be altered too quickly. The illusion that change for its own sake makes things better is often dangerous. Continuity is crucial, and many of our institutions have responded brilliantly over time. Unfortunately, as it turns out, the American high school is not one of them.

Schooling, by definition, must be conservative. It is naturally dependent on an older generation's level of knowledge and sense of values. Educational reformers who construct curricula on the basis of a vision of what in theory may be right for the future can be properly accused of facile arrogance. Their ideas are dependent on prognostication. Schooling for the future means speculation (because one doesn't really know what the future will be like). Reformers who fear the future often make the seductive assumption that inertia will rule the day. The future then becomes a mere extension of the present, just as the present is frequently construed as a mere extension of the past. Those who despise the present invent schemes cloaked in the rhetoric of restoration.

Since they are inherently conservative and rooted in established ideas, all systems of education reflect, even inadvertently, some vision of what ought to be. That vision, too, is rooted in a particular moment in time, in a generation's sense of itself and its values. The vision can take the form of a culture's anxiety about losing crucial habits and ideas. In that case, education becomes explicitly a bulwark against some sort of erosion in values and skills. One of the most powerful systems of education, that formed by the Jesuits, emerged from the Counter-Reformation, when Catholicism, faced with Protestantism, a rival and possible source of defeat, sought to renew itself.

In much of America today, the schools are often expected to cultivate and sustain moral and ethical values. There is considerable ambivalence about this idea. On the one hand, sectarian groups scrutinize teachers, the curriculum, and library holdings for presumably heretical materials. On the other hand, there is a generalized fear, not of religion per se, but of doctrine linked to any particular religious framework. Americans would like to embrace the idea of religion as if it were generic, but in fact religious fervor rarely is. It is narrowly tied to specific doctrine. If merely being Christian were enough, matters would be easy except for Jews, Muslims, and non-Christian Asian Americans. But being Christian does not satisfy everyone.

For all the political exploitation that has taken place over the notion of prayer, trivializing it beyond recognition, the school prayer movement—which appears to be a cynical attack on the deism of Jefferson, modern agnosticism, atheism, and the separation of church and state—is really a symptom of an American tendency to simplify and synthesize irreconcilables. Beneath a thin veneer of allegiance to the secular character of schools, Americans increasingly want the schools to act as if they were religious schools. What they mean by that is indeed not indoctrination, but that schools should teach a sense of right and wrong, humility and thankfulness, which may be applied to everyday life. In our enthusiasm to conserve the values we think are at risk, in the face of the apparent failure of secular authority—the state, the community, the home—many Americans believe that an appeal to the prestige of the divine is the next best thing. The school prayer issue mirrors the hope that schools can be a useful potential weapon against vulgarity and violence. Given this expectation, it should come as no surprise that schools seem to fail most when dealing with adolescents. Elementary schools still succeed in part because children continue to be somewhat shielded from adult life and are treated in America with a sentimental and protective overlay. We still cherish the child as one last metaphor for innocence. But any assumption of residual innocence does not apply to the contemporary adolescent.

But if schooling is to be conservative, it must be clear not only about what it should or might conserve but also about what it realistically can conserve. For example, we transmit through teachers and the curriculum our sense of language, science, and history. In these areas we do not build curricula on the basis of what we speculate or anticipate about the years ahead but on what we believe we know. However, as we are teaching and codifying the world in textbooks, the social and political circumstances in which we educate change continuously. Through schools we cannot entirely insulate the world outside of school from change. For example, in thinking about how our historical circumstances differ crucially from the past, we frequently focus on technology. Going to school before the telephone or the typewriter was invented was clearly a different experience. It may be a trap to try to explain history by linking it to technological change, but at the same time we cannot underestimate the influence of the photocopier machine and most recently the television and the computer, particularly on our habits of memory with regard to ideas and images.

The alterations in the environment surrounding education that exert the most influence on the prospects for learning concern the real circumstances in which people live. Wealth and poverty, social status, family, religion, and health come to mind first. In terms of American adolescents today, the most striking changes are the medical and nutritional advances that have taken place in progressive societies during the twentieth century. These advances are particularly pronounced in the area of child development. A 1992 study of nearly 5,000 adolescent Flemish girls indicated that menstruation now takes place almost a year and a half earlier than was the case during the late 1930s. A drop in the onset of puberty by a year and a half may not seem remarkable, but no parent, much less any former adolescent (which most of us are), can fail to recognize the significance of this change in terms of how we relate chronological age to physical development and to emotional factors, such as the capacity to concentrate and the development of independent interests and self-confidence.

Margaret Reese, writing in the British medical journal *Lancet* in 1993, took the issue of the onset of puberty back into the nineteenth century. In 1840 the average age was sixteen and a half. Historians estimate that the average age of menstruation fell during the later nineteenth century at the rate of about three or four months per decade. Even skeptics of this version of the effects of nutrition and medicine in history concede that the average age for the onset of puberty in the late nineteenth century was substantially higher than it is today. The American high school came into being in its current form at the end of the nineteenth century and the beginning of the twentieth century. It was designed when the average age of menstruation was between fifteen and sixteen. In the late 1990s it has fallen to thirteen. As educator Lawrence Cremin observed, high school became the "dominant mode" of secondary education beginning in 1890. From that point on, high school enrollments doubled each decade. Unlike its continental European counterparts, the American high school was a continuation of a unitary educational system, providing a single avenue of educational advancement. In the past, when maturation occurred later, fewer than half of Americans before 1950 completed more than the ninth grade. Since 1950, that percentage has grown steadily, so that now most Americans go through a system of education designed nearly a century ago for a small percentage of young people whose pattern of maturation was radically different.

The blunt fact is that the American high school was designed for fifteen-to-eighteen-year-olds who were children only beginning their journey to adulthood. It is now filled with young adults of the same age. One does not have to subscribe to a Freudian theory of human development to accept the sharp distinction between the years before and after sexual development. And likewise, one does not need to be a professional psychologist to recognize that the way in which one deals with a prepubescent youngster is quite different from the way in which one deals with one in the early stages of puberty.

The earlier onset of puberty has also changed the relationship between education and late adolescence. Despite all the writing that has been done about the turmoil of the 1960s on college campuses, we still don't fully understand what happened then. One factor behind the enormous generational challenge to authority that erupted was the fact that American undergraduate colleges were dominated by students who were more mature (in physiological terms) than those in previous decades. They were far less amenable to traditional expectations, habits, and regimens of collegiate life established before World War II. Like the G.I.'s who returned to undergraduate life after 1945, the students of the 1960s had difficulty with what they regarded to be the restrictive rules and regulations of universities and colleges. The rebels of the 1960s, like the veterans of battlefields, thought they were being treated like children. But the G.I.'s were a minority in a hurry to get on with life. The more developed modern adolescent constituted a majority without a clear agenda.

The consequences of the acceleration of physiological and biological changes in terms of contemporary adolescent culture have been profound. Sexual activity, particularly among women, begins earlier today than it did a century ago. Earlier maturation, combined with the ease of transportation and the growth of urban and suburban communities, limits the ability of families to control the freedom of movement of young people between the ages of thirteen and eighteen. Consequently, the transition from childhood seems abrupt. No matter when adolescence begins, as parents we find ourselves dealing sooner with incipient adults who are no longer children. Therefore, the gap between the achievement of exterior signs of adulthood and adult habits of behavior seems wider. Not only are we at a loss in terms of basic communication and regulation, we also have not found a means to help adolescents between the ages of thirteen and eighteen to deal with their maturity, intellectually and spiritually. Body and mind seem more out of step with one another in these difficult years of early adolescence than they did in the past, in part because our institutional practices of education do not correspond with the actual course of human development.

In the contemporary consumer culture of America, freedom of movement is associated not only with travel, independence from the home, and control of the use of time but also with shopping and the capacity to exercise individuality and taste through living as a consumer. One of the dimensions of freedom that we properly try to inculcate in our children is a sense of autonomy and responsibility in the use of money. Money is understood as the key fuel of personal independence. Many middle-class parents give allowances to children. Others encourage young people to work part-time in order to earn money, even when such employment is not essential for survival. In many instances, adults let them use that money as they wish. And money is spent by adolescents provocatively. They use it as the self-declaration of independence. Television, Hollywood, and the pop and rock industry are only too happy to embrace the thirteen-to-eighteen-year-old consumer. Clothing manufacturers have set their sights on this age group as well, as suggested by the frequency with which teenage-looking advertising models are used in very adult ways. As young people exercise their sense of separateness from adults through their function as consumers, they inevitably create (or are exploited in the creation of) a distinct adolescent popular culture.

Since the 1950s, popular culture—again partially in response to the earlier onset of adulthood—has celebrated rebellion, anger, and cyni-

cism. Insofar as violence and sexuality in life are presumed to be pre-
rogatives of adulthood, adolescent popular culture has appropriated
them and dispensed with much of our residual framework and rhetoric
of responsibility and accountability. That is why there is so much hypocritical outcry about popular culture. In this context, teachers and parents of high-school-age youngsters are understandably hard-pressed to
keep adolescent Americans at their high school desks in a state of
enthusiasm and relative calm about learning that may have little to do
with consumerism, sex, or violence, and seems blandly affirmative of a
world from which they still feel shut out. Popular culture has filled a
vacuum left by the failure of formal education to capture the imagination of the adolescent. And it thrives on punishing its potentially-
effective rival.

The challenge, therefore, is to find ways to engage the early onset of
adolescence and its attendant freedoms and habits. How can we harness the ages thirteen to eighteen effectively for learning? The irony,
of course, is that all these new realities, which only seem like problems,
are themselves powerful educational opportunities. The very qualities
we deem destructive can be the sources of the motivation to learn. The
juxtaposition of chronological youth and maturation suggests that offering a genuine opportunity for young people to take responsibility for
serious adult learning may work. The capacity to feel like an adult and
move about freely and assume the poses of freedom can inspire discipline and ambition. Sexual maturity ought to be a key to curiosity
about anatomy, physiology, and therefore biology and nature. Too often
the intensity of experience characteristic of young adolescence is dissi-
pated. The infuriating tendency of adolescents to see only the extremes of an issue—black or white—as opposed to ambiguities is itself
a profound motivator. Plato knew this, as the frequency of hotheaded
and stubborn young interlocutors of Socrates in the *Dialogues* makes
plain. The attraction to absolutism and to rigid certainty can force a
young person to search for the new and to overturn tradition and conventional wisdom. Many great poets and mathematicians of the past
were young when they made their first breakthroughs and contribu-

tions. So, too, were the revolutionaries: Robespierre, Saint-Just, Lenin, Trotsky, and Thomas Paine, who formulated their ideologies at remarkably young ages.

The risks and dangers attendant to the way in which this age group formulates its outlook are all too familiar. The fanaticism and solidarity that fueled the Nazi movement were forged in the crucible of adolescence. The failure to challenge the critical faculties of young adolescents can be dangerous. We face that danger today, in part because we have overlooked the fact that, chronologically, these formative years occur one, two, or three years earlier than they did before. What we have traditionally associated with the intellectual awakening during the college years must now occur in the high school. For the older among us, the years of early adolescence may have been unforgettable in a positive sense. In the American system of education they have become totally wasted years.

The consequence of failed high school education is staggering if one considers that since the mid-1960s close to 80 percent of Americans graduate from high school annually, a much higher rate of completion of academic secondary schooling than in other comparable industrial societies. What makes the high rate of secondary school completion possible is the existence of a quite standard and interchangeable basic secondary school format. No matter the local differences, the essential diploma is the same, and access to further schooling after high school beyond local and state boundaries is rendered possible.

At first glance, it might appear that the opening of access to a high school education in America has been achieved at the expense of quality. Before 1945, fewer than half of Americans finished high school. The results of the American system, measured by the accomplishments of high school graduates before access was broadened, were more comparable to the results shown by nations in which access to academic secondary school was limited and still remains restricted. In Europe, for example, the secondary school diploma that assures access to the university is made available to a minority of adolescents.

Many critics of American schools are fond of comparing today's results with those from the past, forgetting that during the first half of
this century only a quite narrow and more privileged part of society
received the chance to finish high school. If one eliminated the lower
third of today's high school graduates—defined not by race or ethnicity,
but by family income—and tested the remainder, American schools
might not look so bad when compared with those of other countries.

The American high school is the unique but logical result of the
democratic ideal of common school. Unlike the other industrial countries to which we are compared, we do not segregate young people in
early adolescence into groupings that are then tracked and placed into
different types of secondary schools. Instead of a common high school,
other countries maintain a variety of parallel options based on interests
and abilities. Some are vocational schools. Even within the secondary
school sector where a subsequent postsecondary education is expected,
there is a division between the humanistic and scientific and technical
curricula. Only a select few of secondary school options in other countries keep the road open to higher education on the university level.
For a German or Japanese child tracked in early adolescence, there is
no turning back or switching tracks.

The question is whether equality in access and excellence in education can be reconciled before the college years. Pessimists and prophets
of America's decline allege that this is a hopeless and impossible goal;
they assert that there will inevitably be an elite and that the educational system should face this fact. Rather than argue about matters we
do not know enough about even to frame the questions properly—such
as whether the ability to learn is inherited, or whether schooling really
can make a difference—we should settle for finding a way to improve
the educational performance of all adolescents.

Let the national concern about education focus on the inadequacy
of what all American adolescents—no matter their differences—emerge
with from school. Universal access to a bad school system that ends in a
useless diploma cannot be a reasonable goal. Precisely because in a
democratic society in which church and state are separate and the pop-

ulation diverse, the capacity to keep the peace, resolve differences, and gain a consensus about right and wrong demands a level of reasoning that makes a high standard of education among all adults imperative. The unsatisfactory and deteriorating character of our politics—particularly the quality of candidates and their campaigns—makes the necessity of a better education for young adults all too clear.

And for the more privileged among us it should be clear that there is no such thing as an elite refuge. Too often those who now decry public education and can afford to send their children to private schools somehow believe that no matter what happens to the rest of the population, the privileged and gifted will manage to do well. In highly stratified aristocratic societies, such as America in the eighteenth century and England and France even more recently, class differences and social status by birth were closely intertwined. One compared oneself with those in one's own class, and one did not think in terms of bridging hierarchical differences. An impoverished nobleman was still a nobleman, and no nouveau riche bourgeois, no matter how liquid in financial terms, could be his equal. Even though American society today is highly unequal in terms of the distribution of wealth, the principle of egalitarianism—of a democratic society in which a one-person, one-vote principle prevails—exerts a significant influence.

The reason American popular culture succeeds so well abroad is that it is designed to adapt to the myth that all people are equal. It has created a leveling aesthetic that is transferable across cultural lines and can pass as an international style. In the context of a commercial mass culture directed particularly at American adolescents, the illusion of solidarity that is encouraged is not one of class but of generations. The population is segmented by age group. The behavior of sixteen-year-olds is influenced by that of other sixteen-year-olds as perceived through popular fashion and trends, rather than by the behavior of those in that age group in one's class or older or younger members of one's own social grouping. In terms of educational performance, this translates into a powerful dynamic within the high school. The best are influenced by the weakest. Insofar as popular culture is directed away from the ethos of learning, it influences the motivations of those with potential in the same age bracket. In the case of literacy, the problems with writing and reasoning in the adolescent age group are spread uniformly throughout the spectrum of income levels, from urban areas to suburbia. The population within an age spectrum moves and acts as a group. No adolescent is immune from the failures of American schooling, since the attraction to a perceived peer culture is so pervasive. The parents of the most privileged and successful adolescent students, in their own self-interest, should be most concerned about how the weakest adolescent students in the schools perform. These students help to set the standards.

Although wealth determines where one lives and therefore one's school district and high school (or, alternatively, which private school one can attend), all Americans, rich or poor, attend much the same kind of high school. Whether private, parochial, or public, American high schools are more alike than they are different. They are broad-based academic institutions offering a diverse curriculum leading to a diploma that theoretically enables its holders to go on to college. The high school's program of instruction is more general than it is specialized. It also represents the last and most important phase of training for citizenship. High schools support student governments, extracurricular activities, and, above all, sports. In American popular culture, sports has assumed a legendary status as something everyone can relate to.

Owing to the uniformity in this educational structure, a much higher percentage of adolescents than elsewhere in the industrial world graduate from secondary school and go on to some form of college. Unfortunately, the fact that we give out more diplomas has not ensured higher levels of competence. The inadequacies of high school and the resultant devaluation of its diploma have only deepened the role of high school as merely a transitional phase in education. It is no longer an end point. In better high schools, an inordinate amount of time and psychological energy are spent on thinking about college, applying to college, and preparing for it. High school is increasingly seen as a way station to the next stage: a two-year community college, a four-year state college, state university, or private college or university.

American adolescence, therefore, seems to end in a bonanza: higher education. The consequence, however, is that until college, the previous phases of schooling are seen, teleologically, more in terms of where they lead than in terms of what they accomplish. The responsibility for learning is passed on by each part of the chain in our educational system to the next like a burning fuse. It explodes in the college years, when remedial work is confronted (or not, as the case may be) and students struggle to make up for lost time. The sad fact is that the age of eighteen is too old to start a serious education, particularly in science and mathematics. Curiosity and the love of reading in particular need to be nurtured well before the first year of college.

Instead of worrying about grade inflation, we ought to be worrying about degree inflation. The comparisons between our adolescents and those in other industrial countries cannot be limited to secondary schools, since in the United States we keep more young people in school for longer. Even though we keep them in school beyond high school, the results are poorer. At a more advanced age, our students can barely do what their foreign counterparts did two to four years earlier. By delaying serious learning, we shut out more people from education than do the so-called nondemocratic systems of other nations. We give out more diplomas to more people who spend more time in school but who have less to show for it in the end.

This may be outrageous, but it is true. About 20 percent of the population never finish high school and have truly little to show for the ten, eleven, or twelve years of compulsory schooling. Most of these are from the lowest economic stratum. For them, ironically, schooling might have provided the greatest added value to their lives. Another 30 percent of the population finishes high school but does not go on to college. They are slightly better off, if only because of the high school credential. But as the surveys show, their skills and knowledge base do not seem to justify the time spent in school. Furthermore, the high school diploma has been so denigrated that its value is dubious as a terminal degree. Of the remaining 50 percent, at best only half of those ever finish four years of college. For the majority of those who go on to some kind of college, what they learn might as well have been gotten in high school. At age twenty they demonstrate levels of achievement that they could have shown at eighteen and even sixteen. America has a more elaborate educational system that spreads over more years, reaches more people, and ends up with results *for the entire population* that are worse than those countries with educational systems that are explicitly not democratic and on the surface offer fewer opportunities for advanced education. The final irony is that the country where the so-called elite receive the best educational opportunity is the United States, because its university system, at its highest level, is designed to accommodate and encourage the gifted, ambitious individual. Yet we prepare students for higher education less effectively than nations with weaker systems of university education. In the name of fairness, equal access, and democracy, we end up defrauding the majority of the citizens. The high school fails everyone. The current system, with its consequences, is a living satire on the idea of democracy in education.

II. THE FAILURE OF HIGH SCHOOLS

The abolition of high school is a radical proposal. Sensible observers of educational reform movements have noted that such sweeping school reform proposals always seem to be doomed to failure. For the most part they are, because too often they are political in the most narrow sense. They mirror a wish list of what groups or individuals seek to impose in the name of one or another ideology. In the United States they reflect real disagreements frequently rooted in religious conflict. But there have been pivotal moments in the past when schools have changed fundamentally. Reforms have worked and have become part of the accepted traditions of schooling because the reforms met real, concrete needs. The Depression in the 1930s was the most recent case in point. Schools and colleges had to adjust to what was clearly a national and international economic and social crisis. In that decade, educators Robert M. Hutchins at the University of Chicago and Stringfellow Barr at St. John's called for reforms that sought to engage young people better so as to inculcate in them democratic values. The rage for John Dewey in the opposing camp of progressive educators during the 1930s was in part a function of the anxiety that Americans, like their European counterparts, might become attracted to either fascism or communism and abandon democracy. Although we may continue to blame (wrongly) educational progressives and bemoan what happened to the progressive legacy during the sixties, no one can dispute that the coming of age of the baby boomers and the huge explosion in college enrollments, combined with the rapid increase in the percentage of young people staying in school through the end of high school, constituted real and not fictitious social and demographic changes. And they have had palpable cultural consequences, which we have failed to address.

Therefore, although education may be inherently conservative, it cannot fly in the face of facts. The high schools are failing not because teachers are bad or kids are bad. No amount of testing or mere imposition of national standards will make the difference. High schools are not failing because we have neglected to hold true to past traditions, and therefore if we just turned back the clock, they would be fixed. As the defenders of our schools correctly observe, given the momentous changes, it is remarkable how good our school system has proved itself to be. But the high schools are clearly not doing the job they need to do, and the reasons have very little to do with politics.

As the history of science teaches, the models we use in our thinking periodically have to be challenged. When we shift the "paradigm" we use, complex problems that seemed insoluble paradoxes turn out to have simple solutions. It is alleged that a sign once hung over one New York University laboratory that read: "Another beautiful hypothesis ruined by a simple fact." The beautiful hypothesis we maintain in our minds is the image of the wholesome, well-run, and successful American high school of yesteryear with its students graduating at the age of eighteen, bright-eyed and eager, ready for college, ready to play by the rules, virginal, physically fit, respectful of parents, and neatly dressed. The simple fact that has ruined this mental picture is the massive change in human development and adolescent culture in modern America. Our high schools have problems not only with intellectual achievement and test scores but with attendance and basic decorum. They are, more frequently than we care to think, breeding grounds for violence, for drug and alcohol abuse, vulgarity, and a totally thought-less, rampant expression of sexuality.

The high school is not the only institution to find itself at a loss in the face of these social and biological changes. Their consequences have taken their toll on colleges as well. Twenty years ago, in 1976, Harvard University changed its undergraduate curriculum for the first time in nearly thirty years. It sought to reinstitute general education in an effort to provide the kind of basic grounding that one might have expected by students before 1976. A representative of the university was quoted at a 1976 conference of high school and college educators as saying that Harvard was not overly concerned about the quality of high schools. After all, once students came to Harvard, the university would take care of everything. It would fill in the gaps. This turned out to be wrong. No doubt, after the 1960s, as Stanford and other universities discovered, there was a need to reconsider the general education re-quirements that had been abandoned or were no longer working. But the mere reimposition in the 1990s of general education requirements on today's college students—similar to those classic courses David Denby recently revisited at Columbia University in New York—will not work the same way. Simply put, first-year college students are not in the same place their predecessors were three generations ago. If one seeks to create a core curriculum, one has to structure it differently for no other reason than that today's first-year college students have lived the external appearances of an adult life for many more years than their counterparts fifty years ago did and have wasted their early adolescent years in a failing high school system. Insofar as the reigning nostalgic image of undergraduate college life is rooted in the experiences of our grandparents, it should be recalled that on American campuses the presumption of adulthood from the vantage point of faculty and administrators during the 1930s was less pronounced than it is today.

Ironically, Oxford and Cambridge, key prototypes for the ideal of the American college, in their dealings with students, place the emphasis on aristocratic birth and breeding and not on chronological age. They have sustained over the years a more stable sense of equality between adults and college students. There the key to equity and respect is social class and high selectivity. Aristocrats treat one another well, regardless of age. At Oxford and Cambridge a gracious camaraderie was cultivated that underscored an intergenerational tradition of respect within an elite. No doubt this respect also went both ways. Students approached adults with deference. American youth, in contrast, prided itself on an attractive and fearless brashness all its own. This tolerance of youthful initiative has been the key to much innovation in science, industry, and business in America. On the other hand, since in democratic societies there is no classic, traditional aristocracy, in its place, age has loomed far more important than we realize as a characteristic by which we separate ourselves from one another. We treat the young with the contempt the British aristocrat reserves for his social inferiors. With the possible exception of our pseudo-aristocratic and pseudo-British Ivy League–style institutions, by comparison to our British counterparts we accord less respect to students and assert the authority of adults more readily in American colleges and universities. This was certainly true before 1960. In part this is a consequence of the imprint of the German university model on American universities, which was quite influential at the turn of the century. In the German university, itself a state institution, the authority of a single senior professor had a kind of dictatorial character to it and set a tone of institutional command toward junior faculty colleagues and students alike.

Today, entering first-year college students, like their counterparts in high school, have naturally outgrown the historic expectations of years gone by. Harvard's conceit of twenty years ago turns out to be misplaced. The presumption of adulthood among entering college students is now overwhelmingly dominant (which is why Brown University, with its laissez-faire spirit and near absence of common curricular requirements, has remained so attractive to many of the best high school graduates). Furthermore, the deficiencies in education created before college cannot be compensated for during college. We cannot wait. The plain truth is that if a young person comes to college at age eighteen without a serious love of reading, without a reasonable comfort level with mathematics, and without a basic concept of science or history, it is usually too late to fix all this. Most important, sloppy habits in terms of concentration and memory are not as easy to correct in an eighteen-year-old as they were fifty years ago.

The younger one is, the easier it is to correct or adjust ways one has learned to do something. Young children often learn a skill—to play a sport (for example, tennis) or an instrument (for example, violin)—with incomplete or deficient technique and form. They have a better chance of correcting what they are doing wrong if retraining is done earlier rather than later. Many aspiring adult tennis players have had the depressing experience of having gone to tennis camp repeatedly to learn how to serve or use the backhand properly, only to discover after returning from their intense retraining experience that they fall back on the bad habits they learned early on. A young person will assimilate a new way of doing something quickly. Moreover, that same person will not require as much repetition to make a new lesson stick, even when it replaces an old way of doing things. The young person will not forget as easily. The pliability, in intellectual terms, of the thinking and learning of entering first-year students today is somewhat lower than it was fifty years ago for the very same cultural and biological reasons that high schools are now failing. The old core courses—general education and the sort of basic training and orientation we associate with the college of yesteryear—are therefore much more appropriate for high-school-age youngsters now in eleventh and twelfth grade. This is the moral of the educational story in late-twentieth-century America. Colleges are no longer able to pick up the pieces of what is broken or left unfinished during the high school years. And because of the clash between the high school and maturity, the last two years of high school, particularly the senior year, are a waste of time.

For those who still cling to the myth of declining standards, all this may seem oddly counterintuitive. We have become very accustomed to thinking that the solution to the low quality of an American high school education is to reinstitute yesterday's standards. The call for the imposition of national standards is now *en vogue*. There is little doubt that higher expectations and some degree of uniformity with respect to basic learning are good ideas. However, the shortcomings of our educational system cannot be explained by the absence of national standards or the failure to test knowledge of essential subject matter. New York State, which has had a tradition of Regents examinations, is no more successful with its high schools than states that have no sensible uniform standards. The problems we face have as much to do with motivation and linking learning to life in age-appropriate ways as with defining the proper tests and standards.

We need to change our basic expectations entirely. The first step is to reinvent grades six through ten. Schooling during these years can be more effective and efficient so that the basic education which is now poorly delivered over a longer time span is accomplished at least two years earlier. The second step is to offer fifteen- and sixteen-year-olds educational alternatives appropriate to their maturity.

The only way to solve the paradox that our eighteen-year-olds know too little despite twelve years of schooling is to create a flexible system with new options that meets the realities facing us. We now place adolescents in a system that simply won't fit. To put it plainly but graphically, we don't bury our dead in coffins built in the sixteenth century, because they would be too short. And when today's churchgoers and opera lovers sit in a restored but unrenovated sanctuary or opera house built before 1850, they often find the legroom excruciatingly small. We generally do not travel, except for pleasure, by horse and buggy or by sailboat. And we certainly shouldn't think of educating our children with curricula, a school day, teachers, and buildings that are as obsolete and useless to the way we are today as old coffins and sail-boats.

Setting aside the question of when puberty occurs, in thinking about high school we need to confront the character of adolescence today, no matter at what age it usually occurs. In terms of what and how they learn, what are the opportunities and challenges presented by young people? Anthropologists and psychologists understand the many ways different cultures and societies deal with adolescence. Fashions change, but certain key insights remain. Rites of passage occur across cultural and historical boundaries. They are social celebrations that mark the transition from child to adult. Some cultures seek to suppress any semblance of a transition period. They prefer to assume that at puberty, adulthood begins immediately. But since the nineteenth century, particularly in middle-class American life, the idea of a special time of life in between childhood and adulthood has become firmly established. However, this does not diminish the usefulness of rites of passage that mark the end of childhood. Religions have understood this best. Confirmation and bar or bat mitzvah, for example, signal to the young person that he or she is now welcome into the body faithful as an equal. While civil and criminal law may not hold the individual under sixteen or eighteen totally responsible, in Christianity and Judaism an individual over the age of thirteen has already taken his or her place as a responsible adult equal to older members in the eyes of God.

Since we embrace the notion of adolescence as a mere transition, we run the risk of not taking the adolescent seriously enough and making him or her feel peripheral. On the one hand, we realize, correctly, that the adolescent is not fully an adult. On the other hand, the adolescent loses the protections and benefits of innocence accorded to childhood. And we are caught in a trap, unwilling to trust adolescents as adults and no longer able to treat them as children. Many young people between the ages of thirteen and eighteen develop the sense of being neither fish nor fowl, so to speak. This easily breeds resentment and insecurity in the relationships between children and adults. That, in turn, can fuel arrogance. Even though we encourage a certain amount of experimentation and try to convince adolescents that they, unlike "real" adults, can take risks and sample many aspects of adult life without having to be committed to them, they are rarely satisfied. And adults themselves are understandably profoundly ambivalent about the notion of adolescence as a transitional period of experimentation. Adults resent the ease with which adolescents display authority without responsibility, particularly in the arena of sexual activity. There is a definite but sometimes indistinct line between encouraging a young person to try this or that sport, or this or that activity (with a full understanding that there are risks for failure involved but also unique opportunities for retreat), and at the same time categorically forbidding experimentation with drugs, sex, and alcohol. Adolescents have a hard time understanding (as do adults) why some things must be accepted on faith (such as not taking drugs) and others not. How do we explain that it is good and reasonable to "find out for yourself," learn by trial and error, and test accepted norms in some cases but not in others? Cultivating the faculty of judgment without incurring too much risk of harm is the key challenge in dealing with adolescents. Voluntary restraint in the use of freedom is a difficult habit to nurture.

The experimentation by young adults with dangerous and alluring activities is not a new phenomenon. Embedded in our cultural myth of adulthood is the legend of each individual's successful journey through temptation. We still subscribe to the archetype best set forth by Homer in the *Odyssey*, in which the hero, Odysseus, passes through unimaginable tests and dangers to arrive at domestic and marital tranquillity. In contemporary America we have ritualized the access to the most dangerous activities, particularly alcohol, drugs, and sex. It is nonsensical to assume that these activities can be forbidden entirely and effectively, but it is equally wrong to believe that one can leave to chance the probabilities of a successful passage through the rites of encounter with these activities. The key will always be the development of countervailing and competing motivations. A young person is likely to handle the availability of alcohol, drugs, and sex in a reasonable manner if there is something in his or her life at stake—such as an intense, sustained engagement with an activity (music, sports, dance, laboratory science, art, artisan skills, etc.)—that competes successfully with those three pursuits, each of which has the attraction of immediate gratification and the inherent flaw of not being in the end a sufficient reason all by itself for continuing to struggle with life.

It is no surprise that frustration is perhaps the most recognizable dimension of adolescence, after one sets aside the endemic insecurity and awkwardness that all adolescents possess. Puberty, no matter when it occurs, doesn't help. For men in particular, it is the age of greatest sexual readiness and capacity. As Freud recognized, that process occurs at a time when the satisfaction of the sexual urge is least condoned and most suppressed by external society. On all fronts, adolescents find themselves betwixt and between, unable to move autonomously and act independently. Unfortunately, the high school in its current configuration solves this problem by resorting to the mere imposition of discipline in a school day marked by routine. Even the flow of traffic and the schedules are overregulated. Attempts to inspire the student are abandoned out of necessity so that high schools can maintain holding patterns.

Adolescents have an uncanny second sense about adult hypocrisy and lack of candor. The truth is, adults do not hold teenagers, despite their sexual maturity, as accountable for their behavior as they do older people. Teenagers know it and exploit this weakness. We must find ways of teaching adolescents to make constructive use of this unique time period in their lives and enjoy the assumption of responsibility. In the classroom that means treating adolescents as young as thirteen and fourteen more the way we do college students and adults and less as children. What is implied by the college model is not lecture hall practices but the seminar class with the intense engagement of students taught by teachers who are highly trained in their disciplines. The curriculum, the teaching materials, and the manner of teaching must be serious, significant, and committed. This does not mean imitating the frequent inattention to teaching many universities and colleges thrive on; neither does it mean the proverbial "throwing the book" at students in terms of the sink-or-swim approach we often encounter at colleges and universities. One must remember that, unlike a seasoned adult (although we, too, often overrate adulthood, especially its stability and virtues), the adolescent is especially ill equipped to tolerate frustration and failure. No one likes criticism—adolescents least of all. Despite this evident fact, adults and parents preach endlessly about virtues they themselves do not possess. Among these are precisely the ability to take criticism and to accept the success of others with grace and good humor. Since we find this difficult, it should come as no surprise that adolescents find it impossible. As we raise our expectations of adolescents in terms of learning, we need to do so with care.

A school for adolescents, therefore, has to sustain the interest and energy of teenagers, even when they find learning complex, obscure, or without any visible, immediate reward or source of satisfaction. One simply cannot expect a young adult to learn without careful assistance. One key component is that teaching teenagers requires a regular and rapid feedback and response. This is why the presence of older adults—teachers, siblings, and relatives—is so crucial to adolescents. Class size for teenagers, for example, must be *smaller*, not larger, than in elementary school. We tolerate altogether too much of a group mentality in today's high schools, which is fostered by the regimentation of the day and year designed to contain crowds, not inspire individuals. The beloved camp counselor, the gifted high school teacher, the favorite grandparent, aunt, or uncle—all nonparental adults who can have a profound influence on a young person—are individuals who can project the delicate and appropriate balance between adult expectations and a sincere respect and tolerance usually reserved for small children. The ideal teacher of an adolescent is a kind of centaur—not, as in mythology, part man and part beast, but a cross between adult and child. That individual is willing to spend time with young people to sustain the sense of individuality and uniqueness naturally found in children but often discouraged and suppressed. These gifted teachers can show adolescents how to be the kind of adults that perhaps even the gifted teacher is not. The image of the centaur as teacher dates from classical Greek mythology in the figure of Chiron, the tutor of Achilles and Jason. A more recent example is John Updike's novel *The Centaur*, a thinly veiled account of the author's own father, a teacher.

Many of the best teachers and counselors of teenagers themselves are far less appealing to adults than to teenagers. They seem strangely less adult to those who have spent their grown-up years exclusively with people over the age of twenty-one. This is not meant to diminish those who are good at dealing with young people. To the contrary, insofar as adults retain part of the eccentric and unpredictably imaginary aspects of childhood, so much the better for all of us. Adulthood should not be defined in a narrow and utilitarian fashion. There is truth in the recent wonderful children's book by Chris van Allsburg entitled *The Polar Express*, in which only children hear the magic of a small bell from the North Pole. Allsburg captures the irretrievable loss that growing up represents. There are few adults who have not felt resentment at the price we pay for growing up. Therefore, it should come as no surprise that adults often transfer this resentment onto children. We should remember our desire not to lose aspects of childhood. And we certainly ought not treat adolescents with a sublimated vengeance or a camouflaged envy of the fact that they are young, energetic, and idealistic and possess the natural advantages of youth. We should capitalize on the fact that adolescents have a unique capacity to learn to love learning for its own sake.

Among the most penetrating observations about adolescence made in recent years are those of the University of Chicago psychologist Mihaly Csikszentmihalyi. In two separate books published between 1984 and 1990, he demonstrated that instead of creating schools that offer a diet of criticism and negative feedback designed all too explicitly to steer young people away from behavior we fear and consider "bad," we need to create schools that establish plausible models and ideals of desirable and good behavior. As Csikszentmihalyi argues, we need to have schools for adolescents that "seduce" them into learning and acting in ways that are helpful and constructive. The curriculum and culture of high schools for teenagers should be defined not by the avoidance and fear of evil alternatives—ignorance and disorder—but by a vision of the pleasure of knowledge and accomplishment.

At its best, this idea has been the optimistic note sounded since the early eighteenth century in the best of American colleges. College, after all, has always been voluntary, not compulsory. It has been viewed traditionally by its best students as a privilege and not as either an entitlement or a chore. It has been associated with an individual's sense of becoming powerful in the world and establishing oneself, and has therefore been synonymous with acting individually and independently. Perhaps that is why marriage used to take place so frequently right after graduation from college. No doubt colleges often fail in delivering on these worthy sentiments. But in their fundamental design, curriculum, and teaching patterns they are by definition better suited to do well by adolescents in the middle years than the high school is. The virtues, once associated with the college years from eighteen to twenty-one, must be made part of the school experience of young people between fifteen and eighteen.

One objection to this position may be that today's high schools seem to work for the best students, those who do well in them. There will always be teenagers who are extremely motivated, who learn easily and with enthusiasm. But these young people remain culturally and statistically a small elite. In the bell-shaped curve, they are at the upper end and not part of the bulge in the middle. And even though they are at the upper end, perhaps our expectations of the best are too low, just as our minimum standards are too low, which in turn makes the definition of the average also too low. Furthermore, if one thinks counterintuitively, one might speculate that this segment of the population will do well no matter what—no matter how poor the schools are. When we wax nostalgic, for example, about the great high schools of yesterday in New York City—Midwood High, Erasmus High, Jamaica High—we ought to give proper credit to external factors: ambitious immigrant families, economic necessity, anticipation of upward social mobility, and the persistence of old-world, premodern values that were relatively insulated from the influences that we now identify with contemporary popular life and culture.

The failure of American high schools may retard the progress of the best students. But the greatest damage is wreaked upon the average and lower-than-average student. They are the most impressionable and most easily influenced by their surroundings. In the so-called good old days, perhaps some were carried along by the best. But back then they dropped out well before graduation. Today they stay in school but are bored. They can't concentrate. They gaze out of the window, dreaming about doing something else. They can't sit still. And they cannot divert the enormous energy they possess into something that makes them feel better about themselves. All this holds true for too many so-called gifted underachieving adolescents. The activities adolescents like to do and can do are understandably those that require no training or study and that easily provide quick and instant satisfactions. Hanging out, engaging in sex, shopping, eating, watching TV, and driving around demand no extensive preparation. However, they possess few lasting benefits. Consumerism and sexual encounters—enjoyable as these are—are transitory (except for the extreme potential consequences of bankruptcy and pregnancy). Isolated from a larger sense of well-being and purpose, these activities fail to sustain in the adolescent a positive sense of self over a long period of time.

These pursuits cannot be considered independent of the political world in which young people mature. The motivation to learn is related to some view about how an individual might take his or her place in the world. Unfortunately, we live at a time when there is very little confidence in government and an extreme loss of faith in politics. A sense of powerlessness is commonplace, not only among adolescents but among adults as well. Insofar as doing well in school is a way of declaring an allegiance to the world one is entering, any lack of confidence in the legitimacy of that world will erode the motivation to learn. As children become adults, they think for themselves but in imitative patterns. They observe adult cynicism and mistrust. Since they do not have the experience or the habit of differentiating between the shades of emotions and attitudes, they assume the mantle of opposition they already detect in adult behavior. The reason to change our schools radically, particularly for adolescents, is that by doing so we might begin to get back on the road of restoring our public institutions. What better place to start than with those that serve the young adult.

This leads us to an equally paradoxical observation. We sometimes lament the loss of the work ethic among the young. We express concern that the so-called American dream no longer works its charm. Is it that our young people do not seek economic security and domestic happiness? From the perspective of politics, consider why societies in which the majority of individuals live in relative prosperity and peace, marry, have children and families, and possess jobs still harbor significant dimensions of rage, envy, resentment, and disappointment seemingly out of proportion with their good fortunes. Why do their lives possess so little meaning for them? Alternatively, why would people not put aside apparent differences in order to work together to create a more stable world in which peace and quiet, family life, and a higher standard of living could be sustained? These apparent paradoxes seem even more inscrutable when one considers how difficult it is for people, particularly in the United States, to debate issues and through that debate alter their own views and those of others. In our search for meaning and identity, we seem to lurch toward hardened and simplified allegiances. The result is an unsettling mixture of rigidity, an absence of communication, and dissatisfaction. Outside of the United States these patterns can help to illuminate the widespread active and passive participation in the irrational and destructive collapse of civility in the former Yugoslavia, the endless strife in Northern Ireland, and the failure to achieve peace in the Middle East.

The education of adolescents can play a crucial role in overcoming such obstacles to developing a more civilized and tolerant world. For the teenager, being able to build something, to play a sport well, to show command of an activity that requires planning, concentration, and sustained discipline that carries with it has some kind of opportunity for public recognition offers more prospects for the building of adult self-confidence and lasting happiness than the activities to which many teenagers are now condemned in part by inadequate schooling. It is regrettable that despite the evident advantages of the computer, it signals an unfortunate but inevitable trend—namely, an excessive dependency on a technological device we do not command entirely or truly understand. Nostalgia indeed might be warranted when we look back at a time when many youngsters could build their own version of the latest gadgets: shortwave radios and audio equipment. Technology today has exceeded the grasp of the individual to come to terms with its mechanisms, making even its most enthusiastic users inescapably dependent and even addicted to what they cherish. Desktop publishing is a great tool, but most of us in school fail to comprehend fully the implements of contemporary information technology. One can adapt a computer system by putting together disparate components, and young people can program their own software, but those possibilities still do not bridge the gap between the raw elements of ordinary existence and the almost magical properties of modern technology. A young person today, by tinkering mechanically, can no longer easily get to the bottom of how and why something complicated works. No person can build a microchip at home. This makes the need for a higher level of theoretical science and mathematics education in adolescence imperative.

Marxist critics of an older sort may wish to attack the objectives of schooling as being dangerously allied to a work ethic that idealizes living by the clock and behaving dutifully as wage earners, an ethic that encourages senseless activity structured to enhance the profit of a very few in the owning class. No doubt there is less concern about the growing gap between rich and poor in America than one might wish. But the critique of schooling as an instrument of so-called socialization to capitalism is all too simple, particularly in an America where factories and industrial labor of the old sort are vanishing before our eyes. In some utopian world, perhaps work can be rendered unnecessary. These critics may be onto something in our culture, but whatever may be wrong with our values, it does not result from schooling. Critics of the status quo are responding to the fact that in the wake of the collapse of the nineteenth-century ideologies of socialism, there is a vacuum of idealism and belief, filled in the United States only by the model of the market, competition, and the bottom line.

Political ideology aside, insofar as having a job and feeling useful and productive remain crucial parts of the way we define ourselves, education will play a greater, not lesser, role in a world with fewer artisans and good blue-collar jobs and more employment opportunities contingent upon learning and skills. In addition, how we spend time away from work is increasingly important. Americans today realize that their sense of themselves and of their happiness is as dependent on how they spend their leisure as it is on how they spend their work life. Shopping and sitting passively in front of a television set are not, by anyone's standards, enough of a foundation for long-term adulthood characterized by a sense of well-being and pride, particularly in a free society.

III. THE SOCIAL RESPONSIBILITY OF HIGH SCHOOLS

In terms of what we want young people to learn, we must provide American adolescents with a school system that encourages ambition, idealism, concentration, and self-discipline. Our greatest success has been in the area of high school sports—but only with varsity athletes. In an age of so-called political correctness, it is truly ironic that it has become acceptable to lash out against "elitism" in our schools when teachers and administrators seek to single out the "gifted and talented" in classrooms. Setting aside for a moment the question of whether such tracking or segmenting is a good strategy for teaching our most talented pupils, we as a society seem to have no quarrel with the nearly exclusive allotment of public money and time to a very few highly select athletes who compete in high school varsity sports. High school students do not benefit equally from the investment in sports; the best qualified get more of their share. Perhaps this is as it should be. But then we need to adopt the same principles and standards with respect to intellectual excellence and prowess as those that apply to athletic excellence and prowess in our high schools.

The goals of high school sports—winning in the public arena and gaining the approbation of peers—are clear. The existence of these clear goals allows standards to fall easily into place. One has to beat out the competition. One must learn to play by rules understood as objective. If the opponents move the ball around better, make fewer errors, and catch more passes, the home team must respond by working harder. In this context, the authority of the coach seems easier to justify than the authority of the teacher in the classroom. The training regimen appears self-evident. It is clearly tied to the results it provides. The more physically fit the team is, the better it can compete. The more time spent practicing a single shot, the higher the chances of getting it in.

Integral to the process of sports training is regular feedback. Coaches are constantly cajoling, shouting, yelling, and praising. They both criticize and extol, "telling it as it is" and lending confidence to raise morale. Each individual on a team knows when he or she is or is not pulling his or her weight. Coaches react to what each young person is doing. Why can't our classrooms work the same way teams on playing fields or youth orchestras do? The motivation and pride visible in well-run youth music programs are directly comparable in technique and atmosphere to our best high school sports programs.

Csikszentmihalyi has documented the extent to which adolescents experience a "high" that comes from sustained involvement in sports. He has called this a "flow" experience. Runners identify a phenomenon they call "breaking through a wall." What these terms describe is what many adolescents feel when they work hard at something in a focused manner, particularly on the playing field. In the circumstances created by musical ensembles, theater, dance, and sports, despite the team effort, the young person feels extraordinary control over his or her actions. Even though individuals must adjust to the group, the paradox-ical result of sports training, team participation, and membership in a troupe or ensemble is the development of a greater sense of oneself.

Crucial to the power of the "flow" experience is the transformation in a young person's perception of time—the sense of how time can be used and spent. For example, for athletes there is an acute awareness that every second counts. The shot clock and the five- and two-minute warnings in many of our sports point to the significance of otherwise small units of time: a game can be won in seconds. That lesson is also critical in life. Obviously, for physicians and airline pilots the same small units of time can mean the difference between life and death. But even in ordinary existence, many crucial and intense experiences with lasting impact have short duration. When we remember key mo-ments, including conversations, sight-seeing, great lines from a speech, images from television programs, favorite moments in a film or a piece of music, it is astonishing to discover how short their objective duration is when measured by a stopwatch in ordinary units of seconds and minutes. Listening and reading can offer the same magical intensity: the sensation that ordinary time has vanished painlessly.

The routine daily experience in high school is an object lesson in the exact opposite. Young people learn how excruciatingly slowly time passes. Yet they are at an age when they can and should spend time without any sense of boredom or irritation. When you enjoy doing something, you lose the sense of time as measured by the clock. Many parents will recognize the frustration of trying to pry an adolescent away from doing something enjoyable because dinner is being served or a chore has to be accomplished. When parents complain that adoles-cents aren't listening, they may be overlooking a positive fact: young people may be so much in a world of their own that they do not notice what is going on around them or how much time has elapsed. This can be all to the good. Daydreaming and wonderment are essential compo-nents of the process of imaginative discovery and invention. The trou-ble is that this happens so rarely. Our image of adolescence is therefore dominated by the idea that they have too much time on their hands with nothing to do or to engage them.

The detachment from the rhythm of time in the ordinary sense—the experience we associate with successful training for sports or playing a musical instrument—can be transferred to the activities of the mind. Reading is the most familiar example. A child who learns to read loses contact with the clock. That child begins to live in the time frame and the imaginary world that fiction creates. That child easily turns into the adult who loves to read. Unlike television, reading requires the active use of the imagination. Neurological measurements show that the only time the brain is more active than when we read is when we dream. Reading generates electricity, as it were, in the mind, inspiring the desire to write and command language in one's own way.

The crucial link between the activity of the mind that reading can stimulate and the conduct of our ordinary lives—particularly for adolescents—is the faculty of memory. Adolescents not only learn more quickly and adapt new patterns of behavior more quickly than adults, but they remember more easily and readily retain in their minds what they learn. Strengthening the capacity for memory can be a useful objective of adolescent education. Traditionalist educators claim that memorization took an unfair beating from progressive educators first in the 1930s and then in the 1960s. Rote learning became a pejorative term: a code word for bad teaching. Memorization requires the individual to hold and keep in the mind language and information independent of any reference materials, whether they are books or photocopies. The problem is how to make memorization seem natural and necessary. Actors in high school plays do not resist having to memorize their lines. Young musicians memorize with ease. When they are doing so, they are programming their memory banks. The brain has a more complex and profound capacity than computer disks. The more of the brain we format in different ways, the more we can retain. And the best time to format the brain is during adolescence, because during those years the capacity for thought can be enlarged and deepened.

The consequences can be astonishing. My grandfather survived the Warsaw Ghetto and a Nazi labor camp. One of the things I remember most vividly from his account of his wartime experiences was how he managed to survive psychologically. Surrounded by death, isolated, hungry, and terrified, he was still able to focus his mind. His capacity to do so was not a function of his being "smart." Without books, a radio, a phonograph, pictures, or writing implements, he was able to hear music in his head, recite poetry, and remember ideas and details he had read and think about them. He was able to travel beyond the oppressive world in which he was trapped. He could contemplate the possibility of life despite the fact that the world he knew was threatened by destruction. He had studied foreign languages in secondary school. He had memorized long stretches of prose in more than one language as part of his old-fashioned European *Gymnasium* secondary education. Slowly, all that came back to him. The cultivation of his capacity to learn things by heart during the years of adolescence had allowed him over the years to absorb long pieces of writing, music, and theater. Imprisoned, abandoned, and helpless, he reached into his memory and reconstructed a new world in his mind over days, weeks, and months. The stuff of book learning and of a school education fueled his imagination. It provided him with a way to sustain a will to live. His imaginary mental life became an antidote to the systematic elimination of all the ordinary things to which, in normal life, he had become accustomed: that which we crave and define as the goals of life. He had been wealthy but was now penniless. He had been prominent and respected but had lost his employment and station in life. He had been part of a community and a large family, most of whom were killed. Yet he constructed a thread of hope when there was no longer reason to imagine any future at all. Many survivors from more recent examples of traumatic and unjustified incarceration, including American hostage Terry Anderson, recount similar experiences.

We ought not educate adolescents in anticipation that they need to survive the worst, particularly the unimaginable horror that befell past generations. Rather, we must show how boredom and unhappiness in ordinary life can be diminished, circumvented, and overcome by the use of our mental faculties. The use of faculties is not contingent on some extraordinary talent. And what we absorb and use later is best cultivated during adolescence. It is at the midpoint between childhood and adulthood that serious things can be learned and remembered for life. Our high schools must find a way to do so.

A good school for adolescents, therefore, must engage the attention of every young person. It must build self-confidence. Insecurity is endemic to this age group. The goals of schools from the point of view of students must be clear. The rewards must be regular and constant. As in sports, rewards are an integral part of criticism and the achievement of high standards. Often we use grades punitively and create a false exclusivity about high grades. Despite the pervasive rhetoric of fairness, students frequently perceive grading as an indication of mere favoritism by teachers. We stress the difficulty of the achievement of grades and emphasize results on standardized test scores, as in the SAT, as opposed to the evidence of learning retained by a young person, which he or she can generate spontaneously on a blank piece of paper. The proliferation of high school advanced placement courses designed to raise standards of learning has not worked to offset this pattern, since the AP courses are explicitly test-driven and overtly designed for specific and intellectually inadequate standardized examinations. Competition over test scores and grades and high-minded reticence about offering rewards in the name of high standards have not translated into either individual or group excellence, much less idealism and motivation about learning.

In the classroom, the balance between self and others must be struck consistently. These are distinct but intertwined elements. Individual performance and attainment are the key, but they must be nurtured in ways that point to the interconnections among individuals. Each individual, in working with others, engages the requirements of our political and social world. As in a game, the value and importance of the enterprise, like winning, must be compelling even if winning turns out to be quite divisive. One wants to be able to lead a young person to discover why it is enjoyable and useful to read classic texts or know about the founding fathers or command algebra. There needs to be ample opportunity for public recognition. It won't do to preach at students that they need to learn something because of its "timeless and world significance." Few adults and certainly fewer adolescents appreciate or comprehend such large-scale historical verbiage. The authority of tradition must be constantly reclaimed and reinvented by each generation in its own time and place. And it must possess emotional significance. Every sports fan, adolescent or not, is capable of becoming fanatically obsessed with whether his or her team has won against its archrival, whether that rival be in the next city, town, neighborhood, or country. Adolescents and local fans know that high school athletes are not "as good" as those playing at Forest Hills or in the World Series. But the local leagues assume as much significance and inspire as much emotion.

We can achieve the same enthusiasm and love for learning. The heart and the brain are not, as the composer Arnold Schoenberg once observed, separated from one another or in conflict. A young person may be eager to understand science without harboring the ambition to win the Nobel Prize or to be part of some historical pantheon of thinkers. Young people can simply want to be part of the effort to prevent pain and cure disease; the sense of satisfaction gained when one understands how things work or solves a problem can equal that of playing well or being on the winning team. Music, like sports, has been magically successful in inspiring intense involvement, discipline, and reward in young people. A person playing in an orchestra or a band has a sense of importance and joy that can leave a constructive residue in life. This applies as well to the theater. It is more fun to play and sing than to listen and watch.

From the start, adults must encourage the sense of localized significance and success within one's own specific world. To do this, we must counteract the emphasis we currently place on excessively idealized "stars." We have developed a culture in which it appears too often to young people that unless one makes it to the very top, working hard

has been a failure. Being enormously rich and famous is paraded before
the young as the only truly worthwhile goal. One of the negative consequences of the "global village" and of the easy access through CNN to
all parts of the world instantaneously is the destruction of the sense of
the importance of individual achievement and the smaller environments in which we conduct our daily lives. The local high school,
therefore, should be considered as important as the NBA. The local
achievements and rivalries should be given more time and energy by
local communities than what is on national television. Respectable and
rewarding levels of skill are attainable more broadly than the star system implies.

The same is true in the arts. We need to create a system that encourages communities to reward and sustain local accomplishments;
videos and recordings of young local performers and venues and facilities in our own neighborhoods, particularly for young people, are higher
priorities than we have made them. This does not mean in any way that
we need to falsify the distinction between world-class and local excellence, but instead of focusing on the gap, we can actually discover how
much the two have in common. The young musician who wins a prize
for piano playing in high school or college has more in common with
Vladimir Horowitz than with the person who doesn't play at all. The
young winner of a science prize in high school has more in common
with a Nobel Prize winner than with someone who has never learned
any science or mathematics.

Millions exercise and run daily, but few exercise their minds. A fit
body and an underutilized mind constitute a paradoxical combination.
By rethinking what adolescents are capable of, and by stepping away
from our star-obsessed scale of judgment, we can help young people
realize how valuable and enjoyable learning can be. This principle applies over the entire spectrum of the bell-shaped curve. Serious learning need not be reserved for the so-called gifted. This, once again, has
been well understood in our religions. The study of holy texts and
theology is not the exclusive province of priests, rabbis, and theolo-
gians. Indeed, not everyone who enjoys playing baseball or basketball

is tall enough or strong enough to compete professionally. The same holds true for learning. Yet we believe that the psychological benefits and the sense of well-being derived from physical exercise and training are applicable to all young people, even the handicapped. This idea has its direct analogy in the benefits of mental training, the development of concentration, and the enjoyment of learning. The mind is parallel to the body. Our national enthusiasm for regular physical fitness must find its mirror image in mental fitness: sustained engagement and curiosity. The time to build the foundations for the proverbial sound mind and sound body is between ages thirteen and eighteen. To achieve this, we have to start from scratch with an entirely new educational approach and structure. We must therefore set aside the obsolete patterns and habits of the past and begin anew.

IV. IMAGINING ALTERNATIVES

If we accept the premise that the high school must be abandoned, and if we start without preconceptions, several opportunities come into view. The school system before World War II was divided into the elementary grades, K–8, followed by four years of high school, 9–12. In the postwar period, in part influenced by the novel psychological literature on the special nature of adolescence, elementary school was redesigned to encompass kindergarten through grade six. An invention that has proved to be a disaster came into being, the junior high, spanning grades seven through nine. The junior high school segregates out the most vulnerable age group in human development, thereby separating them from older and younger peers. By so doing, the young adolescent loses an older, more adult model for the setting of goals, and by being cut off from younger children is robbed of any reminder within the daily life of school of the positive dimensions of incipient adulthood vis-à-vis childhood.

One suspects that the popular reason for extracting children out of elementary school in early puberty is to insulate childhood and prolong it. In our educational system we reflect our culture's excessive attachment to the innocence and charms of childhood. We therefore create a context in our school system in the way we divide the thirteen years of schooling, which deepens the sense of ambivalence and awkwardness that children feel when they reach puberty. The end points of the trajectory of schooling are rendered invisible by the junior high school system. We leave a volatile age group to fend for itself without a framework defined by the memory of where one began and any anticipation of where one is going.

High school has been turned into a three-year experience, grades ten to twelve. There are some variations on this pattern: the division may be grades K–5 as an elementary school, followed by 6–8 or 6–9 as a middle school, and the remainder as high school. In a reform that meets contemporary realities, schools can be divided into only two parts: elementary school, K–6; and secondary school, 7–10. A high school diploma can be awarded at the end of the tenth grade at fifteen or sixteen years of age. Earlier maturation suggests an acceleration in human development from the start. The growth of the day-care movement is an indication that schooling—bringing children into groups for the purposes of learning to do things and to be with one another—can begin productively before the age of five. Our current school system is based on a K–12 model, beginning with the fifth year and ending with the eighteenth year of life. School should begin at least one year sooner, at age four. If kindergarten universally began when children were four, then even in the current system the age of school completion would be one year earlier.

The 1996 Carnegie Corporation report entitled *Years of Promise* came to the conclusion that early care programs have "misinterpreted" aspects of developmental psychology. They have underestimated the capacity of children before the age of five to learn and to benefit from teaching and the curriculum characteristic of "high-quality elementary school practice." Indeed, developmental psychology in this century, using a variety of methodological approaches, has demonstrated that the young child's mind is capable of learning before the age of what we now require for schooling. A long-term study of children in North Carolina showed that early education programs in regions of extreme poverty had lasting improvement in performance reaching into young adulthood. Craig T. Ramay, professor of psychology at the University of Alabama, concludes that "early experience is critical for development of full intellectual capacity. . . . Beginning at age five is too late." Headstart, that much-maligned program, has shown quite definitively that teaching directed at children aged three and four is as effective as kindergarten. If the evidence from humans was not enough, one can resort to animal studies. Marion Cleeves Diamond, from the University of California at Berkeley, used rats over three decades to show that early stimulation in groups resulted in permanent improvement in physical brain structures connected to thinking. What's good enough for rats ought to be good enough for humans.

But starting earlier and finishing earlier are not the primary objectives. The entire system could be more efficient. The clash between the years spent in school and the learning retained is an offense to common sense. If the number of years it took to accomplish the necessary tasks were fewer, then everyone would be better off. There would be less needless repetition, and the total cost of the educational system would be less onerous. If we returned to a system divided into only two basic groups, elementary and secondary, we would increase the possibilities for individual students, as both children and adolescents, to advance in specific subject matters at their own pace. School curricula should not be driven by rigid patterns of expectations defined by grade levels clustered together in narrow age groupings. There should be more fluidity, for both the slow and fast learner throughout the system.

Efficiency is not, by definition, a virtue. In learning there must be some latitude in how we spend time. A certain messiness and absence of clarity can be crucial components to creativity. Not everything moves with mechanical efficiency. But there is a lot of time wasted, primarily that of children and young people. If the entire duration of compulsory schooling could be reduced by two years, there would be some savings. Instead of spending so much money over thirteen years of uniform schooling, we might choose to spend the same over eleven years. Then the expenditure per pupil would be more concentrated. We would enable the schools to do better.

Although there is a clear political significance to reducing the number of years of school, any attendant savings of such an initiative should not be a primary motivation. The key reason for reducing the total number of years in school before college is educational. Children and young adults can begin learning sooner and more quickly. Since they mature earlier, they need to be released from the obligations of compulsory education at an earlier age. The high school diploma as we define it, which is now given to Americans at age eighteen, could be awarded at age sixteen.

Before accepting a reduction in the years of schooling, we must be clear about the minimum standards of accomplishment for which we would give a high school diploma, at any age. Before outlining a reasonable set of minimum expectations for graduating high school, it should be emphasized that arriving at a consensus about what ought to be learned in secondary school need not involve controversy. The needs are obvious. The high school diploma should represent a demonstrable command of written and spoken English. Every student should be able to write and read at a level of proficiency and complexity sufficient to engage issues of politics and civic life. For example, every high school graduate should be able to express an opinion, defend it, and react to the issues surrounding the O. J. Simpson case in a coherent and intelligent manner. This requires a basic knowledge of civics, including the practice and principles of law and justice. A graduate should be able to express an informed response to a presidential campaign; to resist the blandishments of TV political advertisement. They should be able to articulate their position on such issues as a constitutional amendment, school prayer, and abortion. They ought to be able to think critically and analytically on the subject of whether America should intervene in Bosnia, Rwanda, or Iraq. A graduate should also be able to write a condolence letter, a love letter, and an application letter in a way that effectively communicates with its intended reader.

All students should be able to demonstrate reading comprehension of a variety of types of written materials. They should be able to read instructions, the kind that one finds when applying for a job or a driver's license. In the best of all possible worlds, they should be able to read the sorts of useful instructions that are contained in the cars and gadgets we purchase. Most of these instructions are incomprehensible, but it is precisely the necessity to work around specialized language that most severely tests one's ability to read. One should be able to read a variety of nonfiction, ranging from a newspaper article to a biographical narrative. And finally, one should be able to read fiction and poetry with pleasure and insight.

Each high school graduate must demonstrate a fundamental knowledge of the Constitution and should have a rudimentary knowledge of American history, understood in the simplest of terms. Every student must have a reasonable command of geography, both national and global, as well as some demonstrable orientation in world history in order to discover things of interest and place them in a chronological context. Special emphasis should be placed on nineteenth- and twentieth-century history all over the globe—something with which all students should have a basic familiarity. All high school graduates should have demonstrable skill in arithmetic and basic algebra. Geometrical concepts should also be learned.

Most important, every student should have a rudimentary knowledge of statistics and probability. Although this goal sounds too sophisticated and even unrealistic, every day of our lives we are forced to assess risk and take chances. Whether betting on a horse or getting on an airplane, every citizen should have a chance to grapple with how risk is actually calculated and then to assess it. Every politician inundates us with so-called facts and figures. A high school graduate ought to be able to exercise some judgment as to how facts are constructed and articulated and which facts make sense and which ones don't. Before a young American lights up a cigarette, he or she should be able to understand the link between smoking and disease and how that statistical linkage has been proved and described and what relationship, if any, there is between a correlation and cause.

Every high school graduate should have a fundamental knowledge of human biology. It is astonishing that with all the interest in sex that most young people share, they are totally ignorant of basic anatomy and physiology, much less anything more sophisticated. They should have a fundamental understanding of what DNA is and of the structure and function of cells and living organisms. Politics aside, the history of human and natural variation should be taught, together with some ability to think about the environment in larger units. Students should study populations and ecological systems with a view to understanding how their own environment changes. To that end, a fundamental orientation with respect to physical laws, including thermodynamics, should be provided.

High school students should encounter something that challenges the tendency to conform and that is foreign and strange to themselves. This means that they should study language, culture, and history that are not American and not European. Much has been made in recent years of multiculturalism and diversity. These are stock words that have come to signify nothing. Both sides of the debate have proceeded to simplify and obscure the issues, and this should never have occurred. It is obvious that a person graduating from high school in the United States ought to know something about Asia, Africa, and Latin America. This is a matter of self-interest and not any sort of political correctness. Furthermore, that Americans should be encouraged to extend tolerance and respect to other cultures, particularly other religions and nationalities, is also a principle of enlightened self-interest. Most of all, we need to break the habit of thinking about ourselves and others using oversimplified notions of difference in terms of ethnicity and religion. The words white and black, Christian and Jew in their current usage fail to illuminate or represent the actual differentiation that exists. Furthermore, each of these categories contains as much difference as sameness. No shortcuts should be offered that diminish the sanctity of individuality.

Perhaps the best way to inspire interest in multiculturalism and diversity in a lasting sense is to connect them with the study of economics. If a high school graduate can have an understanding of agricultural and industrial production, of trade and commerce, of money and value, then it will become clear that the framework of his or her life and work is global and interconnected and not parochial and local. A respect for others is not a matter of *noblesse oblige*. It does not require abandoning loyalty to one's so-called roots or beliefs. It only requires eliminating the most basic dimensions of ignorance so that a "live and let live" attitude can be developed without doubt that it is right. To this end, every high school student should struggle with the effort to learn a foreign language. For most Americans, Spanish would be an obvious choice, since it is the second language of the United States and the primary language of our southern neighbors. Whatever the language, learning it requires no sacrifice to English. Since humans are not hardwired to be a monolingual species, lessons can be learned about differences between cultures through how others speak. From that perspective one can then build bridges between cultures. Finally, the visual and performing arts must have a central role in the curriculum as active pursuits and objects of analysis and interpretation. A love of the unexpected and unusual power of the human imagination can be instilled before the age of sixteen.

This is a simple, straightforward construct of high school graduation requirements. To achieve it, much will have to change, including the length of in-class time and the shape of the school day and week. This proposal is not dissimilar to efforts by many prominent educators, including Theodore Sizer, to develop a basic high school curriculum. The point of the formulation given here (which is not intended to be complete or comprehensive) is to make it clear that these goals can be accomplished in eleven years and not thirteen. The reason for compulsory schooling is to ensure that all citizens can function in the political and economic life of the country. Basic literacy and civic orientation must be achieved by common schooling. These are the sorts of goals that can be mandated nationally and tested well and efficiently. The state is properly obliged to make a fundamental education available to the children of its inhabitants. Horace Mann, the great nineteenth-century reformer, was right in understanding the common school as a school for democracy. There is no reason, however, to extend such a school experience into early adulthood. Rather, it should end at the time when the founders of the high school at the turn of the century thought it should end, after early adolescence is over.

At this point, the reader will no doubt raise some obvious questions. First, what are we going to do with sixteen-year-olds after the tenth grade? What's going to happen to the high school buildings? And what about all our high school teachers and administrators?

Let's take the last question first. One of the reasons to abolish high school is that high school teaching is the weakest link in our system of training teachers. A 1996 Carnegie Foundation report on the state of American education reiterated conclusions that had been made for decades by one report after another on the profession of teaching. The report confirmed our worst suspicions. It severely criticized the standards, particularly on the undergraduate level, in teacher-training programs. The logical if painful conclusion that must be drawn from this report is that there should be no B.A. degree with a major in education. Every teacher should complete college with a concentration in a discipline other than education. Indeed, the commission urged the "reinvention" of teacher preparation. It decried the inadequate recruitment of qualified teachers, and it repeated the oft-made claim that we are not rewarding teaching enough. In 1990, only about 53 percent of mathematics teachers had a state license with a major in mathematics. In the United States in 1990, teachers earned less than physicians, lawyers, managers, engineers, sales representatives, scientists, accountants, registered nurses, and sales supervisors. Something is wrong with our priorities. Last but not least, the ratio between classroom teachers and other personnel in our educational bureaucracies is the highest among Western industrial countries. We have siphoned off too many of our resources from classroom personnel to administrative and supervisory functions.

When it comes to recruiting and organizing our teachers, for generations we in America have made a catastrophic error. We have segregated and segmented those who would wish to become schoolteachers from the center of the college and university system. There should be no undergraduate schools of education. The Carnegie commission is correct. All teachers should be required to finish an undergraduate degree in a subject in the arts and sciences; their training in education should be done through an entirely separate and additional program. This can be accomplished either by offering undergraduates internships, supplemented by supervision, or by the study beyond the B.A. of education and psychology. What should be avoided is the corruption of the study of English, history, and mathematics by the mixing in of pedagogical science, curriculum strategy, and classroom management. Americans have inflated the study of pedagogy when there is nothing to be taught that can't be better taught on the job.

Consequently, we associate teachers less by what they teach than by the age group they teach. In America, teachers are organized professionally in a horizontal way, by the age group they teach and not vertically by the subject matter they teach along all age groups. Thus, a junior high school French teacher has more in common professionally (in the conventional view) with the junior high school math teacher than he or she does with the high school or college French teacher. We all would be much better off if the college physics teacher had a professional relationship with the high school physics teacher, the junior high school science teacher, and the elementary school science teacher. Instead, the college physics teacher talks with the college English teacher and has no contact with or interest in the high school science teacher, the junior high school science teacher, or the elementary school science teacher. Consequently, teaching in colleges and universities has assumed an inappropriate prestige. We ought to take inspiration from Thomas More's *Utopia* (which divested gold of its value) and turn our reward structure inside out. Perhaps we should pay junior high and high school teachers the most, elementary teachers second highest, and college and university professors the least. We should endow schoolteachers with the high status we now accord our university and college colleagues.

As a result of the discrepancies between the rewards of college and precollege teaching, as early as 1983 it became clear that our *least*-gifted college students were going into teaching. The report *A Nation at Risk* found that half of the newly employed teachers in 1983 were not qualified to teach the subjects they were assigned. When that report was written, the average SAT verbal score of young people going into teaching was around 400, which was below the overall national average. The SAT scores for those intending to enter the field of education rose somewhat by 1993, but they were still below the national average. Daniel Singall, writing in 1991, reiterated an obvious recommendation toward the improvement of the training of American teachers: that certification requirements mandated by the states should be abolished. The state requirements are designed to sustain the monopoly of schools of education, which do not attract the best students. It is ironic that private schools end up having better teachers at lower pay because they do not require certification. The courses that people are apt to take to meet certification requirements are mostly make-work courses empty of content. Despite all the continuing education and in-service training required of teachers, by and large teachers still do not command the subject matters they are required to teach. They are then too tied to textbooks and workbooks and cannot go beyond them. This is particularly acute for the high school years. The results are disastrous when one contemplates the areas of math and science. These teachers in America waste their time studying education and never gain a serious training, so that they are unable to teach clearly and with understanding. No wonder our seventeen-year-olds do poorly in math. Although 48 percent of American teachers hold a graduate degree, a very small portion hold them in subject areas.

A key problem is that teaching school in America is not a valued profession. How many parents desire that their children become schoolteachers as opposed to doctors and lawyers? Perhaps a radical means to change the attractiveness of this profession would be to make teaching in public schools exempt from federal income tax. We should use whatever means help. In many fine suburban school districts, despite comparatively good wages, teachers are unable to live in the district, since the cost of housing exceeds their income. That fact undermines the authority and prestige of teachers in the eyes of children. The teacher is an outsider and second class, neither a member of the community nor an equal. Our communities must find a way to lend distinction to schoolteaching. And we must remove the most horrendous conditions of work. Those are most egregious in the inner city and in the high school.

Once again one comes upon the conflict between a rigid school system and earlier maturation. Too many teachers spend too much time just keeping order. The tragedy is that our best teachers come into the system with a fair amount of idealism. But they emerge cynical, disillusioned, worn-out by the way they are treated and by the way they have to work. They are not to blame for the results. It cannot be repeated too often that no matter how much we may criticize them, high school teachers by and large are the hardest-working segment of the teaching profession. Elementary school teachers have the relative advantage of the age and innocence of their pupils, and college teachers often use their high status and the pretenses of the curriculum to elude the necessity of close day-to-day contact with their students.

If the quality of teachers is a problem, particularly for the high school, so, too, is the way the curriculum is organized and the day structured. Moving from class to class in short, set periods on a daily basis is appropriate to a younger age but not for young adults. The regimentation and routine of high school worked a century ago, and it will still work for ten-, eleven-, and twelve-year-olds. But even there the quality of the curriculum and teaching has to be improved. One of the keys to improvement is clarity and simplification. We must institute a curriculum that is based upon what pupils need and want to learn.

v. Conclusion: Beyond Secondary Education

Now let us return to the young people in school. Assuming that one can accomplish the goals of today's high school two years earlier, what will our younger high school graduates do? There would be four options:

1. Those desiring to go on to college, if they wish to stay at home, would go directly on to community colleges and finish an A.A. degree at the age they would finish high school today. They could continue, as commuters, in four-year programs leading to a B.A. at age nineteen or twenty.

2. Those headed for a four-year college could go directly to a state or private residential college at age sixteen. This is an old idea. It was a frequent occurrence in the nineteenth century when many men and fewer women went to college at fifteen and sixteen after having been tutored at home and gone only briefly to a secondary school.

3. Those adolescents who have little patience with schooling and who barely survived high school could try to enter the job market or national service. Both our civilian and military programs should be re-designed to accommodate sixteen-year-olds. Perhaps with a "real life" experience behind them, some young people would acquire an enthusiasm and appreciation for the value of schooling. The desire to work in and for the community—whether in construction and landscape projects or service to the elderly and needy—can be readily supported and sustained. These adolescents would be more likely to develop a genuine desire to learn. After such experiences, they would then be at an age when they could still get back into formal schooling without too much of a sense of having fallen behind or being too old.

4. For those for whom more academic schooling is unlikely, the earlier completion of high school should create a new opportunity for public and private experiments in vocational education. Community colleges provide some vocational education. However, this is an arena where America has always fallen behind. As a nation we have maintained a commitment to the common school and have been loath to track young people in a way that might lend vocational education a

pejorative connotation. But by bringing the common school to an end at an earlier age, we open the possibility that a new attitude and approach to vocational education can be created that can meet contemporary technological, service, and industrial requirements. Among the new options that would become practical with the earlier completion of secondary schooling is the creation of focused programs not based in public schools—directed at skilled activities including the arts, design, crafts, and trades that permit the adolescent to concentrate on one interest exclusively. The ages sixteen to eighteen are ideally suited to intense training in dance, sports, painting, science, writing, designing, and building, so that concentration and individual achievement in specialized interests and talents can be nurtured. These new programs could be extensions of a variety of institutions, including art schools, conservatories, unions, architectural firms, professional sports teams, hospitals, and laboratories.

In terms of funding schools, which in many states is done on a per-capita basis by counting every day's attendance by each pupil, this system would create the opportunity for a genuine state voucher system. Today's conservative politicians talk about giving a ridiculously small amount of money to create school choice. These proposals are really covert attempts to undermine the principles of public education. As the traditional liberal criticism has pointed out, current initiatives such as vouchers are little more than a gesture toward the middle class and proponents of parochial and segregated education and to ideological opponents of the public system. However, by ending the school system two years early, one could create a real voucher program for young people. Instead of funding the senior and junior years of today's high school, the state could assign the full cost per pupil to the local community college or new programs the high school graduate chose to attend. Such a per-capita contribution could also be added to the state university's funding formulas to account for those sixteen-year-olds who go on to four-year programs. The student who went to private institutions should not benefit in the same way. If, for example, a high school graduate cost $5,000 or $6,000 a year to educate in a high school, that amount of money would be added to the community college's budget or the state college's budget above and beyond any existing enrollment-based funding formula. In terms of further schooling, the essence of this plan is that by ending high school earlier, an education appropriately designed for a young adult begins when it should.

Those interested in going to college will be able to exercise greater choice in the new system. For those who stay at home, the community college system is the most likely option. Already these institutions are dedicated to repairing the damage done in high school or doing what ought to have been done. The basic organization of the community college is more respectful of the incipient adult. Classes are selected and scheduled by the individual. There is a campus. The day is divided so that night classes are an option. The classes are run by faculty with better training in the subject matter. The presumption of the classroom is not rote fulfillment of state requirements, but rather teaching in response to the ambitions of students to learn and get ahead. Community colleges have large numbers of older students, well beyond the so-called traditional college age. As teachers know, nothing better serves the swaggering sixteen- and seventeen-year-old more obsessed with style and the peer group than being in classes with students in their late twenties and early thirties, for whom school has become truly voluntary and serious.

Some fifteen- or sixteen-year-olds can go on directly to four-year colleges, either as commuters or as residential students. No doubt traditional college administrations will not like this prospect. A younger-age population places a greater burden of responsibility on the institution. One cannot get away (as is now often the case) simply by saying that at eighteen one is presumed to be an adult and is therefore on one's own. Colleges used to have rules and were prepared to assume roles *in loco parentis*. While a return to pre–World War II ethos is unlikely and undesirable, some adjustment for the younger-age student will have to take place. The residential colleges, state and private, will have to take on, more than they might wish, the task of helping young individuals outside of the classroom. But the rewards outstrip the negatives. Fifteen-

and sixteen-year-olds are more inclined toward risk-taking and unembarrassed enthusiasms, making intellectual exploration an object of enjoyment and passion. Most important, colleges, in their faculties and curricula, are in a better position to take the young American adolescent seriously intellectually.

For those not immediately college-bound, a space would be created that could be filled by vocational and professional training programs, sponsored jointly by the state and private industry. Yes, some young people will begin to work and will discover, earlier rather than later, that without a higher education there is less chance to move upward than they might have imagined. Many of these young people who finish school and begin to work may return to school more focused and motivated than when they left. They would then return to higher education at eighteen or nineteen.

By compressing the total number of years spent in a common school, the democratic basis of schooling will remain intact, without a sacrifice to what is learned. The opposite of what now happens will occur: young people will learn and retain more. All Americans will attend and finish ten or eleven years of common schooling. There is already a great deal of repetition in the curriculum. What is now done in twelve years could be achieved in ten or eleven with better results. Then, at the initiative of young people themselves, not that of the government, there will be a variety of options in place of the high school. Community colleges will expand. The per-student state expenditures can follow the student. New programs with specific educational goals will develop. A hugely wasteful and anachronistic institution will be dismantled.

In the myriad of possibilities that would emerge through the condensation of common schooling, the abolition of the high school, and the displacement of advanced academic programs to community colleges, new vocational programs and four-year colleges would open up new ways of dealing with those adolescents most at risk. Now we face the nearly insoluble problem of keeping order in urban high schools and guiding their spirit so that teaching and learning and not mere order dominate the building. Furthermore, urban high schools have few ways of dealing with dropouts. And they do not have the resources to hold on to those young people who, despite the odds, show talent and initiative. No journalistic accounts, no matter how eloquently phrased, can convey the impression and shock one gets when one visits inner-city schools, particularly high schools. The dilapidation of the facilities and the inadequacy of the basic tools for teaching and learning are unimaginable. What we, as a nation, tolerate in the name of education in the inner city constitutes a scandal of complacency. The first target of any reform and change must be our inner-city schools.

What can be done with the closing of urban high schools is their conversion into twenty-four-hour educational centers and emergency rooms. The inner city requires a sufficient number of safe havens for young people from the ages of thirteen to eighteen. These facilities should be heavily guarded—surrounded with state-of-the-art security systems to ensure that neither weapons nor drugs enter. Inside there would be recreation facilities and a cafeteria. Both could be open all day and all night. Those permitted to enter would have been registered. Once admitted, they would have a wide choice of instructional programs and opportunities, on demand, all day and all night, for groups and individuals. Many of these could be computer-based, with supervision by teachers. There would be scheduled night classes and also tutorial staffs, made up of college students, graduate students, and other qualified staff and volunteers. There could also be a small infirmary. Finally, there could be a limited number of overnight facilities—dormitory-like beds—that young people could use.

Young people could avail themselves of these facilities for recreation, short-term problem-solving, a return to school, and systematic instruction leading to a high school diploma, as well as nondegree courses and for-credit courses. The key advantage, particularly for younger adolescents, is that this twenty-four-hour safe haven would be a constantly available alternative to the streets. The opportunity to learn and be taught would be there for the asking, all day, all night, all year round, even on holidays. We provide short-term and long-term care in matters of health to citizens around the clock. So, too, for young people the process of learning and their motivation need to be organized beyond the traditional school day and tied more closely to the sense of a need to know at any moment of time. Modern technology, including the provision of computer hookups to participants in their homes, makes the full use of such an urban center plausible as a sustainable, consistent resource.

For our young adolescents at risk, a safe haven free of drugs and violence, with a twenty-four-hour flexible opportunity to learn and to maintain a conversation with a supportive adult, is essential, even though it might appear extravagant. For our inner cities we may re-create in a new way the tradition of the settlement house, which served prior generations of the poor and oppressed so well. The range of the programs of these new centers should encompass the arts, sports, and practical skills, as did the older settlement houses.

But the ills that plague the education of the American adolescent are not limited to the most disadvantaged. The failure of the high school today cuts uniformly across race, ethnicity, gender, and region. It also cuts across income and social class. The twenty-four-hour settlement house model for the education of adolescents and adults can work elsewhere, in suburban and rural America, as well. Only by setting the entire apparatus of high school aside can we create new opportunities to motivate American adolescents to embrace learning and to make their learning crucial to the conduct of their private lives and their public selves.

CHAPTER IV

HELPING CHILDREN LEARN:
TWENTY-FOUR MAXIMS
FOR ADULTS

I. INTRODUCTION: PARENTS, TEACHERS, MENTORS

An undeniable residue of the neoconservative, Reagan-era critique of the liberal political traditions of the 1960s was the recognition that we need to focus on the social and cultural values of family and home. Liberals have struggled in vain to regain this issue for themselves. At the other end of the spectrum, contemporary neoconservatism, like all self-righteous political ideologies, tends to go too far. It has taken a straightforward and constructive idea and used it to attack, bully, and denigrate. By now the words *family* and *values* have become so abused by politicians that they are nearly useless. They are often laced with contempt and hate for those who fail to fit a narrow picture of the ideal family—a white father who works, a white woman who is a home-maker, and two white children, all of whom, of course, go to church each week. This picture resembles more the television programs of the 1950s than it does any past reality. However, such myths should not deter us from trying to encourage adults to reflect on why it is that family and home are so crucial to children and adolescents. To begin with, a family—no matter how it is constituted, by one or more adults, two or more generations, with or without siblings—is indispensable to education and learning. It frames the transmission of culture from one generation to the next. We can use to our advantage the fact that the

131

lessons of family and home are adaptable to a multiplicity of environments that deviate from our so-called ideal picture.

Historically speaking, the political use of the notion of family has been Janus-faced. The positive side derives from the fact that human offspring do not develop properly in a vacuum of intimate human relationships with adults. Since the rise of modern industry in the mid-eighteenth century, there has been a profound concern for the future of the family. A rural model of bucolic togetherness, in which several generations lived and worked side by side on the land, was replaced, of necessity, by a new urban reality. Migration, overcrowding, factories, urban poverty, and the use of child labor contributed to an early-nineteenth-century debate about alternatives to the harsh and seemingly inhuman economic and social reality that was fast emerging from the competitive industrial world of modern capitalism.

Consequently, attempts to defend and define the idea of family for modern urban life did not go unscathed. A theoretical critique of modern marriage and family emerged simultaneously with the agricultural and industrial revolution. Its best articulation is found in the work of Jean-Jacques Rousseau from before the French Revolution. (Later Karl Marx and Friedrich Engels took up this theme in their 1848 *Communist Manifesto*.) Suspicion of historical models of marriage and family is not without its compelling logic. Marriage can no longer be regarded as analogous to a commercial contract in which the woman, in effect, can be transformed into either an indentured servant or an object of property. The sanctification of marriage through religion frequently constituted a high-minded camouflage of radical inequality. In the same vein, parents ought not wield unlimited rights over the welfare of their children.

The critique that developed over the course of the nineteenth century of the institutions of marriage and the family and of the theological justifications that lent these institutions legitimacy was part of an admirable and reasonable reaction against disturbing social facts. Women were not treated equally. Children were exploited. The sanctimonious discourse of preachers and moralists propped up a system of values that secured a monopoly of rights and opportunities for male adults. Before jumping on today's moralistic enthusiasms about so-called family values we should pause to remember some unpleasant facts of history that once gave what we now call liberalism the moral and political edge it struggles to reclaim. And more important, for all the talk of family values, we, in our own time, have still not found a way to make families work together with the values of openness, tolerance, and skepticism, particularly about race and religion.

The wishful thinking of politicians aside, no one can be surprised that we live in an age in which cynicism still thrives about both marriage and family and the rhetoric surrounding them. The redefinition of middle-class marriage in the context of the realities of work and income and feminism has been a complex and not altogether successful venture. Both equality between the sexes and its alternative—a stable equilibrium between male and female in which there may be inequality in terms of who works and who stays at home but also general happiness and satisfaction—elude us. Such hopes for marriage become even harder to sustain when there are children. Motherhood sets up a natural tendency to inequality in the distribution of responsibility for the child's upbringing. No matter the ridiculous lengths to which people may choose to go to offset the consequences of biological differences between male and female, the role of the mother will remain dominant and differentiated.

This fact becomes particularly relevant since the human species is peculiar in that its offspring do not become independent rapidly. Even if one accepts the traditional critique from the radical left of the modern family—that it is in part too closely modeled after an economic and political system based on hierarchies, markets, private property, and the transfer of wealth—and seeks alternatives for setting the legal rights and responsibilities between and among parents and children, every child still requires some form of nurturing by adults for an astonishingly extended period of time.

It is not surprising that the *kibbutz* movement of Israel experimented with a communal alternative to the family. Utopian communities from the nineteenth century, including Owenites and Shakers, struggled to come up with better solutions. They articulated the possibility that perhaps there was a better way to provide for children and regulate sexual relations between adults other than the nuclear family unit. The short-lived commune movement of the late 1960s and early 1970s was a revival of a long-standing search to develop a larger framework than the family. The West has maintained a romance with images from its own past and from non-Western cultures of close communities larger than families. A less radical ameliorative strategy to strengthen the family has involved creating institutions designed to assist in the care and feeding of children. The day-care movement reaches into infancy and has sought to provide a supplement and surrogate for upbringing at home when adults cannot or wish not to remain with their children.

Thinking about these efforts leads us back to a brutal fact. In contemporary American life, particularly among the poor, but also throughout our social structure, marriage and family seem in trouble. A staggering percentage of children from families below the poverty level are born out of wedlock. While some extended family safety net that can take the place of mother and father still exists in a society in which people live longer and remain more healthy, single parenting and the abandonment of children are on the rise. Since the American middle class has not seen its real wages rise significantly during the past two decades, middle-income families, in which mother and father live together, increasingly require that both parents work in order to maintain a middle-class standard of living.

Therefore, for the foreseeable future, the home may not readily provide the necessary supportive context—much less the intellectual and moral nurturing—of the child through the years of elementary and secondary schooling. William Bennett's effort to shift the focus away from government overstated the argument that education was ultimately dependent on the family. The truth is tending increasingly to the opposite. Schooling and institutions are still becoming more, not less, crucial. Among the affluent and privileged, the aspirations of adults frequently take precedence over the requirements of children. Even when one member of a two-parent combination (usually the man) may earn enough for the other parent to remain at home, few educated women who choose this option remain happy for long. Whether we like it or not, most Americans do not believe that bringing up children, in and of itself, is a sufficient accomplishment with which to reach the end of life. And there is no reason to quarrel with this view or complain about it. It is a cogent, realistic, and honorable stance.

The competitive world in which we live makes it difficult, at best, to start a professional career after children are grown-up. In the absence of the gift of irony so brilliantly displayed by Jonathan Swift, it is still worthwhile to imagine radical and socially unacceptable proposals to social dilemmas that appear intractable. One such modest proposal might be to encourage men and women to have children between the ages of thirteen and eighteen so that the most strenuous period of child-rearing is behind them by their early twenties. Then they can start out on careers without being concerned about either delaying having children or, in the case of women, racing against the biological clock at the same time they pursue a career. Men and women could have children at an appropriate age in biological terms without placing themselves at a disadvantage on a second-class career track. But this clearly won't happen. It is a provocative, if not perverse, thought experiment.

Even though the nuclear family held up by proponents of so-called family values may indeed be a highly idealized and misleading historical model derived from a very short segment of human history, it contains a powerful dimension of common sense. Mother, father, and child constitute an intergenerational unit that transcends culture, time, and place. However sanctified and organized, it mirrors not only a biological necessity but an educational one. Yet throughout history, particularly among the aristocracy of the eighteenth century and in the worlds of classical Greece and Rome, it was understood that the care and nurturing of children by adults did not have to be done by parents themselves. When we speak of adult surrogates in terms of bringing up children, we need not imply something less desirable. The nineteenth-century novel has made tutors and governesses familiar examples. What is needed, family or no family, is sustained, close attention to a child by an adult.

This brings us back to the Janus-faced character of the contemporary discussion of the family in American politics. The vicious side of it uses family values as a way to attack any constructive effort to create alternatives in the task of bringing children and adults together in a social reality that does not conform to a given stereotype. Our children, left to themselves, are in need of help. But any effort to respond differently to the needs to which the family seems to respond naturally is denigrated as secular and liberal. Family values become an instrument of intolerance directed against the legitimate search for a plurality of options that might rescue the millions of children who, to lesser and greater degrees, are born only to be prematurely abandoned and ignored by adults.

This widespread abandonment and lack of attention has one central cause that underlies all the difficulties encountered in creating a healthy environment for children. We are not more self-centered than our predecessors. But even when mother and father are living together under the same roof, we have to consider the consequences of the widespread instability evident in the intimate relationships between men and women. The frequency with which individuals feel comfortable enough to engage in sexual relations in a manner that can knowingly lead to pregnancy and childbirth has not diminished. But we have come to regard the obligations of that level of sexual contact as essentially short-term. Divorce without children can be brutal and scarring, but it does not wreak the same consequences in society as does divorce with children. Cynically speaking, the frequency of divorce and remarriage has its positive side. It offers increased employment and income to psychologists, lawyers, ministers, priests, rabbis, judges, restaurants, clothing manufacturers, gift shops, and record-keepers. If the social cost of divorce without children is comparatively trivial, it seems abundantly clear that despite liberal pieties to the contrary, divorce with children is devastating more often than we are willing to admit. It has become commonplace to argue that children are better off with one parent than in a hostile and deteriorated relationship. But no matter how hard we try, children inevitably take the blame for the breakup of the family upon themselves. Whether we like it or not, having children robs adults of the flexibilities and privileges to which they assume they are entitled with respect to changing their lives. Divorce with children profoundly exacerbates the already limited possibilities facing parents in search of a nurturing environment for children and adolescents.

A well-worn cliché and psychotherapeutic truism of our times that may actually be false is that children are not a sufficient reason for an unhappy couple of husband and wife to remain together after romance has passed beyond retrieval or revival. Perhaps children are the best reason. Our self-indulgent, psychologized contemporary view of personal happiness and marriage clearly privileges the needs and desires of adults. It has made life for schools extremely difficult. It has diminished the chances that any scheme of education will work. One reason education has been the object of intense criticism during the past few decades is that with single parenting, and the economic necessity in two-parent homes for both parents to work, the need for effective systems of teaching and learning outside the school has become acute. In the absence of external supports we will continue to place too great a burden on the schools. Schools were never designed to function alone. During the nineteenth and early twentieth centuries, children of the privileged social classes with access to schooling did not think of the school as the *exclusive* source of education. They did not believe that attending school alone was sufficient for an education. Even in cases in which schooling beyond the elementary level was a first-generation experience—where adults were unschooled and illiterate—home and community outside of the school were understood as providing fundamental information and lessons about life that bolstered the ambition to learn and achieve in school. These ranged from moral values gained through religious groups to the recognition that skills and hard work were indispensable in a brutal and competitive world. Pride experienced by the poor, illiterate parent in the schooling of a child was a crucial motivating factor that provided a key psychological reward for the child. It helped make the schools seem effective.

What we face in late-twentieth-century America is a vacuum of values when it comes to the world children encounter beyond the walls of school. Some children have neither a parent nor a functional adult alternative. Others have parents who are too busy to pay attention. Many have parents whose definition of their own lives, despite the fact that they have mothered and fathered children, does not make room for paying attention to children or being concerned with their development. These adults construe the obligations of life narrowly as providing for their own pleasure and amusement. Despite the improved life expectancy and health of the grandparental generation, a multigenerational support for children is rarely the norm.

The very poor and the very rich have something in common. As parents they turn to the schools to do something they were never designed to accomplish: to be a complete, comprehensive source of values and habits. No school, no matter how good, well staffed, and inspiring, can function without external reinforcement outside of its own educational framework. School is not life, and life is not school. Schooling at its best is a socially efficient system by which habits of mind, information, skills, and a sense of social and civic responsibility can be cultivated within the population as a whole. In some measure, school attendance is a training ground for time spent later at work. But school alone cannot develop in a child or a young person the motivation for learning and an attitude toward life that nourishes the habits of reason and inquiry. School is an essential but limited instrument. At the same time, however, given the contemporary state of family, home, and marriage, schools must try to compensate. One way to do so is for schools and other institutions to find ways of placing children into contact with adults outside of school and home to provide the external reinforcement all classroom education requires.

Waxing nostalgic about family and home will not help. We cannot afford to underestimate the difficulties parents face in trying to act responsibly—whether their relationship to children is biological, adoptive, or the result of an extended family structure. Before the society can develop incentives and programs that get adults to interact with children and young people in ways that provide an essential support to what goes on within the walls of elementary and secondary schools, the prevailing attitude of adults in contemporary America toward schooling has to be changed.

That attitude is a mix of bad faith and contempt. We assert rhetorically that we want better schools for our children, but we ourselves do not live lives that demonstrate a respect for schooling. As has been alluded to already, we do little in our lives to lend prestige to learning and teaching. Pay scales in our society make it clear that the tasks that value learning for its own sake—from schoolteaching to scholarship and research—are less well paid. Doctors and lawyers earn well, but within those professions the highest paid are not law professors or full-time faculty in medical schools who are also researchers; rather, the highest-paid lawyers and doctors are those who place business and profit first and the contemplative or active fascination with law, justice, illness, and disease second. A Supreme Court justice makes less than a successful partner in a Wall Street law firm. The physicians with the highest incomes are not necessarily those who practice the best medicine or who honor the highest ethical standards in the treatment of patients and eagerly serve the sick without regard to the ability to pay.

Society's enthusiasm for education is too often tied to certification and to its utility. We may acknowledge that a degree is essential for getting a job, but few Americans continue the habits of learning and study once the degree program is over. Too few adults read serious books. Despite admirable exceptions, even fewer Americans are members of voluntary groups that get individuals together to discuss ideas, arts, politics. Adults often wait until they become senior citizens to join programs that foster learning. The Elderhostel program on campuses around the country, which offers seminars and classes, and similar postretirement opportunities try to rekindle the values of education in the older population. Even though we could use the senior-citizen population better in terms of how they might assist children and adolescents, all this is too little too late. Children and young people do not grow up watching adults in their prime years, between the ages of twenty-five and sixty-five, even those who hold advanced degrees, living lives informed by a joyful embrace of intellectual curiosity and the love of learning. When American adults want to enjoy themselves, what they choose to do rarely connects with the agenda of any school, either elementary or college level. The one potentially bright spot on the horizon is the conscious use of the Internet as an educational tool and means of entertainment. The trouble is that, like television, the Internet will be only as good as what it contains, beyond its basic facility as a means of communication.

As a parent, imagine sending a child for religious instruction on a regular basis and living a routine in daily life that ignores or undercuts the precepts being taught by that religious instruction. The issue here is not one of doctrine or belief but of authenticity and consistency. Every child wonders about the idea of God. The parent who is an agnostic or atheist but who thinks about the question of faith and sustains curiosity about religion, even in doubt, is more helpful than one who thoughtlessly goes through the motions of allegiance, ignores such questions, or does not think about them at all. So, too, it is with education. If the child gets the idea that doing what he or she is being asked to do by teachers in school is merely a childhood exercise, the importance of which expires in the life of the adult upon graduation—a rite of passage whose utility becomes invisible in the adult world—then why bother? Why should children do something that seems unpleasant to adults and is forgotten?

Thinking is hard, the saying goes, which is why so few do it. But American adults tackle hard tasks that they rarely master with elegance or excellence because the doing of that task seems like fun. Once again, consider physical fitness, golf, or any form of sport or physical exercise. These are hard to do and few people do them really well. Yet millions of adults try and have fun in attempting to improve. Millions spend time running, sweating, lifting weights, just to feel fit and look good. If only the same regular discipline and training were applied to the use of the mind. In contrast to sports, learning and study of the sort encouraged by school are activities practically no adults voluntarily do as amateurs.

Yet, children and adolescents learn through the imitation of adult behavior. Two examples suffice. In music, whether in rural villages before the existence of recorded sound, or in an urban setting with CDs, radios, and television, young children have learned to sing, play, and dance because they observed adults entertaining themselves by doing those things. The Czech composer Antonin Dvořák was first encouraged to play an instrument by the adults around him because the local band of adult amateur musicians needed players. It was as if an ongoing regular pickup basketball game needed more participants— though in the case of music, age, height, and weight are irrelevant. Very young musicians can play with older musicians. Every young musician knows from the start that there are adults who do what they do and like it, whether these adults play well or not. In those situations, children practice their instruments in anticipation and imitation of adult behavior. There is no segregation by generation, only by quality, much like the way golfers are grouped according to their handicap.

The second example demonstrates how foreign a voluntary love of learning and the habits of reflection are to the cultural values of adult Americans. A first-year student was astonished when she received a C on a paper in a required college humanities course. The five-page paper was on the relationship between might and right in international politics. The required text was the "Melian Dialogue" in book 5 of Thucydides' *Peloponnesian War*. The assignment asked students to evaluate the arguments made by the Athenians, who represented an imperial, seafaring military superpower, and those of the Melians, who represented a presumably neutral, small, and relatively defenseless island. The Athenians needed the island for strategic purposes in anticipation of their attempt to conquer Syracuse. They confronted the representatives of the Melians with the choice of submitting without a fight or engaging in war without any chance of victory. The Melians objected to being faced with a choice between enslavement and defeat with honor. Thucydides eloquently outlined the arguments on both sides; the Athenians defend the privileges of power, and the Melians express their commitment to honor and faith in providence. The end result is that the Melians are defeated and all the grown men executed and women and children sold into slavery.

Students were asked to reflect as Americans on Thucydides' provocative way of posing the issues of how one ought to weigh the imperatives of national self-interest and power politics on the one hand and issues and principles about right and wrong and justice in international relations and times of war on the other. After all, the college students in question were American citizens; and America, like Athens in the fifth century, is a superpower whose naval and military presence in the world demands that its citizens be able to reflect carefully about such questions, whatever conclusions they may come to.

The paper handed in by this student was perfectly clearly written. There were no grammatical errors and no mistakes in usage. But it was equally clear that the writer had not thought about the issue. The student simply went through the motions. She did the assignment without thinking, using stock phrases and routine strategies, including a topic sentence and a conclusion, placed conveniently on the very bottom of the fifth page. It was written on automatic pilot, I suspect the way the same student had written papers in the fine high school from which she had graduated with high grades. When she complained that the grade C was punitive and unfair because the paper was the right length and was free of surface blemishes, the teacher explained that although that was true, given that she was a literate citizen with the right to vote and the privilege of higher education, she had some obligation to think seriously, particularly about such a relevant and important issue. Her retort was that this was not so; that the professor, in contrast to the student, was paid to think about such matters. The student, on the other hand, was going to go into business and had no intention of ever thinking about these issues. Since it wasn't going to be her job, it was unreasonable to demand anything more than what she had done. Furthermore, the course was required; she would never have signed up for it voluntarily. This student's pragmatic and strategic attitude toward education and learning mirrors the habits of the affluent, highly credentialed, and literate adult world in which she grew up and in which learning is seen only in terms of its vocational advantages rather than its potential influence on thinking and living.

This state of affairs helps to explain why television has become so powerful a force in political life, despite the growing numbers of Americans who finish high school and attend college. Why is it that in recent years our electoral campaigns, despite advances in rates of schooling, are more and more dependent upon vacuous, bland, orchestrated political rhetoric, and on truly grotesque, simplified, and trivial media advertisements? If one measures a nation by the tests it has passed, we should now have the most sophisticated electorate and the most profound political debates in our history. But the reverse is true. Our political campaigns are not substantive, but they are vulgar and avoid a serious airing of issues and differences.

The reason cannot be ignorance or the failure to educate in terms of schooling. The cause is bad faith, the same bad faith with which we approach education. Americans know that the advertising to which they are subjected is manipulative and trivial. We hide behind the admittedly alluring surface of television. We permit ourselves to act as though we were hypnotized, but we know very well we can invest ourselves more actively in the formation of opinions. The process is subtle. Although we could do otherwise, we let television set the terms of our politics because it is convenient and it offers us a plausible excuse for our lack of will. We are perfectly capable of resisting and ignoring what we see and hear on television. And we do so regularly. Television is not the enemy, we are. We want to blame some powerful force outside of ourselves; we are too lazy to think and to argue and to question. Yet we also assert that the very habits of self-reliance and independent thought are those we would like our children to acquire in school. Why should a young person do something for twelve years that he or she does not see adults do except for those who can be identified as being paid to do so?

One way around this dilemma is for adult individuals, no matter their jobs or professions, to try to combat this attitude in the conduct of their daily lives. We must find ways to encourage adults who have relationships with children and adolescents to interact with them in ways that show that adults like doing the tasks institutionalized by schools. Going to school should be like taking swimming and driving lessons: preparation for something adults continue to wish to do. The key point is that schooling cannot and must not be viewed as the sole purveyor of learning. Schools work only when learning also happens in the world outside of school. School then can accelerate and deepen well-established and honored habits of everyday life.

The twenty-four maxims in this chapter, one for every hour of the day, are designed to be adaptable to a wide variety of adult-child arrangements. They are intended to be suggestive and not prescriptive. There is never one right way when it comes to parenting or mentoring. These maxims are not contingent on a nuclear family in which one parent stays at home. They do not require any particular social or marital relationship. They are not based on any particular religious doctrine. But they all demand that the child from early on have someone who takes a profound and emotionally believable interest in his or her development. The closer that adult person is, the better. The more long-lasting the relationship, the more profound the influence.

Adults who take on the responsibility of parenting, for whatever reason, must be prepared to run parallel to the distance traveled by the school system. We expect, as a matter of right, that our children have access to schools from age five to age eighteen, from K to 12. Similarly, all children born in this country have the right to expect that an adult of his or her own free will seek to nurture and sustain them, not only from K to 12 but from birth to kindergarten. Without this parallel support system, no educational reform will work. Fortunately, this system does not have to be elaborate or complicated. It is not necessary for the mother to be at home at three o'clock when the children get out of school. It is not essential that parents help children with their homework. There are many ways for many adults to fulfill the obligation of reinforcing in children habits of the mind. Children are naturally curious. Adults must find ways of keeping that part of childhood alive in themselves as an example for their children.

There are four fundamental attributes that should govern any supportive relationship between adults and children outside the school with respect to education: believability, availability, continuity, and regularity. Regularity can mean twice a week, but it cannot mean once a year. Continuity can mean contact over four years, but it cannot mean only one week in isolation. Availability does not mean any time and any place, but neither does it mean rarely or "by appointment only." Believability means credibility. The child must observe the adult doing what the adult asks of the child, or behaving in ways that bespeak respect for learning.

There is a fifth principle that applies both to adults outside of school and to teachers in the classroom: the ability to transform each moment in time and place to be useful to the pursuit of knowledge. In dealing with children and young people, no experience in life is too small, unimportant, or trivial not to offer an opportunity for learning. No second, minute, much less hour or day, passes without inherent significance for the experience of wonderment and reflection. Every moment is, by definition, significant. No doubt there are degrees of importance. There are moments that become transformed as evidently significant and life-changing, and it cannot be predicted when and where those will occur. On the other end of the scale is not a void. In all learning, the unexpected, the counterintuitive, must be taken into account. Since one does not always know ahead of time when teaching or learning is possible or what will be remembered—much less understood—or what may have a profound impact, seemingly transitory experiences demand attention. We sometimes use the phrase "the devil is in the details." By the same reasoning, the sacred, the profound, and the true are also in the details. The devil and God—good and evil and truth and falsehood—are in competition in the arena of the specific. Therefore, every interaction with a child counts.

II. MAXIMS

1. Listen to children. Follow their ways of thinking. Do not short circuit them or impose your thoughts. Respect the child's world.

Literature is filled with the adult's romance with childhood. Lewis Carroll's *Alice in Wonderland* is the most famous and perhaps notorious case in point. Playacting in a childlike manner on the part of adults has taken its own peculiar place in the adult conception of intimacy. Contemporary culture is particularly obsessed with the boundaries between childhood and adulthood. The fault line is sexual maturity. On the one hand, in popular culture and in the visuals of commercial advertisement we celebrate early pubescent adulthood. We fantasize more like Humbert Humbert, the protagonist in Vladimir Nabokov's *Lolita*. On the other hand, in our public policy we flip to the other side. We revile and focus on the abuse of children as the worst form of social deviancy. In all of this we don't actually respect the imagination of children. From the start, in the acquisition of language and the discovery of the world by children, either we condescend to them by the use of baby talk, or we ignore them. The way to respect a child is not to act childish, but to treat the child with the same seriousness with which we treat adults. This means following them in their flights of fancy. A fine example of how this is done well with very young readers can be found in the children's writings of *New Yorker* cartoonist William Steig and, for older children, the work of Daniel Pinkwater. They think like children, with unerring seriousness.

Among the most common mistakes committed in daily interaction is the reflex of interrupting the logic of the child. For example, children imagine the world and how it works differently than adults, often completely bizarrely. Correcting them is not enough. One needs to encourage their counterintuitive speculation, and at the same time get them to see why, in fact, what they imagine to be real might not or could not be real. Adult cultivation of the child's own imagination is a crucial dimension of adult interaction. The worst damage of television is that it short-circuits a child's instinctive capacity to amuse her- or himself by invention and generate an internal visual fantasy and story. Adults can reward that habit of creating mental pictures and stories, not only by paying attention but simply by letting children be and formulate their own worlds.

2. Help children figure things out and find answers for themselves. Do not always simply respond with facts.

Parents often feel obliged to respond to children's questions briefly and simply. No doubt clarity is essential. However, the first thing a child should witness when a question is asked of an adult is not the adult's authority or confidence but curiosity and self-criticism. Children do not need to know that Mom and Dad have the answer; rather they need to see how Dad and Mom arrive at answers and defend them. Unless you happen to be a physicist, answer questions about the sun rising in the morning in an open-ended way. The facts you may know are, by definition, incomplete. Since the words "rising" and "falling" (or "setting") are euphemisms, let the child realize that fact. For example, point out that the sun is setting in one place (at home, perhaps) and rising elsewhere at the exact same moment. When something seems absolutely cut-and-dried—that Paris is the capital of France or that a piece of paper will burn when you put it in a fire—the larger significance of that fact or the other questions it relates to have to be woven in, even in the briefest answer. From the start, every child should know that there is nothing beyond the reach of further inquiry. Asking questions is the most important habit we can nurture.

On the difficult matter of right and wrong, confusing an assumption about ethical behavior (love thy neighbor as thyself) with a fact (babies come from humans and are not delivered by storks) is a dangerous shortcut. Above all, do not falsify or lie in the service of simplification, thinking that an answer "is good enough for children." The Ten Com-

mandments—for example, thou shalt not kill, or thou shall honor thy
father and mother—may seem to be true, as true as the fact that the
earth revolves around the sun. But defending each of these propositions requires a different logic. The ways in which we answer the question "Why?" in both cases do not resemble one another. In the case of
the sun and earth, we cite proofs, experiments, evidence, and logic. In
the case of the commandments, they are not about pure logic and
experience, and living by them is clearly a different proposition. A child
often witnesses anger between parents and grandparents, as well as a
great deal of disrespect between the generations. And as far as killing is
concerned, the violence in history on our screens and in our present
culture makes the truth of the commandment hard to understand. It is
not difficult to live according to the laws of physics, but it is very
difficult to live by the Ten Commandments. Pontificating by authority
in both spheres without reflecting on the meaning and difficulties of
understanding why different things can be true and how things can be
true in different ways deters reflection and encourages thoughtlessness.
And thoughtlessness is a crime itself, with devastating consequences in
the way we conduct our daily lives.

The most important aspect of any easy "fact question" (where does
milk come from?) is, once having given the child the answer, to help
the child arrive at the answer him- or herself. Play scientist if you have
to. Always point to the next level of learning. Milk production, in the
end, is a question of complex biochemical processes. Take a small piece
of paper and show how it burns. Then help the child figure out about
heat and combustion. In complicated matters, incomplete understanding is better than deference to authority. The memorization of facts
and learning by rote are essential in school, but they work only when
the child has developed the habits of musing about questions that
begin with "Why?" Only then are frameworks created in which facts
make sense.

3. Reflect on the exercise of authority.

This is among the most difficult things for parents and teachers to accept. We have an uncanny attraction to authority and certainty, to which we are tied in two ways: we love to possess it, and in an odd and disarming way we love to be subject to it. Communism and fascism did not succeed only through terror and fear. Dictatorships and absolute monarchies thrive through voluntary adherence. Communities bound together by absolutist beliefs, where dissent is frowned upon—for example, truly fundamentalist religious groups—provide clarity through certainty and authority. Authority gives comfort to its membership. We like to have children because for many of us the family is our only arena for the exercise of authority. We can be kings and queens in our own homes.

At the same time, much as we love authority, we resent the monopoly of power that the government, the police, and the military represent. We like to work, but we don't like our bosses. Americans in particular have a heightened sense of not being ordered around. "Don't tread on me" remains among the most memorable Revolutionary War slogans. From the point of view of a teacher and parent, encouraging skepticism with respect to government and a resistance to the imposition of authority is healthy. However, it is difficult to help young people to make the distinction between willful and self-serving criticism of authority and dissent, which reflects an understanding of the necessity of a compromise between individualism and reciprocal obligations in the context of a social contract with others. The Aryan supremacists are anarchists among us who defy the authority of anyone but themselves. They do not accept the premise of the social compact in which individuals exchange natural rights for social rights and responsibilities. But more important, their aims are at odds with the fundamental principles of democratic government. Likewise, those groups that simply want to avoid paying taxes and seek to elevate greed into a principled position of resistance against governmental authority cannot be held up as models. By the same token, there should be no doubt that the abusive government authority and the needless exercise of violence—as in the case of the Waco disaster—represent the danger of intolerance to sectarianism and fanaticism when they are possibly benign and harmless, except for the fact that they threaten our own sense of decency and rationality.

When we return to the matter of families, the issue of authority turns out to be no simpler. Political theory contains a tradition in which political authority is justified by analogy to the unquestioned legitimacy of parental authority. The key to maintaining authority in the family is not in the end the threat and the use of force. That is why, when we talk about families, we often think with pleasure about that brief moment in early childhood when the authority of parents remains respected, unquestioned and unchallenged, making the issue of force unnecessary. The mere assertion of arbitrary will is usually sufficient. When the age and size of our children gradually erode that ease of authority, we try to retain it by displaying superior knowledge.

In contrast to the last century, a large percentage of today's adults will have a longer relationship with their children as adult beings because of extended life expectancy. Therefore, we would be better off developing patterns of relationships that can readily thrive in adulthood. We can best nurture respect for ourselves as parents by stressing the integrity of what we say and how we think. That can be helped by emphasizing from the start what we don't know. When a child encounters a parent or teacher who answers a question by saying, "I'm not sure," or "I don't know," a memorable opportunity is created. The adult can then say, "But I think I know how to find out." Even better, when parents take the risk of hypothesizing an answer, they can indicate how they will try to make sure that it's either right or wrong. Perhaps no clear answer can be found. It may even be that the question is unanswerable or illogical. There are few lessons as long-lasting as the self-confidence displayed by the parent who says, "I guessed wrong; here is the right answer." By imitating the parent, the child can begin to discover how answers can be found, evaluated, and challenged. It's important to stress how tentative our state of knowledge is and how much is yet to be discovered; how what we now regard as true will be revised, refined, and replaced by the work of future generations.

4. Do not encourage children to disparage what they do not know or understand. Find ways to appreciate that which is foreign to you.

Prejudices mirror what we think of ourselves. Hostilities among ethnic and religious groups are, in the final analysis, reflections on how poorly people think of themselves. In America, each competing ethnic group in conflict with another has created a mythic image of the other that overtly highlights sharp differences but reflects fear of their own worst selves. Those who define themselves as white know nothing about the black community; anti-Semites invent a caricature of the Jew that is nothing more than their worst fantasies about the evil in themselves. Too often we fill in the blanks of our own empty pages of personal knowledge with those things we fear and despise that we do know about ourselves but might wish to suppress. Recognition and the embrace of ignorance, therefore, are the first steps to tolerance. The next step requires diminishing the scope of one's ignorance. Since that process never ends, the recognition of one's own fallibility and one's receptivity to new ideas and information become crucial virtues to cultivate in children. The child needs to see, in adult behavior, the link between knowledge and judgment. This maxim applies particularly to the way children learn to respond to and live with people who are quite different from themselves and the adults around them. Adults communicate the decisive cues.

5. Show that you enjoy thinking. Exhibit curiosity in the presence of children. Show a love of learning that parallels what they are being asked to do in school. In this way demonstrate that learning, curiosity, and study endure beyond the years in school.

Learning must be linked with life. Each person can find some way to do this. There are no formulas. We often hear about parents helping children with homework. Showing interest in homework is indispensable, but helping with it can be a double-edged sword. Children need to learn to do work by themselves. Adults don't dribble balls with their children on the court during the game, but they do sit on the sidelines, play with them informally, attend practice sessions and games, and root for them. What is even more important is that schoolchildren should see adults and their parents learning and liking it. This can be accomplished by children observing adults read, hearing them ask questions, witnessing their excitement at discovering something. We need to be as much a nation of learners as we are a nation of consumers. For generations, children have learned to love to shop because they see how much pleasure it gives the adults. Musicians understand this principle readily, since, whether in classical music or in jazz, when one sits down to play with others, what matters are skill and enthusiasm. If we are worried about having a nation of people who sit passively by, watch too much television, complain too much, and don't vote (to cite three of the most common criticisms), we have to change our own behavior and not blame schools, the media, and politicians. Learning should not be a process we connect only with immaturity and childhood. This linkage is particularly nefarious in American culture, where age segregation—distinctions based on age groupings—is so pronounced. The arts and crafts offer great opportunities. Many adults have discovered that they can begin to play an instrument (consider the late John Holt, the educator, who took up the cello as an adult and wrote wonderfully about it), paint, photograph, and make objects. These undertakings should be started by adults as an example to children while the children are young.

6. Encourage children to spend time alone. The time spent alone in childhood and adolescence can be decisive. Resist the emphasis in our culture on group experiences and group acceptance. Fight against the tendency of individuals to judge themselves primarily in terms of how they are seen by the majority of their peers.

The home-schooling movement in America is growing. Much of its momentum derives from families who are dissatisfied with the moral and religious content of the public schools, and even the private schools, from which they might choose. But there is a second factor behind the appeal of home schooling. The balance in the lives of our children between time spent either with others or alone productively has shifted excessively toward time spent with others. We have become a nation that brings up our children with more of a concern about how they appear to others than how they might think of themselves as individuals. America's greatest philosopher, Ralph Waldo Emerson, wrote an essay, "Self-Reliance," that celebrates the ability of Americans to cultivate their own sense of judgment and autonomy.

What has happened, however, is that we have exaggerated another countervailing American virtue: egalitarianism and the desire to belong. Americans have a healthy disregard for people who consider themselves better than others. Furthermore, a nation of immigrants is perpetually insecure about belonging. As outsiders eager to enter the supposed "center" of a culture and society, we exaggerate that center, even invent it, and certainly elevate its significance. The diversity in the origins of Americans leads, ironically, to the intolerance of highly individual differences. We seek to disappear as distinct characters in order to justify our legitimacy as Americans. The success of advertising and mass marketing is based on this drive to assimilate into an indistinct average that we ourselves formulate as a necessary corollary of the ideal of equality.

One of the objectives of a common school is to teach Americans that as citizens and before God, everyone is equal. This absence of a perpetually stable multigenerational aristocracy constitutes the essence of democracy. There is no landed gentry, and inherited wealth lasts only a few generations, as new money always enters the picture. But the price that is paid by too great an emphasis on egalitarianism and conformism in terms of education is unacceptable. From the moment children hit the school classroom, fitting in and getting along are stressed at the expense of the cultivation of personal independence. The tendency is exacerbated by the outside culture. The peer group dominates, and the intolerance of those who are different or who disagree starts from an early age. Children learn to subordinate what they think to a group whose leadership is often based not on wisdom, but on physical prowess and good looks. Bullies succeed all too often in our schools.

We fear that our children will be lonely. In general, Americans are terrified of loneliness. But the only effective antidote to loneliness is the ability to spend time alone, to be content and happy by oneself. We confuse loneliness with solitude. Solitude is a virtue. The capacity to relish spending time alone, doing something with a sense of accomplishment by oneself, and experiencing for oneself, is an important survival skill. It indicates that one is comfortable with oneself. Parents need to support the idea that their children can cultivate their own distinct personalities; that they can be by themselves, think for themselves, and stand up for themselves. Respecting the group and accepting one's place in an egalitarian political structure do not require submitting to a dominant point of view or submerging one's own self into a collective consensus. One teacher admonished a mother at a parent-teacher conference by expressing concern that her child wasn't fitting in. The teacher, however, had no good answer to the parent's retort: "To *what* is my daughter not fitting in?" Merely going along with a group is not a virtue.

In a densely populated world, people live close to one another, as in cities and suburbs. This only makes cultivating independence and autonomy—crucial corollaries to freedom—all the more difficult and essential. It was easier when one's nearest neighbor was miles and hours away. We often ask why so many seemingly decent people sat idly by during the rise of Nazism and permitted an otherwise civilized society to systematically exterminate a specific group of human beings in their midst. All Germans in the period 1933–45 were not murderers. The majority would probably pass as decent, ordinary people. But the fatal flaw in their ordinariness was their thoughtlessness and timidity in relation to what was a wildly popular set of beliefs. Too few individuals had the courage to think independently, to speak out, and to stand up to prejudices and practices that even without critical self-reflection literate people might be presumed to realize are unacceptable and barbaric.

Even though America is a diverse society that now celebrates, in the name of multiculturalism, how different we are, the danger to democracy and civility is not difference, but horrifying sameness. Even the way we define ethnicity and gender has an intolerant uniformity to it. Our differences themselves have become standardized into routine, generalized labels that deter and obliterate individuality. The melting pot was a useful image in the past. Assimilation today need not necessarily breed only uniformity. Yet if we eat the same food, put on the same clothes, think little and in the same way, we won't need to protect free speech because there will be no real dissent. The object lessons of the late twentieth century are not about excessive diversity, but about uniformity. That overarching uniformity transcends ethnic identity or religious belief; it spells the death of all individuality. It is the responsibility of parents and schools to encourage the pride and courage of the individual. A key to achieving this is to help young people enjoy spending time by themselves and thinking for themselves.

7. Do not make too sharp a distinction between small matters and large issues even when questions of right and wrong are at stake. Principles of behavior—issues involving fundamental values— should not be reserved only for apparently weighty matters. Help children see that there are few things we do, particularly in daily life, that are genuinely trivial.

We all love to speak in generalities. The politicians are not the only ones who spew forth well-rehearsed platitudes. Too often we interact with children in an effort to distinguish between right and wrong by citing general principles. One doesn't have to take a course in philosophy to recognize that the use of language to indicate general categories requires a complicated mental reasoning process. Such words as *justice*, *beauty*, and *truth* are, no matter what anyone says, complicated, amorphous, difficult, and imposing. If one is a follower of Plato and believes in the existence of a metaphysical realm, one must concede Plato's view that there are perhaps only a few in society who have the intellectual capacity to grasp such higher general truths. Consider the classical philosophical disagreement between nominalism and realism. Nominalists believe that our general categories are human inventions and are a function of language. Realists believe that general categories might exist, even though they are not knowable by ordinary procedures. The essence of particular things in the world, therefore, can be grasped. But from a parent's point of view, it is probably better to follow Aristotle than Plato and to believe that general principles are only learned from the specific. It is in the encounter with the specific that important lessons are taught.

Most of us are not equipped to hold our own with philosophers and the realm of abstract principles. The things we know best are quite specific. When it comes to values and ways of thinking, children should not copy our assumptions that some things in daily life are obviously less important and even irrelevant. No doubt we all have to make choices and weigh different things in our lives differently. Children need to learn to create and justify hierarchies in the exercise of judgment and value. Therefore, we should encourage children to pay attention to all details and not simply adopt our scheme of things. This will enable them to discover new ways to understand and formulate larger truths. For example, parents are frequently baffled about how to get young children and adolescents to be polite and adopt manners that display our standards of civility. When challenged about politeness, most parents retreat to authority and to the proverbial "Do as I say." Authority is an indispensable technique, but like all forms of coercion, it should be the course of last resort. A much better opening strategy might be to inspire the pragmatic but ethical recognition that in the seemingly small, irrelevant acts of politeness—saying "please," giving up one's seat on a bus, opening a door for others, lending a helping hand, sending thank-you notes, etc.—there are small but significant results that, however fleeting, mean someone momentarily feels better or smiles.

Both the small acts of politeness (which are obviously less potent than saving someone's life or offering a life-changing benefit to someone) and their results can easily be related to larger issues about doing right and wrong. After all, one important issue about believing fundamental values concerns how one achieves some measure of consistency in a complex and chaotic world. If it is wrong to harm someone else, and if it is wrong to be excessively selfish, it is also wrong to hurt someone gratuitously or trivially. Instead of making impoliteness a minor part of a larger framework, we should build up the larger framework by the pregnant possibilities inherent in the seemingly insignificant details of the way we conduct daily life.

The same habit of paying attention to apparently unimportant details can be used to relate to gaining knowledge. How things work and the petty details of day-to-day existence possess opportunities for thinking about larger questions. That's why children are so fascinated about how ordinary things work. They want to know the reasons behind what appears to us to be routine occurrences and unreflected habits in everyday existence. After all, the answer to the question of why the ball rolls downhill can be a beginning point for all of physics. A consequence of this strategy is the validation of a principle that children might well follow. Consider the admonition "not to suffer fools gladly." This phrase is usually misinterpreted to mean that intelligent people rightly have little patience for stupidity. But it is a mark of the truly wise person that he or she does indeed "suffer fools gladly." The opposite of this clichéd admonition is actually the case. One can learn from anyone, if one listens carefully, no matter how obvious or wrong that which someone says seems to be. If someone belabors the obvious, it is interesting to understand why and in what formulation that person accepts conventional ideas so readily. People are wrong and mistaken in interesting, curious, and fascinating ways. There is no encounter that cannot help to strengthen one's powers of observation and reasoning or deepen one's grasp of the world we live in, particularly with respect to the psychology and attitudes of our fellow human beings. Teach children to listen to others empathetically, to follow the thought patterns of others, if only to sharpen their own convictions.

8. Help children to see.

When we let our children move about without looking up, down, and around, we deprive them of one of life's joys. One tradition in Romantic nineteenth-century thought held that our eyes are the source of all understanding. Perception and sight were a unique way of knowing, of taking in information and ideas: a subtle but indispensable adjunct to the use of language. Obviously, we connect what we see with language. We inevitably talk about images and reflect silently on what we see using language. It seems redundant to stress the faculty of sight in a culture dominated by movies and visual advertisements. Pundits tell us over and over that we are living in the age of the supremacy of visual culture. But being inundated and influenced by images is not the same as possessing visual literacy. Visual literacy is about seeing beyond surfaces and appearances with a critical and receptive eye. It is most useful as a means to expand the meaning of daily experience.

Parents can easily play games with children about what can be seen. When moving about with children, always ask them what they see. Encourage them to look beyond, to notice, to compare, to generate mental pictures, and to remember. They should think self-consciously and photographically about the various frames and angles of images, the frozen moments in time that can become the building blocks of visual memory. In conversing with people, children should notice not only what people are saying but how they present themselves physically. Sherlock Holmes is the quintessential symbol of the mastery of the visual observation of details. Details are clues that let us discover how to construct what really might be going on. One excellent experience is to ask children about what they noticed and remembered and to return to the same places and help them expand on what they can see. A senior colleague taught me that when visiting someone's office or home, one should try to take in as much detail as one can about the visual environment. When walking on the street, one should look around at design and architecture, at the way the light falls, at people and the way they move and gesture, at colors and shapes.

Encourage children to use sight as a trigger for asking questions. Help them link what they see to daydreaming and imaginary worlds. Cultivating in children the faculty of sight in the mundane, every day, makes it much easier to encourage them to like looking at art and to think independently about the character and significance of beauty. The way one looks at the world at large easily influences the way one responds to being in a museum or in a gallery looking at new art. Opening up sight creates an entirely fresh avenue for taking pleasure in both the apparently ordinary and the exceptional, in the natural environment and the world created by human intervention. A generation with independent visual imaginations will see to it that art—in movies, in objects, on canvases, and in industrial design—will not atrophy.

9. Encourage children to hear.

Hearing is much like seeing. There is always a foreground and a background, which we, the hearer, create by discriminating among the myriad of sounds around us. We hear selectively. Therefore, it is important to train young children to listen. The imperative to pay attention is one key to making sense out of the objective chaos of noise around us. We should also reflect on what we respond to in a seemingly effortless manner. Listening requires noticing and separating what is happening around us in terms of sound. Children should think early about the tone of a voice and the color of a sound. They should notice the space that sound occupies and concentrate on that which they take for granted, such as the wind, the street, the hum of appliances. Too often we make too facile a distinction between noise and meaningful sound such as speech and music. Children should consider all of noise as musical events. They should learn to concentrate on the rhythms of the subway, the patterns of birds, the pitch of the scratch on the black-board, the timbre of a creaky floor. All children should be encouraged to play with found objects and fill time with sounds they make using pots and pans, their hands, spoons, and other objects. A heightened sense of the beauty and variety of sound allows the child to create a wide palette of sound events, which in turn can make aural memory more acute. An ear for accents, for habits of speech, and for words is an important adjunct to literacy. Listening critically helps concentration and the power to sit quietly. All this has little to do with musicality— the ability to discern and reproduce pitch and play music patterns. Above all, learning to listen permits all children to appreciate silence.

One of the major differences between our contemporary world and that of the past lies in the changes in acoustic environments. There were always noises and ambient sounds. The nineteenth-century city created its own new sound world. But there is little historical precedent for the extraordinary density and diversity of sound in which we now live. Apart from the sounds of nature, technology, and industry, we have recorded sound. The ease of sound reproduction has made us very uncomfortable with real silence or quiet. In turn, this impatience has robbed us of the true sense of excitement we might have when we encounter music. The overdose of sound and noise makes us less able to respond to or focus on music. Helping the child early on to appreci-ate silence, to discriminate among sounds, to enjoy the process of se-lecting and using one's ears to discover, and to resist sound as well, increases the chances that young people will appreciate the very special world created by music. One residual benefit of encouraging very young children to be aware of the power and subtleties of hearing and controlling sounds is that the more one can listen in a discriminating manner, the less loud something has to be to grab one's attention. Too often rock music is accused by such conservative pundits as the late Allan Bloom of being a key source of contemporary cultural decline and moral evil. The only authentic downside to rock on which there might be agreement is that it is unnecessarily loud. It can damage hearing. It is often designed to take too easy a shortcut to getting and holding attention. Cultivating a child's capacity to listen well can put voluntary brakes on the delight taken in brute force in the form of sheer volume; inventiveness in rock music flourishes more readily at lower decibel levels.

10. From the start, encourage children to write.

The simple fact is that we measure educational performance in our schools nearly exclusively by testing the passive use of literacy. The question "Can you read?" is not sufficient. There is a lie implicit in the separation of reading and writing skills in the American school curriculum, which is that one can read well without being able to write well. That simply isn't true. The best readers are those who can write, because only they can easily go below the surface by asking how and why any piece of writing is the way it is, whether in a newspaper, a magazine, or a letter. The difficulty is that children do not grow up in homes where they witness adults using writing just for fun or for the solution of important tasks in daily life. The one exception, of course, is the computer. However, with the popularity of Windows and the use of the mouse, the necessity of using explicit written commands has been bypassed. Certainly, chatboxes and interactive programs and e-mail will bring more children into contact with each other and with adults who write. This is one of the finest contributions the computer can make. The restoration of the visibility and prestige of being able to express oneself in writing may remain on the horizon. But most of our schools and homes have not yet caught up with this. And the voice-activated computer may reverse the progress already made.

Today we communicate largely by telephone and in person. Since we travel easily, we visit the relatives and friends we like. We call and drop in. The only relatives to whom we write are those we really don't want to see. When we want to avoid confronting something or someone, we resort to written communication. Bureaucrats specialize in this. And in the worst instance, when we have deep conflicts, we hire lawyers who do the writing for us.

The antidote to this is for more adults to keep personal diaries and journals and to make their entries while children can watch them doing it. Children need to see that adults use writing as it should be used: as a means of discovering what one thinks. Anyone who writes knows that what teachers frequently say is not true. One doesn't really know what one thinks before one begins to write. Rather, as in a chess game, one begins to write with an opening gambit. The endgame is not yet in sight. Often we begin to write on a hunch. Now that editing and revising on computers have become easy, we can write more spontaneously, drafting what we once might have said aloud. Particularly in the keeping of journals and diaries, the act of writing triggers a process of association. Ideas and connections that didn't exist before one began writing emerge. Writing is not an act of documentation. It is an act of invention and creation open to all, a way we continue to define ourselves and expand the range of that definition. Writing should be a crucial part of the voyage of self-discovery. Every adult can benefit from it. But the most powerful benefit is that if adults enjoy writing for themselves on a daily basis, they teach children by example the power and joy associated with active literacy. In this way the home not only can support the school but can force the school to raise its own standards.

11. Connect children to adults through reading.

Having established that writing is an important activity for the home (and as will be argued, television should be rationed and put in its proper place), we come to an easy piece of advice. Adults should read on a regular basis and be observed doing so. Children should get up in the morning and see adults reading newspapers. They should see you read the mail. And most of all they should see you read for pleasure at home in the evenings and on weekends. The notion that one should read to young children is widely appreciated. But nothing is more effective than reading to the whole family. Children are even more impressed when adults read aloud to one another. Americans spend a good deal of time in the car, where some people listen to books on tape. Like radio drama, listening to recorded readings of books sparks the visual imagination. It cultivates concentration, because in order to follow the story line one listens and imagines simultaneously. But for those who can handle the motion of the moving car, reading aloud to one another while traveling is better. You can stop to reread, to react, and to talk. Reading becomes personal. And when you read, show emotion. Laugh aloud. Show displeasure and anger. Don't seem impassive. One of E. B. White's finest moments in the classic *Charlotte's Web* is the death of Charlotte. (Like other works of great literature, it is a story for both children and adults.) Children marvel at the fact that their parents can hardly keep their composure when reading about Charlotte's death. A writer has shown himself to be so good that the reader has made one type of transfer from fiction to reality and cries over the death of a spider.

Last, vary what children see you read. On some level, it makes little difference what one reads. On another, it is important to read not only fiction and journalism but a variety of nonfiction, including philosophy. Read books from other times and places than your own, particularly the great classics of European and American culture. Reread books you love. There is always more and something different to be gotten out of good books. Among my most precious memories is my awareness that my grandfather read and reread *War and Peace* many times. He also read it to me.

12. Don't demonize television, but don't rely on it yourselves. Compete with it, do not artificially replace it.

Television is attacked unfairly. It has become an easy scapegoat. It is not responsible for what is wrong in our culture, our schools, or our society. On the matter of violence, if television were really as influential as it is supposed to be, there would be much more violence, given the extent of violence on the screen. Television is, however, the most alluring form of entertainment ever invented. It is spellbinding because it combines sound and picture with a compelling mix of illusionism and realism. It's a richly orchestrated, fast-moving magic trick that never stops. Because it is mesmerizing, it's hard to turn off.

What television is not and never will be is a serious tool of learning. Educational television is an oxymoron, much like corporate philanthropy. Educational television—such as Ken Burns's fine documentaries or *Masterpiece Theatre*—is essentially higher-grade entertainment. If one is well educated, television (particularly CNN and news programs) can add marginally to what one thinks about and remembers. But without an education and the capacity to sit still without TV, television is useless as a means of learning. *Sesame Street* is helpful and amusing only to those children who know how to read or are learning how to read without television. All the programs about public affairs, history, and biography, as well as the dramatizations of literature, are best suited to those who either already read and think about politics or who have read the books involved: those who are genuinely literate. Teachers who use television in the classroom as a surrogate are cheating.

Once we accept the idea that television is great entertainment, we can proceed to deal with it constructively. The first step is to realize that television-watching is not a childhood disease. It is so magnetic that if children develop the habit of watching it early in life, they can fritter away endless hours with little to show for it later. The way to avoid having children watch television is for adults not to watch it themselves. Television does incline one to passivity and speechlessness. One consequence of parenthood is the necessity to internalize self-restraint. With children around, someone is always watching you. Every parent knows that freedom and flexibility are reduced during the years of child-rearing. That principle applies particularly to television-watching. Second, television should never be used as a baby-sitter. Third, it should never be watched regularly, even for a limited period of time. There is no need to ration it on a daily basis. Two hours every day can be worse than fourteen hours in a single day. Television should be treated like ice cream: as an occasional harmless event. But the worst sin of all remains the illusion that television can be harnessed for good purposes. It is to the intellectual and spiritual development of individuals what a diet of milk shakes is to physical health. There are two notable exceptions to this principle. The first concerns video and television that an individual makes him- or herself. As an active medium of expression, television holds great potential. Recent video technology makes shooting and editing increasingly easy, affordable, and accessible. Perhaps today's near monopoly on programming, particularly in the area of news and public affairs, will be undermined by local and individual initiatives.

Second, in moments of political crisis and in conditions of censorship, television has and will continue to be indispensable. Television played a role in the downfall of communism in Eastern Europe, particularly in East Germany. The traffic in underground video material continues to be a force against state control of the media in countries with authoritarian regimes. Television will clearly remain a medium for the rapid worldwide dissemination of events and information, particularly in cases where the anticipation of television and its actual intervention are part and parcel of the events themselves.

13. Show children that you change your mind, and how and why.

Children need to see how adults connect thought and action. One obvious way to show this link is to let children in on the process of how, by speaking and doing and by being explicit about why, we change our minds. In their relationships with children, adults become models. Imitation can and must be a key part of learning. We don't want to and can't always give reasons for what we think or do. But when we change our minds, an important opportunity is created. Reasons become vitally important. Since every child, from the very start of consciousness, should learn why and how we act, there is no better moment for teaching and setting an example than those times when we change course and direction. It opens up ways to show the influence of other people's ideas and arguments; how new information changes assumptions. It exposes, unfortunately, the nature of arbitrariness. Whims become harder to camouflage. Most of the things we choose to do or are maneuvered into doing fall into that immense gray area between good and evil and absolutely white and black choices. Life is made up of compromises and less-than-ideal options. Most often we do not choose between what is unequivocally right and what is unequivocally wrong. Negotiating the waters of ambiguity and complexity is the hardest thing to teach. Despite our best intentions, all actions reveal unintended and unforeseen consequences. That experience deepens our uncertainty and doubt. A leap of faith is frequently associated with taking a position and doing something.

The more children see how all this works, the more they will be able to take risks and weigh alternatives well. Children should be encouraged to take risks in thinking, and to be original. Adults can teach the courage necessary to take a stand and hold fast to one's beliefs. Ironically, the best opportunity for teaching this process is when children can appreciate that we are inconsistent. Those are the moments when children need and want an explanation most. One obvious residue in such cases is the child's awareness that adults do not fear change or the idea that they have made mistakes and misjudgments. The worst habit to display in front of children is the moralization and self-justification that adults engage in when they are faced with awkward circumstances. To assert high-minded principles when we know they do not totally apply or to conveniently downplay the ambiguity of a situation is all too human. But if we are concerned with teaching children to think, seizing the high ground should be done sparingly and only when it is truly important and thoroughly valid.

Therefore, seek to explain yourself. Do not imitate God or the Ten Commandments. Limit the use of brief categorical claims. Following this segment of advice may lead us as much to the danger that we all talk too much. But much of human communication is nonverbal. Nonverbal explanations exist: a gesture, a wink, a smile, a scowl, even a pat on the back. Adults must be sensitive to when it is inappropriate merely to proceed without explanation, particularly when adolescents are concerned. Too often adolescents misread silent cues and gestures. Democracy thrives on the rule of law. Not only is the proper and fair application of law crucial, but so is the ability to challenge the legitimacy and fairness of laws. The mere imposition of dictates of authority is too dangerously analogous to the application of force. The "do it because I say so" prescription without justification in families is a bad model for the way we conduct ourselves as citizens. Being explicit and showing why is an obligation, even if it refers to one's irrational sensibilities and wishes.

14. Tell children stories, knowing that more is at stake than entertainment.

In fifth-century Athens, the Homer texts were a key source of education. Homer's magic in part was his greatness and skill as a storyteller. Children love to listen to stories. Tell them real tales—from history. Tell them imaginary stories and display your own inventiveness and playfulness. Tell them about your youth and childhood. Do not keep unnecessary secrets, and choose the proper time to tell them about tragedies as well as triumphs. Do not exaggerate your own exploits in a manner that erodes the development of a child's self-confidence. Self-confidence is often inadvertently diminished by the way adults present themselves in stories. All children should know as much as possible about their ancestors and the origins of the adults around them. The circumstances of birth and death—the places and people of the past—should come alive to children. Truth is more often than not the best defense and the least harmful way to proceed, even when the truth seems painful. Older adults should continue the practice with grandchildren. And they all should write down their memories. Stories can be embellished (as they often are) to lend them excitement and mystery. And do not fear repeating the same stories. Children love the familiar and are more intrigued than you think by how you alter or do not alter the same tale in its retelling.

15. Avoid complaining constantly in the presence of children.

It ought to go without saying that most of our life demands a tolerance for the constant personal confrontation with a daunting and unpredictable mixture of failure and success, pleasure and pain, satisfaction
and disappointment. Life is frustrating, and so, too, is work. We never
live in the best of all possible worlds; we live in the only world in which
we can live. Since we have no choice, it makes no sense to denigrate
our times, our century, the world in which we live. That's foolish. But
more harmful is the constant complaining about one's lot in life. This is
especially the case when it comes to work. Americans talk a good game
about the importance of a work ethic, but it is hard to cultivate that
ethic when adults complain about how hard they work, how much they
don't like to do it, how bad the pay and conditions of their work are,
and express little else than cynicism. If the only point of work is the
relief from work that earning money provides—leisure and retire-
ment—then it is hard to imagine that children will grow up eager to
work. Why not simply pursue leisure without work? Simply saying that
it's unrealistic to get something for nothing is not convincing to the
child if, in fact, you believe that in an ideal world you are owed something for nothing. There is nothing wrong with complaining about what
is. Everything could be better. Complacency is no virtue. Ambition to
improve things is essential. But we often don't realize that a balance
between complaint and appreciation fails to be struck.

One of the most devastating distortions to come out of the shock of
the Holocaust is the ease with which we had expanded the notion of
who is a victim. Those who died and those who survived the concentration camps are unquestionably innocent victims. However, they do not
constitute a general metaphor for how life works. We would like to
avoid taking responsibility for our lot in life. We would like to ascribe
our failures and unhappinesses to forces larger than ourselves: the society, the culture, the economy, our employers, our teachers, our parents.
The generalization of victim status has gone well beyond its reasonable
application. Children must learn that we are willing to take responsibil-

ity for our lot in life. If we take responsibility, we may be less inclined to complain, because if we do complain, then we inevitably have to blame ourselves. If we accept responsibility, we would then be more inclined to do something about that which we complain about. That, in turn, might lead to having less to complain about. Children, like everyone else, have a tendency to remember bad news more easily than good news. So it is not the number of minutes we spend time complaining or expressing satisfaction that counts; it is the perceived balance and the emotional weight we give to complaining and the expression of satisfaction. Optimism and a sense of possibility must be part of what we impart to children. They must help children hold their own against cynicism, mistrust, and anger.

16. Discuss "adult" topics, particularly politics, with children.

No doubt we need to deal with children both as children and as young adults from the very start. The magic of childhood, which has been referred to before, needs to be kept alive. But there are dimensions of being in the world, where the image and reality of childhood do not apply. Parents should locate those areas and from the start begin to treat children as incipient adults. Concern for others and the realm of politics is one important case in point. From an early age, children should be part of discussions about politics and society. When talked to about those things, the same seriousness and tone of voice and attitude displayed with friends and relatives should be directed to children. If the love of reading can be cultivated best in childhood, so, too, can the love of citizenship and the pleasure of holding political opinions and acting on them.

17. Cultivate a sense of humor.

This seems self-explanatory but bears repetition. Children love to see adults laugh. Sometimes they will understand why, and sometimes they will need to accept the irrationality attendant to the sources of humor. Perhaps the most important part of displaying a sense of humor is being able to laugh at oneself. Laughing only at the expense of others does not qualify as having a sense of humor. If one is humorless about oneself, one is in trouble. Furthermore, one needs to show how humor can be interjected when it is most necessary and least expected. Humor is an important way to defuse tension and to shift moods. Many parents cultivate wonderful ways to make children laugh when they are out of sorts or unhappy. Children must observe adults doing that among themselves. Humor is related to playfulness, and while we take many games seriously, we ought to show children we play games that lead us to laugh—once again, at ourselves.

18. Avoid inexplicable double standards.

Double standards and inconsistencies are the stuff of life. It is impossible to avoid them and to create a circumstance in which children never witness them. The best advice is to be honest about them and to clarify why imposing a double standard or being inconsistent was an unavoidable consequence of the lesser of evils. Candor about the inability to get out of a difficult situation is another example of how in very sensitive and complex circumstances the simple truth works best. Do not camouflage the persistence of awkward and murky circumstances.

19. Do not sacrifice complexity for convenience.

We all are busy people. Perhaps because of their size, children often bear the brunt of our being in a hurry. We also assume that in dealing with children it pays to keep it simple. However, it is better to allude briefly to the idea that things aren't as simple as they appear. Putting the child on notice that most things in life bear close scrutiny encourages the idea that such scrutiny is rewarding. The best of all circumstances is to make the time to explain something. Children are the last of our interlocutors who should be given short shrift. The world should stop so that we can answer the questions of our children. Part of answering is, of course, paying attention. In the Jewish tradition it is alleged that the indentation above our lips comes at birth. All knowledge is contained in the newborn child, but an angel presses a finger on the lips of the newborn so that each child can keep the secret. This idea in part justifies the saying that from the mouths of babes can come the truth. Abrupt exchanges with children prevent us from hearing the truth in a new way from those who are younger. Passing children over deprives the adult from learning from them, from drawing out the truth the angel has placed in them. The new perspectives on the truth children offer us deepen our sense of how rich and many-sided life is.

20. Foster a genuine concern for the welfare of others.

This piece of advice is a cliché. But it is in this arena that a gap between rhetoric and reality is most pronounced. Ultimately, the consequences of learning should be evident in the quality of our interactions with our fellow human beings. Even the most abstract speculation can have its ethical consequences. So-called mere speculation or the appearance of spinning one's wheels (for example, about how many angels can dance on the head of a pin) is actually a celebration of the human imagination and can be linked to a sense of well-being on the part of the person who speculates and the person who listens. But most of what we can teach has consequences that are less abstract or amorphous. If a child grows up seeing adults paying attention to those around them, being concerned with the well-being of others, and doing things for others, the need for knowledge and expertise becomes all the more evident to the child. And we should not hide the satisfaction we get from being helpful and concerned.

We should bridge the presumed gap between self-interest and altruism. It may not exist, and therefore the key is to define one's own happiness partly in terms of the well-being of those around oneself. We are in the habit of citing the pursuit of happiness as a right of each individual. But remember that Thomas Jefferson's phrase in the Declaration of Independence was a moral claim. The right to pursue happiness, by definition, involves a reciprocal obligation. We can't search for happiness entirely alone, and therefore our capacity to find happiness is contingent on others permitting us and helping us to do so. That is in part why institutions in civil society, such as schools, museums, and volunteer organizations, are crucial to us all. The possession of knowledge is a key part of this dynamic. Free speech is, likewise, a reciprocal virtue in society. In an environment of openness the benefits of truth and the exposure of falsehood are shared. Learning, therefore, is part of how we must define doing something for others. Every child should understand that his or her achievement in school is, in and of itself, a contribution to the welfare of others. In this way the child should recognize that doing something someone else does not do can constitute something extraordinary. Self-cultivation must be understood as an integral part not only of one's individual existence but of that of others.

21. Teach the value of holding convictions. Admit to stubbornness and even willfulness when they occur. Do not rationalize or equivocate.

Lawyers are trained to function in a closed adversarial system, the law. We frequently adapt this model so that life appears to run parallel to the way legal disputes are framed and adjudicated. In this mental picture, life becomes an adversarial system. This, in turn, leads to the notion that extremes rarely represent the truth but are only strategic ploys. The truth, therefore, always seems to rest, as the saying goes, somewhere in the middle. This is not usually the case, because the law is not a comprehensive or complete prism through which life can be understood. The law is about winning, but life generally has more to do with convictions and truths in a context without final outcomes. One's convictions need not always be tempered by the need to compromise or to accommodate. Compromise and accommodation may be necessary and realistic at the same time they can be fundamentally wrong. It is, for example, never right to lie, but one might contemplate the expediency of doing so in the real circumstances of life.

Children not only should see compromise and accommodation; they should know where adults stand. They should see them defy the majority and cut their own path. That is the necessary prerequisite for discovering how they might be convinced to follow or how they might agree to disagree. Much in the same vein, there are moments when stubbornness and firmness are necessary—for example, when adults stand up in public to speak their mind and defend their ideas and actions. We can find ourselves in circumstances in which, in seeking to explain something, we are forced to make bad arguments. Such arguments shouldn't be made knowingly, and in cases when one has no appeal for an explanation beyond irrational and personal judgment, then that should be made clear. Rationalization is a pejorative term because it is "misleading" and unnecessary. And when one does it, one should avoid making it seem a virtue. Children should see bad habits when they exist and see that the adult knows that they are bad. Smoking, for example, is a bad habit. There is no need to rationalize it. There is a virtue in facing it for what it really is, and even in admitting personal weakness in not being able to control it.

22. Stress the evolutionary and open-ended character of knowledge, interpretation, and inquiry. Teach children not to judge too harshly or quickly.

The corollary to the above maxim is that even when one is entirely certain and takes what might be assumed to be an extreme or absolute and unassailable position, always hold out the possibility of being wrong. This is particularly important in confronting one's own beliefs and prejudices. No doubt there are truths that seem certain, but in fact the linguistic claims that a truth is absolute often are only expressions of high probability. If the probabilities of disproof are minuscule, there is no reason to shut the door unequivocally. The child should always have the sense that every question is open for reconsideration and that there are no taboos. A sense of one's own fallibility and the possibility that what we now believe to be true can be revised is not the same as relativism. Relativism in its extreme form admits of few possibilities for hierarchies of value or even for reigning hypotheses that function as true statements. A sense of fallibility is an essential human characteristic. It is a tacit admission of the possibilities in the progress of knowledge. There are, after all, statements which are nonsensical and wrong.

Therefore, introduce children to the habit of making responsible judgments and to the inevitable encounter with the risk and doubt that come with choosing and making decisions. What we think and what we do have consequences. Taking responsibility for those consequences is an indispensable lesson. Whether or not we truly believe that we are in control of our own lives, we must act as if we are. Even when we are not sure, it is better to err on the side of stepping forward to take responsibility for what happens around us than the opposite. Many decisions are the result of predictions we make that are rarely complete or entirely accurate. The gift of foresight, which Prometheus presumably gave to the human race, is not the gift of prophecy. Rather, it was the ability to think and to plan ahead. That was the essence of the Promethean gift of knowledge in the form of fire. Knowledge triggers the dignified opportunity to be held accountable. As knowledge increases, so does the sense of responsibility. Children should know that responsibility is not a burden, but a source of excitement and meaning. Further, they should see that we must act even when we are not certain. Doubt and risk are central to life and are no justification for inaction, passivity, or paralysis. Doubt, however, does not absolve the doer from taking responsibility if things go wrong after the fact.

23. Resist conventional wisdom. Balance a respect for tradition and authority with skepticism.

It is ironic that in creating maxims an author should warn the reader of clichés and conventional wisdom. There is no necessity to be original. What is new might be good, and what is good may not turn out to be new. But if one is going to adhere to convention and to well-worn truths, one should do so having carefully considered the alternatives. Maxims and facile claims are like spurs in the side of a horse. They are useful to get one going on one's own train of thought. The composer Gustav Mahler is reputed to have said that the appeal of tradition is a bad excuse in the form of sloppiness. He was only partially right. A facile appeal to tradition is insufficient. But if one travels the journey of thinking and questioning and comes out on the side of what is already widely known and understood, there is no shame in it.

Likewise, merely being skeptical is no virtue. We are often subjected to a school of investigative journalism that operates on the assumption that nothing that appears to be good or honest is really so; that under the proverbial rug there is always dirt. A permanently suspicious view of the ideas and actions of others is no more superior than blind faith and is as arrogant. Children should question what they hear and read. But even the radical skeptic must admit the fallibility of skepticism. And encourage children to think counterintuitively. A nation of educated individuals who think and are curious might find its way to accept that what is commonly held to be true is what passes for conventional wisdom. The reverse is equally true. In that sense, the progress of science can be a model for us all. For all the ills attributed to modern science and medicine, the refinement and alteration of conventional wisdom in those arenas has led to ongoing advances against disease, pain, and premature death.

24. Use games that engage children.

Games offer the chance to join in with children. They show children that adults are like them. They create an encounter with chance and mystery and provide opportunities to escape the routine of the everyday. Games are self-contained worlds that define and occupy time in unique ways. They mirror the indispensable play element in all cultures. Among the most powerful aspects of play are word games. Language, in its varieties and possibilities, is an inexhaustible source of playfulness, ingenuity, and fun. The philosopher and writer Fritz Mauthner recounted that as a child surrounded by many different languages, his favorite pastime was playing with words and experimenting with their possibilities. Comparing uses and meanings and even combining languages lead to inventing uses, meanings, and patterns. Word games lead to discovering not only subtleties and novelties but also originality and insight.

Do not only teach children to play games but let them create and choose games. Games enable adults to teach children what they know and can do. Let children win—without cheating, but give them a head start. Level the playing field. Show them the pleasure of winning. Most of all, show them that you, too, know how to lose, especially to them.

CHAPTER V

THE AMERICAN COLLEGE

I. TRADITION AND UNIFORMITY

Once the prestigious end point of education and the province of the few, college is gradually becoming a pivotal intermediary step in our essentially democratic system of education. It forms a necessary bridge to graduate and professional education. The American college has retained some of its glamorous aura even though its role has expanded and despite pressure from below by the shortcomings of high school preparation and from above by the expectations of advanced study beyond the B.A. degree. College is now as indispensable as high school was a century ago for advancement beyond blue-collar employment. In an economy based on technology and human services, college has become today's minimum standard of schooling. Half of the population that reaches eighteen and finishes high school now starts college, a figure that represents nearly 40 percent of all American eighteen-year-olds.

Even though the two-year community college program is the fastest-growing part of American postsecondary education, the image of college that the public still holds up as exemplary in its collective imagination is that of the private, residential New England college. We imagine college as a place with ivy covering the walls of Federal style or Gothic Revival buildings. These structures form the ubiquitous campus quadrangle with its well-kept and carefully edged lawn. Nearly every college prospectus—the brochure sent to prospective students—features some sort of a scene showing happy, smiling faces framed by the bright colors of fall leaves. Harvard, Princeton, Yale, and the College of William and Mary were the first to help shape this ideal. The pretensions of these elite American residential colleges harken back to their English progenitors and examples, notably Oxford and Cambridge. In the Northeast, the South, and the Midwest throughout the nineteenth century, this Anglophilic model was imitated with variations. One thinks of Bryn Mawr, Vassar, Kenyon, Grinnell, Duke, and Vanderbilt.

The great, huge land-grant universities founded in the late nineteenth century also drew inspiration from the eighteenth- and early-nineteenth-century American college and its English predecessors. These land-grant universities were novel. They also integrated aspects of the nineteenth-century German research university. By the twentieth century, the American university and college had evolved into a distinct and highly competitive offshoot of English and continental European traditions. The most prominent aspect of the English inheritance is the special place maintained by undergraduate education. The idea persists that the college years are crucial, since they prepare an elite to exercise leadership in society. This claim lies at the heart of the standard speech given by most college presidents to each year's entering class.

Habits reminiscent of a feudal European aristocratic past linger on in American colleges and universities. Each college has its own seal: a sort of coat of arms. Like a clan or aristocratic family, each has its own motto. Universities have their official songs, their school colors, and frequently their private clubs and societies. Every institution seeks to cultivate a nearly exclusive sense of loyalty and obligation among its members, past and present. Colleges justify this effort by making claims to unique heritages, customs, and legacies. They hope that students will internalize a lifelong sense of identification somewhat akin to membership in a tribe or an eighteenth-century Masonic lodge. The

generalized expectation is that the years spent in college will be trans-
formative and decisive to one's life.

Like competing feudal baronies, colleges maintain active rivalries
and jealousies sustained mostly through intercollegiate sports. No analysis of American colleges should be permitted to gloss over the scandal
constituted by the collegiate emphasis on semiprofessional athletics.
Sports are an essential part of college life, but as a participatory learning
opportunity. It is an embarrassment that so much time, effort, emotion,
and money are expended on gladiatorial exhibitions by state and private institutions. They corrupt academic standards and institutional
integrity. We should support athletics in the Greek ideal—that of amateurism and general participation—not in the Roman model in which
training is lavished on a few and the rest of the community is relegated
to being passive spectators. The investment in and image of excellence
and superiority should be reserved for teaching and research, not the
playing field. The threat of negative alumni/ae reaction should be faced
head-on as part of a national movement that highlights the civic support needed for the educational mission at the university. We do not
need the university to provide sports entertainment on television for
the general public. In the end, the public will respect the university
more if it separates itself from prime-time sports competition.

Sports feed the endemic territorialism of American colleges. Not a
year goes by at Harvard without some ritual in which clever jibes are
directed at Yale. Anti-Harvard jokes crop up each year at Yale. Williams
and Amherst, Smith and Mt. Holyoke, Carleton and St. Olaf's, all seek
to maintain a competitive tension, vis-à-vis one another, among their
staff, students, and alumni/ae. Colleges treat current students as part of
a mythically continuous and coherent organism that can pass on particular rituals and recognizable principles from one generation to the next.
While much of this sounds, and in fact is, somewhat childish and
anachronistic, the investment in sustaining a ready-made institutional
sense of identity works as a psychological device. A sense of place and
belonging becomes available immediately to entering students. This is
a compelling strategy, for it offers to every vulnerable adolescent a

facile and reassuring response to the inevitable sense of doubt about one's self-worth and place in the world that adolescents, often away from home for the first time, periodically feel. Unfortunately, too many Ivy League college graduates have been overwhelmed by the allure of the official institutional image, which later in life often signals the high-water mark of an individual's own sense of personal distinction and achievement.

But despite America's uniquely colorful and apparently highly var-iegated assemblage of public and private institutions, each with its own identity and traditions, there is an underlying and terrifying truth. Most American institutions are complacent and intellectually uniform. American institutions are largely indistinguishable from each other, in-terchangeable in terms of curriculum, faculty, and basic campus atmo-sphere. The number of truly distinctive and genuinely unique institu-tions is actually rather small; the list might include the California Institute of Technology, the University of Chicago, and St. John's Col-lege in Annapolis.

The reasons for this predicament lie in the economics and demo-graphics that colleges and universities have faced since World War II. During this period, public higher education grew at a staggering rate and was, comparatively speaking, well funded. The best state universi-ties now compete easily with the Ivy League in all respects, particularly in the recruitment of first-rate faculty and students. At the same time, the competition for students and philanthropy both within the private sector and among all institutions has become fierce, particularly in light of the gradual erosion in the rate of growth in state and federal support, a process that began during the 1980s. Optimistic pundits suggest that we are on the brink of a new age of private philanthropic largesse as a result of the recent massive accumulation of wealth by individuals and that American higher education need not worry. Philanthropy, how-ever, is too often fickle and not adventuresome in terms of higher education.

The economics of colleges and universities remain an unsolved puz-zle. The expenses rise at rates greater than inflation, owing to the need to keep up with advances in science and technology. At the same time, the cost of attending both public and private institutions has risen, and the availability of financial aid has declined. The nation still awaits a rational system under which Americans can obtain what is now essential for the economy: a good college education. Despite all the rhetoric expended on the virtues of efficient and businesslike management, a university is only partially a business. Much of what it does best, the encouragement of thought, is not susceptible to efficiency standards. Furthermore, even when they are poorly run, the basically inflexible and labor-intensive structure limits the damage so-called wasteful management can incur. And few sectors in American economic life are as aware of the limitations on resources.

On the institutional side, the response to decades of increased competition and public scrutiny has been largely managerial and not entrepreneurial. In order to underscore the validity of one's product (and justify the seemingly extravagant price tag) beneath the veneer of a unique institutional character, trustees, administrators, and faculty have systematically cultivated a conservative, risk-avoiding, look-alike character. A quite stable set of institutional arrangements and requirements has resulted. The deviations result primarily from the effort on an individual campus to develop some marginal differentials in terms of particular fields where superiority and excellence can be asserted. Selected investments in programs and specialties help vary an otherwise interchangeable and common product delivered in comparable terms by all institutions.

The scramble for support, prestige, and status, therefore, has led colleges and universities to imitate each other and at the same time cultivate the image of difference. Institutions fear that breaking away may result in having a currency, as it were, that does not convert beyond the confines of a single campus. Credits may not be accepted and degrees may not be recognized if programs of study do not seem to cross institutional boundaries. An elaborate superstructure of regional accreditation and state regulation further helps to ensure conformity and depress innovation. This is justified in the name of quality control and the application of shared standards of excellence. Harvard remains the most frequently cited model for private institutions. The University of California at Berkeley, the University of Michigan, and the University of Texas help set the standard in the public sector.

The fact that most undergraduate programs of study are organized in much the same way as graduate faculties are designed has created a parallel momentum in the college curriculum toward sameness—toward an elective course and credit system based in departments and majors. This pattern, augmented by a few so-called distribution and general education requirements, is replicated in all but a few colleges. To some extent the fact that the history department at, for example, Dartmouth resembles the history department at the University of Arizona is a good thing. Local pride and traditions ought not interfere with an institution's taking its rightful place in an international world of research and teaching. No doubt there will be some notable differences in emphasis. Arizona, for example, will have expertise specific to the culture and history of the Southwest, in part because it is a public institution funded to serve the state and its citizens.

But going to college and getting an undergraduate education are not exclusively about specializing in a given field or about professional or preprofessional training. Most liberal arts graduates do not earn their living in a manner directly connected to their major. The justification for majoring in English, history, or mathematics as an undergraduate does not primarily reside in the idea that the major will be directly connected to some obvious employment opportunity. In cases where there are preprofessional undergraduate programs of study—in business, engineering, and education—not only is there still some pretense to general education, but these preprofessional programs often condemn their graduates to a short-term advantage and long-term disadvantage: the first job is easier to get, but advancing beyond middle management turns out to be harder.

The college years are the first encounter in the American system between serious learning and reflection and the presumption of adulthood. College is where many young adults mature and refine their adult personalities and therefore their fundamental attitudes and skills that extend beyond the range of the first job. This fact alone has lent the question of where one goes to college enormous significance. College is the last link in the chain of general education, where the purposes of education legitimately reach beyond the narrow but crucial objective of preparing a young person for work and employment. Undergraduate vocational programs fail to capitalize on this opportunity and spend too much time in technical training that quickly becomes obsolete. The reason why the four-year liberal arts tradition has displayed greater lifelong utility is that the courses offered in four-year programs are not narrowly utilitarian and stress skills of reasoning and inquiry that emerge from an encounter with discrete fields of study. Unfortunately, it is in the arena of undergraduate education that the sameness and uniformity in institutional practice have become damaging and have prevented the finest ideals of a college education from being realized.

Parents and students oppress themselves and each other in the process of trying to get into a competitive and prestigious institution. The last two years of high school are often dominated by the issue of getting into college. Colleges, in turn, manipulate the insecurity and ambitions of parents and applicants in ways that are harmful and entirely disconnected with any reasonable notion of encouraging curiosity and intellectual ambition. Institutions compete with one another and use the reality and appearance of exclusivity to inspire misplaced awe, fear, and desire. They are very effective in doing so. Students and parents are convinced that going to Berkeley or Harvard, Amherst or Bryn Mawr, as opposed to UC Davis, Tufts, Hamilton, Goucher, or the local state institution will make the decisive difference in one's life. Given the extent to which most institutions are interchangeable, the obsession with getting into the so-called best college is odd if not irrational.

The plain fact is that too much is being made out of getting into college and too little about what happens to individuals once there, or about what it takes to graduate from college. Doing well and learning in a college of standing (of which there are sufficiently many) is far more important than the name of the college from which the degree comes. No doubt there are classes of institutions that might reasonably be ranked according to unambiguous measures of quality in terms of faculty and students. Consequently, there are significant differences between Harvard and the local community college. But there are far fewer differences between Tufts and Harvard. And even in the case of the local state institution that does not have the history, resources, and reputation of the University of Wisconsin–Madison, individual achievement and ambition by a student can compensate, on the undergraduate level, for the institutional differences. Since World War II, the leading nine hundred or more institutions have been able to recruit and maintain a superior faculty trained in good graduate schools. Indeed, the whole spectrum of colleges and universities has benefited from the post-1945 growth of the American research university and the quality of its graduate programs and students. Despite the evident influence of the very popular and highly publicized rankings of colleges and universities by weekly newsmagazines and consumer guides, the gaps between institutions are not as significant as the rankings suggest.

Too much, for example, is made of an institution's wealth, on the assumption that wealth equals quality. No doubt research universities of international standing with, for example, medical schools legitimately depend on extensive resources. At the same time, many of our most wealthy institutions are, frankly speaking, overendowed. There is no measurable increment in the quality of teaching and learning between Swarthmore, Smith, and Macalester on the one hand and Reed, Mills, and Haverford on the other, even though the former institutions are three to four times as wealthy as the latter group. Many well-endowed private institutions behave first as investment trusts and second as centers of learning that confront the challenges of contemporary culture. They act much like the giant Fafner in Richard Wagner's music drama *Siegfried*. Having obtained through hard work a coveted treasure of gold possessed of magic powers, Fafner turns himself into a dragon in order to protect it and remains passive and inert; he can do nothing with his wealth and power but guard the gold. Too often, misplaced complacency and arrogance, after a competitive level of quality has been achieved, are the result of long-term institutional good fortune in the private sector.

This is not to suggest that institutions do not exhibit contrasts in style. These differences derive from an institution's location and local culture. Campuses often display their own peculiar hierarchy of stylistic values and a special range of student culture. Furthermore, the quality and ambition of students and the distribution of their interests define a campus more than the quality and character of the faculty do. Yet Harvard and Yale no longer have a monopoly (if they ever did) on America's brightest or most motivated college students. Most Americans, including the best and the brightest, attend public colleges in their home states. The private institutions enroll fewer than 25 percent of all students bound for college.

What private institutions can offer is a significantly greater degree of geographic diversity in the student body. They also have more institutional freedom and flexibility, which unfortunately they rarely use to their best advantage. Geographic diversity can be important insofar as it is the student culture nurtured on campus—the values espoused— and the links between learning and daily life evident in the dormitory and dining commons that can recommend one campus over another to an applicant. Each prospective student has differing reactions to the culture of a specific campus (even when the differences are ultimately superficial), no matter how trivial the point of contact may be. It is amazing and telling that students often choose where to go to college on the basis of incidental and fragmentary impressions that are nevertheless sufficient to give them a sense of how they will feel as a student at a particular college.

All entering college students suffer from a natural mixture of ambition, insecurity, hesitancy, and courage. One bright and gifted student may thrive at MIT; another of comparable ability and preparation may be undone by that institution's scale and density of talents, ambition, and competitiveness. A student who flourishes in the self-consciously Quaker setting of Haverford might have languished at Williams. The key, from the student perspective, is to find an institution where comfort and discomfort can coexist effectively so that one is both inspired to work harder and yet put at ease. And good institutions are known by the quality and ambition of the students who attend, which is why in every state and region there are excellent choices that can prepare any ambitious and able student willing to work hard.

II. THE MORAL OBLIGATIONS OF COLLEGES

Whatever the on-campus stylistic differences between two competing and essentially comparable institutions may be, the intellectual uniformity and low standards in the undergraduate curriculum visible throughout American colleges predominate and constitute an unnecessary catastrophe. Despite a reasonable shared minimum standard of academic resources in terms of faculty, computers, and libraries, most undergraduate programs of study do not offer as much high-quality teaching as they could and should. They do not adequately meet the broad expectations of a first-rate college education and do not challenge the minds of our best young people as much as they might even within the strict confines of specialized and preprofessional training. In short, the level of general intellectual aspiration and idealism nurtured during college is far too low for comfort. And these shortcomings are the result of lack of will on the part of the leaders of our institutions, not the lack of adequate resources.

In their ideal form, the undergraduate years of college ought to be the time when an individual, as an adult, links learning to life. The original impulse that gave rise to the high-minded rhetoric with which educators regularly surround descriptions of college curriculum and college life—the sort of vague but noble-sounding language that graces nearly every college catalog—needs to be remembered once again. We need to focus on the unique opportunity that the college years provide to inspire young individuals to try to understand and reflect on the world in which they live and their relationship to it. The ages between sixteen and twenty-one represent the last formative stage with radical potential in a person's intellectual development. What distinguishes these from the earlier years of adolescence is the fact that speculation and curiosity coincide with a more stable and sustained adult experience. The college years can be the crucible in which a lifelong pattern between thinking and acting is established by each individual. Insofar as the traditions of learning and inquiry can and do influence the way we conduct our daily lives, it is in the college years that the linkage can be established. Where those connections are most important are in that classic Freudian pairing, love and work.

Since the mid-1960s, it has become increasingly unfashionable for institutions to consider the impact of colleges on individuals beyond issues of academic performance. Before 1960, colleges assumed, as a matter of course, a role in the explicit task of character building. As a result, there were extensive rules regulating behavior, particularly sexual mores. One spoke of the college as being *in loco parentis*—as playing a guiding hand. The emancipation of college students from this approach was the result not only of cultural movements (for example, the so-called Beat generation of the 1950s) and the political agitation of the mid-1960s but of the earlier maturation and extension of freedoms visible in the high school age group after 1945.

Colleges welcomed this change. The undergraduate faculty that came to teach in the 1960s saw themselves less as college teachers and mentors and more as scholars and teachers tied to a particular discipline. They were, in short, more "professional," if by professional one means a closer resemblance to the research faculty of a graduate school. The result was that colleges explicitly declared the existence of adulthood on the part of entering students, most of whom, at age eighteen, qualified legally as adults. This relieved institutions of potential liabilities and obligations with respect to personal behavior and the conduct of private life. Depression, illness, accidents, and infractions of the law all became primarily individual issues, not institutional questions. The college students of the late 1960s and early 1970s eagerly took on the mantle of adult responsibility and rejected any residual efforts on the part of colleges to intervene in their conduct of life and regulate their behavior.

What no college president could have predicted from the standpoint of the early 1970s was the striking change that would take place at the end of that decade and during the 1980s. Two factors created a reversal in attitude. First, the women's movement altered the landscape of American higher education decisively. Not only were many venerable all-male institutions transformed into coeducational ones, such as Amherst, Princeton, and Dartmouth (and some all-female ones such as Vassar, Skidmore, Sarah Lawrence, and Wheaton), but the rapid increase in numbers of female faculty and the political organization of women changed the standards and expectation of college life. A subsidiary fallout of the women's movement was a heightened consciousness with respect to sexual preferences. In the wake of the struggle to achieve equality between genders came the awareness that homosexuality and bisexuality were increasingly in the forefront of how some young adults chose to identify themselves publicly as members of a college and university community. Sexuality became a pivotal item of political consciousness on campus. Concern regarding discrimination, inequities, and prejudice on issues of gender and sexuality became a dominant theme of campus life.

Second, the American campus began, albeit slowly, to reflect more fairly the demographic character of the country. Beginning in the 1950s, much to the understandable chagrin of the founders of the newly created Brandeis University, the doors of the elite private institutions in the country began to open to Jews. Then came the post–civil rights agenda. Greater numbers of African Americans, more Cubans, Puerto Ricans, and Mexican Americans, and later Asian Americans, went on to college. Diversity became the hallmark of institutional rhetoric. Institutions were forced to become more evenhanded and less discriminatory in their admissions policies.

Tragically, partly out of reaction to this diversity, a misguided debate has arisen concerning affirmative action. Affirmative action has been a resounding success and should be continued. Without it we will not continue the progress we have made in the rates of college completion among African Americans, which is now at 12.5 percent of the population, still only half that of the rate among whites. The fact that high standards of admission—particularly the use of SAT scores—inherently favor high family incomes and therefore the privileges associated with wealth and membership in an upper social class seems conveniently forgotten. "Need blind" financial aid in a highly selective college is a flawed system of fairness. It rests on admissions criteria that favor prior exposure to a good education, which in turn is the result of economic well-being. Affirmative action in admissions has helped to restore an emphasis on ability, not experience.

If one includes in this picture of increasing diversity on campus the steadily growing numbers of foreign students in the American university, particularly in science and engineering, one can readily appreciate that most, if not all, colleges and universities in the late 1990s are far less culturally, racially, ethnically, and religiously homogeneous than they were in the 1950s. Consequently, in the face of diversity—particularly ethnic, religious, and gender diversity—the imposition of standardized rules and mores seems unreasonable and arbitrary. But the opposite has happened. It turned out that college students were no more able to handle real differences among themselves than the population as a whole can. The equality of women and the equality of ethnic difference seemed rhetorically convenient but hard principles to live by on campus day in and day out. Issues of sexual violence, including date rape, and incidents of racism and hate speech, both verbal and printed, engulfed college administrators. Suddenly, the authority of the institution as moral legislator was recalled from near oblivion. Colleges were asked to set and enforce ethical standards of personal behavior at levels higher than the minimum standards established by law and convention outside the walls of an institution of higher learning.

Although in the early 1980s conservatives began to poke fun at these developments and claim the high ground of freedom of expression as the highest and most important governing principle on a college and university campus and raise the battle cry of censorship, the new obligations faced by institutions have significant precedents in tradition. When a young man was disciplined at the University of Pennsylvania for directing insulting epithets at African American women, there was outrage at the idea that one could be silenced and expelled merely for speaking. The phrase "political correctness" came into ubiquitous use. This cliché has been coined and used in a manner that cloaks two false historical claims: (1) that for the first time, there is a dominant point of view on our campuses that dissenters are loath to confront; and (2) that institutions have never imposed standards of behavior on students. Such legislation of behavior has historically been the norm. What has changed over time, however, are the values that make up the official dogma.

The fact is that an individual such as the one disciplined by Penn might have been dismissed many years ago without controversy for merely breaching a minimum standard of civility and honor expected of an undergraduate at an Ivy League school. In the "old days" honor, decorum, manners, and dignity were assumed to be the mark of any member of an elite club. The sheer vulgarity of the man's conduct in this case would have placed his status as a student in jeopardy. Colleges, after all, were places where exemplary "character" was built. Therefore, excessive drinking, cursing, and improper behavior toward women (understood in the old paternalistic sense of the dignified behavior of a gentleman who pays homage to the delicacy of the "fairer" sex) were legitimate grounds for disciplining students. This was the unique role colleges played *in loco parentis*. The antitraditionalism and hypocrisy of today's conservative critique of modern political correctness are ironic and remarkable. The defense of unvarnished crudity and vulgarity in the name of free speech at a university seems not to square with rhetoric about declining standards on our campuses and the need to reassert a culture of traditional moral values.

Furthermore, each age and generation has displayed a dominant mode of thought on campus. In the 1930s it was isolationism, in the

1950s it was anticommunism, in the late 1960s it was antiwar sentiment. Historically, students, administrators, and faculties have never
been appreciably more tolerant of serious dissent in the face of leading
modes of thought than the external community has been. John Dewey
would not have come into conflict with Columbia University nearly a
century ago if that had not been the case. Academic freedom is a phrase
more easily invoked rhetorically than enforced. It has rarely been defended successfully. The problems of group thinking today termed
"political correctness" are no different than they were decades ago.
Only the fads, fashions, ideology, and politics change, not the pattern
of ostracization and defamation of those who think and speak with a
different voice.

As a result of the two key factors—the more assertive presence of
women and ethnic diversity—colleges have been forced to step in and
adjudicate and regulate campus life. Two subsidiary factors have made
this imperative. First, the changed patterns of child-rearing have de-
stroyed any illusion that there is an unspoken agreement throughout
the country as to what constitutes a civilized code of conduct. Even the
question of what constitutes violence no longer seems to have a self-
evident answer. Students do not arrive on campus with shared mores.
For example, on the issue of date rape, it should come as little surprise
that in a culture in which sexuality and violence on television, in pop
music lyrics, and on the big screen are frequently allied and even con-
flated, students seem unclear as to the boundaries between right and
wrong. If one adds to that the popular assumption that there is something unspontaneous and overly intellectual and unsexy about articulat-
ing desire verbally, the young, inexperienced, and nervous adult can
legitimately be confused about what consent means. Neither family,
community, nor culture has made it clear that consent means the explicit and unimpaired verbal expression of assent and that ethically
there can be no substitute. Furthermore, no one seems to have made it
clear that talking about having sex in no way reduces its appeal. The
nonsense that lurks behind commonplace and popular notions of mas-

culinity, femininity, and courtship is nearly unimaginable and makes the frequency of unethical and vulgar behavior among young and relatively inexperienced adults utterly predictable.

And the adult public needs to recognize as well that many of the worst cases of unacceptable behavior on campus in terms of gender relations and race relations are linked to alcohol. We live in a country obsessed with a desire to regulate through law mores and morals of everyone but ourselves. We go about our own lives as adults without preparing the young for adult life except to prohibit certain activities. No doubt the raising of the drinking age to twenty-one has reduced the fatalities from drunk driving. But the forcing of college-campus drinking underground has not helped. Alcohol remains the central social problem of the American campus, and older adults are now prevented by law from attempting to teach or regulate its use because it is simply against the law for most undergraduate students to drink. The scene in the popular film *Chariots of Fire* in which the master of an Oxford college drinks sherry with students has become impossible to emulate. A controlled example of civilized conviviality involving alcohol—the responsible use of alcohol as a social ritual—has vanished from the campus. If a faculty member or administrator were to serve alcohol to a student today, not only is the law being broken, but should something harmful happen, the institution could be held legally responsible.

This points to the second subsidiary factor. In the late twentieth century, Americans have developed a love affair with lawsuits. Individuals wish to place blame not on themselves but on others, preferably institutions that are well insured. If one can be compensated financially for any and all misfortunes by holding institutions accountable, so much the better. Administrators have a healthy fear of the possibilities and probabilities that students who fail, who are dismissed, who are hurt or hurt others while drunk will sue the institution. Either the college should have been more vigilant in eliminating alcohol (a practical impossibility), or it should have seen to it that nothing untoward occurred under its watch, even though most campuses are run informally, with a primary expectation that students, as adults, must take responsibility for their own personal behavior. Outside the framework of a residential college, in the so-called real world, there is usually no one to sue or place blame for unwanted sexual advances, drunken behavior, and racist outbursts except individuals.

As is no doubt clear, the developments of the 1980s changed the life of college administrators. They now oversee extensive semijudicial procedures and grievance statutes and arbitrate disputes that in the late 1960s had been shifted to the protected private province of individuals. Administrators intervene in matters of sexual behavior and other aspects of interpersonal conduct. They also find themselves held responsible for everything and anything that happens on the campus, whether it is academic or not, even the comings and goings of the public. Administrators spend much more time on police issues and police personnel—an activity known as "campus security"—than any administrator twenty years ago could have imagined was possible. The society at large, including parents and communities, which has failed to instill standards of behavior and mores, now turns to colleges to enforce such standards among unfettered and free autonomous young adults.

The positive side of these developments is the fact that in order to conduct a serious program of intellectual development and academic learning, a higher standard of civility and decency than is ordinarily required in daily life is indispensable. In this regard the old traditions of character-building during the pre-1945 institutional histories of colleges were on the mark. There can be no physical violence, vulgarity, bullying, and verbal hate if serious research, teaching, criticism, and debate are to be conducted. Free speech in a university requires that statements cannot be shielded from careful scrutiny and cannot be of a nature that instills authentic fear.

III. THE COLLEGE MAJOR

The new but yet old-fashioned expectations now facing colleges are a welcome change precisely because implicit in these revived arenas of concern is the issue that should properly occupy colleges and universities and on which John Dewey focused recurrently: the relationship between learning and citizenship. The way we encourage students in college to think and act can influence the way they choose to conduct themselves as citizens later in democratic life. It is all well and good to connect the methods of learning in early childhood education with democratic behavior. Dewey's conception of the narrow space in which individuals have genuine freedom of action led him to be committed to a belief in a trial-and-error, experience-based approach to learning. It led him to be critical of the extremes of authoritarian education on the one hand and total laissez-faire schemes of self-development on the other.

But when Dewey and his followers approached the college years, they shifted their focus more narrowly onto the issue of how a young adult could integrate training for a career and general education with participation in American democracy. That shift bequeathed to the American college three junctures beyond the curriculum at which learning and life could be connected: (1) the economic arena, the areas of employment and career; (2) the personal arena involving sexuality and family; and (3) the political arena, the functioning of individuals in the environment in which they live, both human and physical. This third dimension, which justifies the efforts on campuses to encourage community service, legitimates various attempts to connect the subject matter of courses in the social and natural sciences with public policy.

The linking of learning to life in the young adult is harder to achieve than one would like. In the first place, young people come to colleges in America often with a single-minded focus on career and preprofessional education. Parents and students often harbor the exclusive illusion that college, in contrast to high school, is about preparing oneself for the practical business of life, a phrase that is often reduced to the earning of money. Too many educators overreact to this legitimate utilitarian claim by preaching about learning for its own sake. This is a sort of high-minded, old-fashioned special pleading that is actually counterproductive. Learning for its own sake is wonderful, desirable, and enjoyable, but only after an individual has found a way to connect learning and life in a manner that influences everyday life, including earning a living. There is the danger of an inadvertent concession to the irrelevance of sophistication, the kind of gap between culture and ethics that makes the example of the behavior of the educated German elite in the Nazi era so terrifying.

Once again, we confront the tragic and ironic sojourn of eighteenth-century ideals, such as those of Thomas Jefferson, through history. One of the central lessons from research on the Holocaust is the unreliability of the Enlightenment prediction (which was not shared by all eighteenth-century thinkers, particularly Jean-Jacques Rousseau) that culture and education would naturally lead to a greater level of civility and ethical discrimination. The functionaries and killers of the twentieth century have not been illiterate boors bereft of the knowledge of either literature or table manners. Quite to the contrary, in twentieth-century regimes of extreme oppression, witting and unwitting collaboration by intellectual and artistic elites has been shockingly commonplace. The paradox facing educators dealing with young adults in our post-Holocaust age is precisely how to come to terms with the collapse of the pre-twentieth-century premise that lay behind both English and American liberal arts college curricula.

The traditional Enlightenment premise held by David Hume and Thomas Jefferson was that by providing education to young individuals on the university level, moral and political progress would be assured. Therefore, the expansion of access to higher education would broaden the opportunities for individuals to realize their potential and become not only more sophisticated and productive in technical terms but better citizens and neighbors. The fact that this once-plausible and noble prediction has not been realized lies behind the insecurities that the postwar generation of college educators have shown regularly when confronted with the task of forging a link overtly between undergraduate education and citizen behavior in a democracy. At stake is not the eighteenth-century premise itself, but rather the way it has been acted upon and not acted upon in America and also in Europe. The experience of the twentieth century should lead rather to a renewal in the effort to redeem the eighteenth-century Enlightenment claim. We cannot merely conclude that it has been proved wrong.

Consequently, the plea for learning for its own sake doesn't come across very well to most parents and students. In the contemporary context it implies that learning in the sense of a more sophisticated understanding of literature, history, and philosophy—the kind of thing one ought to obtain in college—by a young adult is indeed an irrelevant luxury without even an obvious civic benefit. Therefore, we would do well to make it clear that such learning in college must absolutely be considered useful. Any college educator who resists the demand that college make a difference in the future lives of students in terms of work is making a grave error, particularly if that educator works in what is called a liberal arts context.

The key to this problem rests in the definition of utility. It turns out that when it comes to education, virtue is its own reward. Learning for its own sake is the best preparation for functioning competitively and creatively. Therefore, any responsible professor of business or engineering or any other practical course of study on the undergraduate level errs by denigrating learning done by students that on the surface seems unconnected to becoming trained to do a particular task. The study of philosophy, for example, might be just the thing an undergraduate engineering major needs to do to become an innovative engineer. This point of view has helped to make Harvey Mudd College as distinctive an institution as it is. The essential training engineers get in problem-solving, using mathematics and the procedures of basic science—not applied science—turns out to be critical in the workplace later on. So, too, is an education in complementary disciplines, including history and philosophy. Likewise, a solid understanding of psychology and literature, not to speak of American economic and social history, will serve an undergraduate business major better than a course in marketing, especially if that student has the ambition and instinct to recognize its value.

A second barrier to realizing the promise of the college years is a more general skepticism and anti-intellectualism inherent in the popular culture surrounding American adolescents. Being an adult is symbolically understood in America in many ways. It is not primarily understood as a status that implies learning as a central personal habit. The result is that in the way most campuses are organized there is a staggering gulf between the classroom and after-class life. There is, in short, a sort of Jekyll and Hyde phenomenon. In very good colleges students work diligently and are attentive and ambitious. But the moment class is over and the assignments completed, an entirely different pattern emerges. American colleges are noted for their vulgarity in terms of extracurricular social life. There seems to be no connection between what students are learning and the way they go about living.

A college ought to be measured by the extent to which the curriculum influences dining hall conversation and the kinds of entertainment students choose. It should be defined by the way learning transforms the definition of play. Not only should learning be enjoyable, but what we, as adults, consider enjoyment should be transformed by what we discover through study. Having a good time (eighteenth-century philosophers would not have permitted us to use the word *happiness*, which, as has been noted, was understood as a moral category, more like what we might term individual or collective well-being) is a perfectly reasonable objective in life. The question then becomes what kinds of things one considers play and part of having a good time.

No matter how rigorous the curriculum, no matter how stringent the requirements, if what goes on in the classroom does not leave its mark in the way young adults voluntarily act in private and in public while they are in college, much less in the years after, then the college is not doing what it is supposed to do. This is the reason why when prospective students visit colleges, they need to look at the student culture and activities and life in the dorms. It is the transformation of peer-group values and behavior that can mark a first-rate college education. But one ought not underestimate the obstacles to achieving this goal, given what students bring from their homes and their high schools with respect to the presumed connection between learning and everyday life and what constitutes play and fun.

A third barrier to realizing the potential of the undergraduate years is specific to the way colleges organize their curriculum and faculty. Since World War II, since colleges have become professionalized, most faculty must have Ph.D.'s. All universities and colleges apply some standard of scholarship to their recruitment and tenure procedures. That is why so often one hears complaints about the "publish or perish" syndrome. On the one hand this professionalism is beneficial because it ensures a level of competence and sophistication in a subject matter that ought to be a minimum standard. Furthermore, the key difference between high school teaching and college teaching is in the realm of love of subject. Love of subject is measured by the extent to which a teacher spends time, of his or her own accord, working on scholarly endeavors in his or her chosen subject. No college teacher who does not experience criticism and evaluation of his or her own written work by peers deserves the right to assign a paper to a student.

On the other hand, the increased professionalism and emphasis on scholarship and research have inadvertently led to the organization of colleges along the lines of graduate schools and to the devaluing of teaching. Teachers are hired in undergraduate schools along structural patterns that mirror the specialized fields of the graduate schools. The college English department looks unfortunately and inappropriately like a miniature golf-course version of the eighteen-hole graduate school department. The same holds true for mathematics, physics, and psychology. This pattern of imitation is especially harmful currently, since graduate training, most noticeably in the humanities, encourages young would-be college teachers to specialize in ways that bear little relevance to the task of teaching undergraduates. In the name of encouraging "new" scholarship and establishing a professional reputation for oneself, fashionable texts, elaborate methodologies, and peripheral questions are favored in dissertations over careful study and interpretation of central issues, texts, and traditions. By the time a graduate student reaches the classroom as an independent instructor, he or she not only has had no useful guidance in how to teach, but he or she is not prepared or inclined to teach legitimately canonical texts and recurrent issues that undergraduates need and want to study. This redefined pseudoprofessionalism has crippled most efforts to reinvent general education. The irony is that this prescriptive procedure delays and inhibits scholarly originality, particularly in the reconsideration of well-established methods, canons, and traditions.

Furthermore, undergraduate "majors" inevitably privilege their best students, defined as those who hold the most promise for a scholarly career. No department wants to become a "service department" without its own majors, relegated to teaching skills and materials to students primarily interested in other subjects. It does not seem sufficiently dignified to have as one's purpose in an English department, for example, the education of a literate physician. This is unfortunate. Every department functions as if it were in a stereotypical Arabian bazaar, hustling undergraduates to become majors. Administrations, in turn, measure success by counting heads in terms of enrollments that derive from majors. The more majors, the more successful the department. This pattern even spills down to the college applicant, who is asked a ridiculous question: "What would you like to major in?"

The truth is that life is not divisible into majors. Neither is work or, believe it or not, learning or scholarship. Asking a high school graduate about a major defined in terms of a university department is usually pointless because the student has no reason to have any notion of what the question might mean or imply. The right questions to ask the prospective student are: "What issues interest you? What kinds of things would you like to study? What would you like to know more about?" If one starts with the problems that young people formulate about the world, one would discover that answering them requires the expertise of individuals defined in ways that do not correspond neatly with the departmental structure of a graduate school. And the search for answers to old questions and the framing of new questions demand an encounter with the full scope of intellectual traditions conserved by the university.

The graduate school can easily defend itself because it has a very specific and legitimate agenda: the training of scholars and researchers.

Despite all the efforts of such individuals as Derek Bok, the training of college teachers is best left as a secondary item in our graduate schools. It is usually an object of contempt and is viewed as a necessary evil distracting the would-be young researcher from his or her rightful task. Some critics of the way college teachers are trained would like research to be massively reduced as a priority in favor of teaching. But that standpoint is in error. There is no inherent conflict between scholarship and teaching. No doubt in science and in the humanities most of what is published in research is frequently trivial, bloated, repetitious, or forgettable. But that does not make it unimportant. It is only in the context of an enormous volume of research pursued internationally and exchanged extensively and openly that the rare jewel and epoch-making insight emerges. And the ambition to write and engage ideas with colleagues is, in principle, viable and a healthy companion to good teaching.

In the case of science, for example, the wide-ranging support of basic research is indispensable, even though in retrospect much of the money might appear to be wasted. One cannot predict on the basis of a proposal, a peer review, or the reputation of a scientist which set of experiments will lead to breakthrough results. Often the most important discoveries and so-called paradigm shifts come as unintended consequences. The huge apparatus of scholarship and publication is an essential, ongoing structure if one is concerned about improving and advancing knowledge. There may be many generations in which a particular field is dormant and unpopular but kept alive by mediocre talents. But that continuity is essential because it creates the possibility for a future generation to innovate. When the need for an obscure field emerges once again, there will be something with which to connect.

But what narrowly justifies the graduate school research structure has less to do with the recipients of undergraduate teaching and learning. A nasty debate continues in our postsecondary institutions about undergraduate general education and survey courses on the college level. The most recent example was at Yale, with the return of a $20-million Bass gift designated for "Western Civilization." Stanford University experienced a controversy over curricular content several years ago. There the questions were posed: Should all students still be required to take so-called Western Civilization? What should constitute the basic requirements that all college students be asked to complete?

The sad part of these debates about general education and the so-called basics is that faculties and the public get caught up in bitter and vicious quarrels over crumbs. If one looks at an undergraduate student's program at the point of graduation, in retrospect general education and the fulfillment of distribution requirements account for less than 20 percent of a student's time. In all these debates around the country—the "culture wars"—the arguments have been too often about the icing (i.e., general education) on the cake, not the cake (i.e., the major) itself. The cake consists of the courses a student has to take to fulfill a major in a field. That occupies the majority of the student's time, and no one has yet proposed tampering with it. No doubt there are bitter controversies within majors, such as whether to require Shakespeare in English literature, an idea whose evident logic has been questioned. One suspects that such challenges to conventional wisdom are as much displays of temporary ideological bravado as they are of sincere reasoning. That fact, however, does not make dealing with such attention-getting strategies any easier.

The reason why competing interests on the subject of general education come into conflict is that too little time in undergraduate education is allotted to general education. So-called Western Civilization must be taught, but in the late twentieth century there also must be an introduction for all students to the civilizations and cultures in the Far East, Africa, and America. The agenda for general education has widened, not narrowed, but the time assigned to it has eroded gradually and steadily since World War II. The departments that are the power centers at colleges and universities will not relinquish their hold over students' time because time means enrollment and enrollment means money and faculty positions, and those two items together constitute power and influence. This is why most American colleges and universities are happy to have managers, not educators, as administrators. The central power, intellectually speaking, in the university has been short-circuited in favor of a system controlled by professional schools and departments which sustains the status quo.

Two anecdotes may be appropriate to give the reader a sense of what is at stake in the task of forging a connection between adult learning on the college level and the conduct of life. Colleges possess an opportunity that has civic consequences and is entirely independent of a system of specialization. Within the last ten years, I experienced two incidents in sections I taught of a required first-year "great books" class that illuminate the intellectual challenge facing colleges. One of the advantages of general education courses, especially those that concentrate on great texts, is that those who teach them are not usually experts in the material. The overwhelming majority of historic creations—whether from India, China, Europe, or America—including the Bible, *The Federalist Papers,* and the works of Dante, Shakespeare, Beethoven, Marx, George Eliot, Tolstoy, Du Bois, and Georgia O'Keefe—were not produced for specialists but for a literate general public. By guiding undergraduates in close analysis and interpretation of works of indisputable quality and significance without being a specialist, one sets an example for the activity of well-educated individuals and citizens.

The first incident concerns a young man who encountered difficulties when faced with a paper topic. The paper topic, which was assigned and required of all students in the class, asked for a commentary on the concept of "tacit consent" in John Locke's *Second Treatise of Government.* This assignment was given in the mid-1980s, before the collapse of the Soviet Union, during the Reagan presidency and therefore in the last years of the cold war when the President still talked of the "evil" empire. Students were asked to write on a fundamental principle of democracy, the notion of consent. In social contract theory, the basic creation of government took place in a far-distant past. Yet the point raised in the text of the Declaration of Independence—that governments are not necessarily permanent—raises the specter that there may be conflicts between the conscience, safety, and self-interest of individuals and the rule of law that demand a radical response in political action—namely, the reconstitution of government.

The issues we discussed were: What are the reciprocal obligations between citizens and an existing government? If we, as adults, are not part of the group that originally formulated the fundamental laws, but instead have grown up under them, have we really consented? What are the limits to our dissent? Does each generation need to be asked to legitimate explicitly the constitutional rules and principles of government? The relationship between individuals and the power of the state in a democracy was raised by Locke's notion of tacit consent. Tacit consent was one way of justifying continuity, if not permanence, in political obligations and arrangements on the part of succeeding generations.

The paper assignment asked students to fashion their own views of how an ongoing democracy, from the point of view of the individual, could be differentiated from any other system, particularly one that was viewed at the time as the epitome of unfreedom and the absence of citizen voice. For example, in class discussion, the matter of which options one has if one has a principled objection to a law came up. As in the Vietnam War years, what might justify conflict and defiance in the face of government behavior? When is rebellion—even the use of force—and the reformulation of a new political system legitimate and when not? Why is it not possible for an individual simply to deny any obligation to law simply because it may be inconvenient? Why must citizens be law-abiding? When is defying the law—as in South Africa under apartheid—a greater ethical obligation than submitting to the accumulated residues of years of tacit consent? When is revolution justified?

The young man handed in a paper of sufficient length, which was little more than a summary of what he had read, punctuated by meek efforts at commentary. The paper had all the hallmarks of a late-night affair. Perhaps the student had finished reading the book at 2:00 A.M. and had begun writing at 3:00 A.M. for a paper due at 9:00 that morning. The student had little idea of how to think about the issues. The young man was the successful graduate of a good suburban public school in the East. He, like many others, had learned how to play the game of school well—a game whose rules involve obtaining a precise sense of what the teacher and school require. Apparently, in this high school, providing some indication of the capacity to recognize, passively, an argument was sufficient for praise. The student had found the most efficient way (which included the free use of pretentious and polysyllabic words) to deliver what would get a good grade. The sad part of the story was that the student obviously did not have the discipline and self-confidence to do more than appear "smart." Developing discipline and self-confidence seriously beyond mere appearance often means favoring one subject over another. This means that students would follow the natural course of their own interests. However, in high school and college good students must continue to balance subjects despite differences in the difficulties encountered in fulfilling the external expectations. To play the game well, however, one must not be distracted by curiosity or court failure by taking hard courses. One must balance all subjects efficiently according to the difficulty encountered in fulfilling the external expectations in terms of good grades.

One way out of this bind is to take very few risks and remain detached. This strategy is pursued to perfection by many students who test well and adapt well to the routines of schooling. One of the keys to this game-playing is to care for little other than the grade and not to be caught up in thinking too hard about what one is learning and reading. Our best colleges and universities—and our law schools, business and medical schools—have traditionally thrived on such students. At some point the earning of money replaces the system of grades and credits as the essential objective and criterion of successful work.

I gave the young man a B for his efforts. I borrowed a teaching strategy from the best teacher I ever had. Instead of dismissing what the student had written as thoughtless, I attempted to make the best of it. I sought to unravel his halfhearted foray into thinking by reformulating what might plausibly have been the points he was making. He was taken aback and profoundly embarrassed, in part because it appeared to him that I had taken more time with his paper than he had himself. The point I was trying to make was that as an American citizen, he had the ability and the obligation to think about issues of consent and participation, particularly the notions of rebellion and civil disobedience, in a manner befitting his intelligence and educational opportunities. He was, after all, going to vote and live in a country where presumably citizens with an education can and should influence the shape of the laws. He therefore had a greater obligation to all the rest of his fellow citizens to figure out what, in his own view, were the justifications for obedience and resistance. I suggested that he look at Martin Luther King Jr.'s arguments written while in a jail cell in Birmingham, Alabama. I tried, with a bit of success, to suggest that the difference between high school and college was that in high school the rules of the game of school applied. In college, since college presumed that the student was an adult, learning and the game of life were at stake and their rules and consequences were neither so neat nor so circumscribed. He therefore should not be frightened of spending the time and taking the risks of engaged thought. The curriculum and his response to it were connected to serious issues with formidable power for creating pain, pleasure, good, and harm.

The young man responded by asking whether the sort of effort I was encouraging him to embrace had any practical significance or was it merely the kind of activity in which only future academics would revel. He was planning to enter medical school and although he might vote, he had no deep interest in politics, history, or ethics per se. In a quite charming way, designed to flatter me, he concluded by saying that I was being idealistic in my attitude. I, after all, seemed to like to muse about such matters. I had voluntarily chosen my form of entertainment. Like others before him, he argued that thinking about politics, history, or ethics had become an area of specialized expertise. For example, only those intending to take neurosurgery seriously should be much concerned about it. Furthermore, any notion of amateurism or citizen participation in thinking became, by analogy, as ridiculous as it was in the case of neurosurgery. My response was to urge him to consider the possibility that his own career in medicine, let alone his private life and his membership in his chosen community, would all benefit from thinking and even daydreaming about issues, texts, and questions that overtly had nothing whatsoever to do with his stated plans and objectives. The utility of serious learning and thinking rests most often in its unforeseen consequences. Furthermore, there was a fundamental civic obligation that the privilege of his education placed upon him.

The second incident took place in the fall of 1996. In a similar first-year general education course required of all entering students, we read *The Republic* of Plato. As part of a plan to help students read the text carefully, we looked closely at the first book, in which Socrates' conversation quickly wears out a wealthy, elderly, and pleasant gentleman named Cephalus. Socrates is left to argue about the nature of justice with only a group of young men. (This point was made to encourage first-year college students to follow in the footsteps of Socrates' young friends.) Explicit in the way *The Republic* opens is the rapid but remarkable three-part transition from (1) normal bantering and pleasantries to (2) the expression of commonplace clichés about old age and the value of being wealthy to (3) the beginnings of a closely argued exchange of views on the good life governed by some notions of reason, logic, and truth.

The class time was designed in preparation for a paper topic that would ask students to relate Plato's theory of knowledge as outlined in *The Republic*, particularly in books 6 and 7—the description of the divided line and the famous "cave"—to some other element in the text, one that argued for a particular way of doing things in, for example, education or politics. The idea behind the assignment was to ask students to link theory and practice. I wanted them to come to grips with how one's beliefs about the nature of truth and knowledge—particularly with respect to how one obtains knowledge—can influence one's ideas about what is right and wrong in the arena of everyday behavior, private and public. I wanted the students to probe beneath their opinions to locate their own basic philosophical assumptions.

I hoped they would begin to reflect on the basis on which one might prefer one point of view to another. What were the grounds for beliefs about right and wrong? Were all opinions equal? Were opinions about ethical behavior merely a matter of taste, or were there, as Plato suggests, objective criteria of truth? Were there different levels of knowing? Are all people equally capable of grasping the truth? What are the consequences of believing in a metaphysical realm of truth and an undemocratic distribution within the population of those who can reach the highest plateau of knowing? One's views on the nature of truth and how learning happens, to whom it happens, and how learning can be influenced all have decisive implications for one's ethical, moral, and political convictions.

An amazing discussion ensued in a class of fourteen bright, highly selected, and engaging first-year college students from all over the United States. It revealed that not a single individual present was comfortable with making any sustained argument on behalf of a universal truth. Even when hypothetical and historical cases were put forward concerning the legal incarceration and extermination of minorities (in Nazi Germany), legal segregation and slavery (South Africa and America), the radical limitation on freedom of movement and expression (in the Soviet Union), or assisted suicide and abortion, there were many different opinions, but no common language by which to compare and contrast the merits of one view over another, which is the process by which opinion is transformed into persuasive argument. Students were ready to hold a view that something was wrong, but they could find no way to defend that view rationally against others so as to make it superior to its exact opposite.

The issue here was not lack of ability or any failure to be articulate, idealistic, or even a tendency to be detached. The neoconservative critique of culture has long held that the American university has been in the hands of relativists; postmodern theorists are accused of spreading a gospel of extreme subjectivity, undercutting all claims to objectivity or value neutrality on the part of reason and science. Claims to universal validity are viewed as little more than elaborate rationalizations of culturally determined and historically contingent views that have no legitimacy over time and space. Western outrage about aspects in the treatment of women in countries governed by fundamentalist Islamic theocracies is just that: the illegitimate effort to impose one set of cultural values on another culture. Yet these students had never spent any time in college. Rather, they were the products of a precollege culture of extreme but superficial subjectivism. They came to college with a deep mistrust of politics and authority. They were willing to admit that the only plausible way to hold on to any truth as absolute or universal was through blind faith and a voluntary but irrational submission to an authority such as a church and its doctrine.

When confronted with the high reliability and universal applicability of the methods and findings of science, they could not find a way to explain the gap between the way we deal with physics and the way we talk about ethics. There were no extreme cultural relativists who argued against the physics and engineering of jet planes as valid only in certain cultures, even though they were quick to point out, along the lines that sociologists of science might argue, that scientific and technological truths were the products of a particular culture and society and were expressed in the terms of that culture and society.

The point in this extended discussion was not that these were amoral or immoral individuals. Rather, they had no motivation or training to defend their quite sensible personal values and therefore no way in which to consider or reconsider them seriously. In addition, there was no common ground for communication and argument. Finally, everything seemed equal to everything else; therefore if, by majority vote, a neo-Nazi Aryan supremacy movement were to be elected, the dilemma as they construed it would be what to do vis-à-vis one's own personal preferences. Since everything was reduced to a matter of equal opinion, prior to such a mythical election there seemed to be no language and logic available by which one could attempt to dissuade people of one idea as opposed to another. There was no way, short of "selling" techniques—the habits of television advertisement—by which to reason with people. It was all a matter of luring them, not making superior or convincing arguments. Holding firm ethical views and accepting basic principled political ground rules beyond majority rule were reduced to preferring Coke over Pepsi. This experience might constitute an argument for teaching the *Nicomachean Ethics* of Aristotle, a text that would help students explore issues relating to daily life in a systematic way. However, the success of teaching that text is as dependent on prior sensibilities as the teaching of *The Republic*.

Insofar as American educators like to claim John Dewey as their inspiration, they fail to realize that the circumstance encountered teaching *The Republic* would have shocked and depressed Dewey. Dewey had an old-fashioned confidence in science. He construed the premises of reason and language in such a way as to presume a common ground in democracy on which disagreements and differences could be debated and adjudicated. He believed that through education, a more ethical, just, and rational society could emerge, without any appeal to authority. Reason and not irrational passions could eventually govern the behavior of individuals, which was why he felt that a democratic system of education was essential and that a democracy could create a more ethical world.

The first irony in this situation is that the only certainty that seems to remain absolute is one of skepticism. All individuals seem equal in their views, and all claims to trans-subjective validity by definition are flawed. Gone is any self-critical notion of the fallibility of the individual's own skeptical constructs of truth. And even further removed is any notion that through thinking the individual can escape from some vague but ever-present determinism. We all are somehow prisoners of our environment without the mental freedom to stand apart and really consider critically what we think. While students today can and do derive from this an admirable tolerance of all and any views, that tolerance is so extreme as to eliminate any motivation to engage one another. The result is that small groups of like-minded individuals gravitate to each other without any hope or desire that they can develop an extended conversation with those who think differently, except to locate and label differences in views. No debate takes place, only the mere identification of points of view.

A further irony emerged when this class was later assigned a paper asking them to imitate the essayist Michel de Montaigne. They were asked to write an essay on a commonplace subject citing an intellectual tradition of their choosing. The argument had to be self-critical and yet espouse a contrarian point of view. The example given them was an argument against the conventional wisdom that visiting a bedridden sick friend in a hospital was a good deed. The contrarian view might be that when healthy individuals go to the hospital to comfort the bedridden, all they do is make the sick person feel worse by heightening the contrast between illness and health. The healthy person sits for an hour, then goes into the world to have fun. This only serves to remind the sick of what they cannot do. And it heightens the pride and joy of the healthy individual who emerges relieved and grateful that he or she is not ill. Therefore, visiting the sick, from the point of view of the feelings of the sick person, is an act of cruelty whose only virtue is to make the healthy visitor feel more lucky and privileged.

All the papers that were written were fine but remarkable for their conformity. For all the talk about subjectivity, relativism, and tolerance for diversity, there was little capacity displayed to think differently. What became apparent was that the corollary to the inability to sustain a rational argument about right and wrong was the inability to dissent. The result of extreme tolerance and the individualistic assertions of the equality of each subjective point of view was sameness and uniformity.

To me as a teacher, the explanation for this state of affairs seems twofold. First, with respect to discussions of ethical and political values, one observes a widespread sense of powerlessness and pointlessness. These young people have grown up without any confidence that the sort of discussion suggested by a Platonic dialogue can be held in a civil and useful manner. There is little to be said beyond the expression of an opinion. That sensibility then connects with the second explanatory cause: pessimism. Once again one can see the consequences of the collapse of any faith in the potential for social and political progress in history. Neither is there much sense of the power of individuals to make important differences beyond becoming successful in purely private terms, in a chosen career or lifestyle.

These two anecdotes can serve to pinpoint the unique task of colleges and their curricula. It is precisely at the moment when society extends the presumption of adulthood to young adults, when they go through the rite of passage and become college students, that one can address the vacuum of confidence in the role of language, learning, and thinking to influence oneself and one's community. The college curriculum in the 1990s must directly address this gap and forge intellectual habits that can help to constitute a common ground for the clarification of beliefs and adjudication of differences, the debate over principles, and the formulation of new ideas. This agenda does not fit neatly into our current university structure of specialized fields.

The same absence of confidence about any common ground and the same failure to try to forge alliances about shared intellectual goals dominate the faculties of our universities and colleges. The issue is not, as the neoconservatives argue, the hegemony of relativists and left-wing radicals in the university. Rather, the problem is silence, detachment, and mistrust. In this environment of nonconversation among scholars and teachers across political and ideological lines, one obvious common goal is lost: the need to teach young adults to know more than they might, to express themselves, to argue with one another, and to be able, in their adult lives, to remain curious, to learn, and to be self-critical and do so in ways that obliterate boredom and propel them into their communities.

IV. A Curriculum for the Future

If one sought to address this educational challenge explicitly, one might be able to find considerable agreement and fashion an effective general education curriculum. A well-worked-out grounding in the conduct of philosophy, in history and historical explanation, in the character and range of science, and in the achievements of the human imagination in literature and the arts seems desirable. So, too, is an exposure to the ways the individual and society can be understood, from psychology to economics.

To fulfill this objective, materials from many cultures and historical periods must be used. The strange, distant, and foreign must be integrated with the familiar, the contemporary, and the local. The curriculum must mirror and constitute a differentiated and dynamic sense of tradition to which a new generation can react and add. The achievement of such a goal will require more than a few token general education courses. It may require that the "major" in college occupy less time or that it become both more efficient and more connected to other disciplines. For example, an economics major should be required to study a considerable amount of history. No history major should go without studying art history and literature, and so forth.

General education should start in the first year, but it should continue through the final year of college. General education stimulates the habit of connecting issues and sustains the interest beyond one's specialty. It should be encouraged as the student becomes more advanced in a particular discipline. Thinking about justice, for example, ought not remain either the memory or province of one's first year in college. A more sustained role for general education does not diminish the importance of getting students to specialize as undergraduates.

Choosing a major and delving deeply into some area of interest must still remain the pivotal part of undergraduate study. It should teach the young adult what it means to get below the surface of issues. It should open up the excitement of being close to the current cutting edge in the way problems and issues are researched and solved. It helps to put a young generation into contact with the evolving character of scholarship and research. And it helps to solidify a student's sense of competence and expertise. However, the undergraduate major or area of specialization need not be defined along the lines of graduate specialties. Two of Harvard's best undergraduate majors—social studies and history and literature—do not possess graduate school departmental equivalents.

Such a curriculum would transcend the current clichés in the public debate about college. It would still be as conservative and basic as is called for by critics, but it would also be multicultural. Insofar as it would seem "Western," it would legitimately be so because the American college and university is, in the final analysis, culturally part of the post-Enlightenment history of Europe and America, where the self-critical traditions of free inquiry, openness, and rational judgment have become institutionalized in the best instances. In this sense, like John Dewey, we would be well to remember the indisputable and common-sense career of science. For all the popular criticism leveled at science, there is little dispute that there has been and continues to be progress in this field. The advances in physics, information science and technology, biology, and medicine are testimonies to this fact.

For all the current skepticism, revisionist theoretical challenges to reason and science, and critiques of organization, origins, and social consequences of research, few of the academic critics of rationality, objective truth, and modern science forgo a CAT scan when they are sick, refuse modern biochemical analyses of their blood samples, or resist the latest established interventions against disease and pain. Nor do they travel by horse or communicate by carrier pigeons or submit to a surgical procedure believing that they are making a concession to a privileged but biased set of assumptions that mirrors the power of either a particular culture or gender. There is, in short, more than a bit of hypocrisy in the contemporary academic debate over the absence of a legitimate intellectual common ground on which to build an undergraduate curriculum. As one legendary professor of philosophy counseled a student who wanted to major in philosophy or some other branch of the humanities: "If you really are serious about cultivating your intellect, study math and physics first." The same advice in reverse needs to be given dedicated science majors who contemptuously regard the arts and humanities as "soft." Einstein had no shortage of respect for the arts and humanities.

The adult engagement with both basic general education and specialized study is so crucial that the number of years spent in college should not be reduced to three, as some—including the former president of Oberlin College, S. Frederick Starr—have recommended. Rather, since in the ideal circumstance college would start earlier, it might even be extended to five years, taking the place of part of the high school years freed up with the elimination of high school and the reduction in the years of compulsory schooling.

Perhaps the easiest way to highlight the character of general education as it ought to be is to detach ourselves as if to create a hypothetical circumstance distant from the context of the contemporary debate. Let us imagine a future decades away, when the specific points of disagreement and enmity in and among scholars and teachers will have been long forgotten. What, then, might still remain as curricular necessities after the fog of the current controversies has cleared? The sequence and type of year-long general education courses one might propose for a college curriculum directed at students of the future might look like the following hypothetical set of nine courses. In this sense, these courses are a bit utopian. They make assumptions about how the world might change in terms of technology and social development. They mimic the kind of language that might be found in a future college catalog, augmented by arguments in defense of that description from the point of view of today.

1. Cognition and Communication: Logic, Rhetoric, and Argument.

This course is about language and thought. It teaches written and oral argument. It is the moral equivalent of what often are English 101 and Philosophy 101 (frequently entitled "The Problems of Philosophy"). There is less emphasis on issues of style and more on logic and the philosophy of knowledge (diminishing any emphasis on mere style).

The use of technology in information gathering, processing, storage, and communication is dealt with, including the command and destruction of all high-tech jargon. Key to this course is learning how information and ideas can be understood, formulated, and interpreted. The bulk of available facts continues to expand exponentially. In this course, for example, students learn how to distinguish causality from correlation. Remembering and repeating facts is less important than framing questions, evaluating issues, and judging ideas.

With today's advances in technology, one might fear (or perhaps hope, depending on one's point of view) that the skill of writing will become obsolete. But it won't. Quite to the contrary, the written word may or should hold more sway as we communicate more rapidly and frequently with total strangers by machines over wider distances. Writing well and succinctly will be a highly prized virtue. Books and libraries will survive. But students may eventually be able to draft and write papers by speaking into machines. Editing will become even more important, as will high standards for logic, structure, and clarity in written arguments.

Since speaking, reading, writing, and the command of language will remain central, elective courses in history, philosophy, and literature will continue to be much the same as they are now. The inherent conservatism of universities and systems of education—mirroring a healthy professorial skepticism about facile claims to progress—will prevail. Therefore, this course is a first-year requirement and a prerequisite for all subsequent courses.

2. Modern Language: Chinese, Japanese, Hindi, or Arabic.

Most foreign languages popular today—French, Italian, German, and Russian—will become gradually less relevant to college students, if for no other reason than that with modern technology students could learn them without courses, classrooms, or teachers. Only instruction in non-Western languages should be required. Spanish ought to be taught in all elementary and high schools as a precollege requirement, since it will remain the indispensable second language of a bilingual America. English will become more and more what Latin was before the Renaissance: the undisputed international language of scholarship and politics. An introduction to linguistics could be an integral part of the study of each of these foreign languages. However, students may opt to study an ancient language—Latin, Greek, or Sanskrit. These should remain highly valued dimensions of the curriculum.

3. The Individual and the Community.

This course covers the territory that ought to be covered today in courses of political science, sociology, and social and economic thought. (Psychology as we know it now may disappear. As a result of progress in neurobiology, Freud, Jung, behaviorism, and all other current theories of psychological development and causality may soon be looked upon condescendingly the way we now regard astrology: as noble episodes from our past that we—thankfully—have transcended.)

This course deals with how we think about who we are; about our individual identities and our relationships to others, as part of families and cultural, ethnic, political, and religious groupings. This is also a course about work, wealth, gender, sexuality, and intimacy. The nature of the private and public spheres—government, homes, and cities— and our rights and responsibilities as citizens locally and globally are key topics. The ethics and politics of the life cycle from birth to death, including issues of genetic manipulation, aging, the prolongation of life, and euthanasia, are part of this course's curriculum.

4. History.

This two-year sequence is often designed to teach students how to interpret historical documents and generate and criticize historical arguments. The curriculum reverses the way we usually teach history. Starting with the recent past, history would be taught from modern to ancient.

a. History 101: The Paradoxes of Modern History. Students in the next century will need to grapple with what happened in the twentieth century, which began with optimism about progress and ended with widespread pessimism. Starting with the late nineteenth century, this course in global history focuses on patterns of prejudice, injustice, conflict, war, and destruction. The central topics are World War I, fascism, communism, the Holocaust, race relations in the United States, the cold war, the problems of ethnicity, nationalism after the cold war, and the rise of mysticism and religious fundamentalism. The course analyzes the economic changes which have taken place, inequality, despotism, and the failure to create a world of tolerance, freedom, and prosperity despite scientific, technological, and economic progress. Particular emphasis is placed on the history of the Far East.

b. History 102: The Premodern World: Europe, Africa, and the Americas Before 1914. Instead of separating history by nations, this course covers the ancient and premodern history of both sides of the Atlantic, focusing on those cultures with significant European ties and roots. It is here that students may encounter what now passes for traditional American and European history.

5. An Integrated Science and Mathematics Sequence.

Mathematics as an independent subject of general education may continue to recede in importance as an autonomous discipline, but it will certainly persist as a necessary component of science. The mathematics required of all students should center on statistics and probability theory. The teaching of math might focus on computational methods as opposed to proofs and derivations of theorems. This multiyear course has four parts, each of which stresses the processes of science, experimental design, and the general conduct and character of science.

Part 1: The physical world, including astronomy and cosmology. Here students encounter the epistemology of physics, the study of time, space, and the laws of the universe (including relativity, thermodynamics, and atomic and subatomic theory). The origins of the universe and the sorts of issues Stephen Hawking and other students of chaos and systems theory have helped to make so popular are touched upon.

Part 2: Biology and chemistry. Included are cell theory, genetics, and evolution, studied from a molecular point of view. The benches and glassware of today's science labs may ultimately be replaced gradually by experimental techniques using minuscule samples and rapid high-resolution instrumentation. For example, students might be able to look at the effect and response of each gene in the human genome to specific diseases, thereby dealing with a set of 100,000 variables that can be studied simultaneously.

Part 3: Ecological science. This section explores nonmolecular dimensions and provides an introduction to the macro level of analysis. How do we perceive the world and the outcomes of scientific interventions? The study of the environment, particularly the impact of human behavior, is a primary focus. Evolution, economic behavior, demography, and epidemiology are included. The ability to assess statistical reliability and measurement will be crucial here.

Part 4: Technology. Students receive an introduction to the tasks of engineering and information science. How do we design the gadgets and instruments we need without using the old methods of building actual physical models? This course leads to an understanding of technology and how basic science is applied. A look at the social consequences of science concludes the course.

6. World Religions.

A century from now there will surely be varieties of new religions. The millennium years between 1990 and 2020 will spawn alluring mystical and metaphysical movements. This course, however, looks backward, at the old religions. Required texts: the Old and New Testaments; the Koran; Maimonides' *Guide to the Perplexed* (part 3); selections from Confucius; the Bhagavad Gita; and the Dhammapada. Readings also include works by Augustine, Aquinas, Luther, Calvin, Kierkegaard, Barth, and Buber.

7. Philosophy and Politics.

This course is based on readings from Plato, Aristotle, Thucydides, Cicero, Tacitus, Machiavelli, Locke, Rousseau, Kant, Hegel, Marx, Emerson, Nietzsche, Freud, Weber, Dewey, and Wittgenstein. The classic texts of American democracy, from Jefferson and *The Federalist Papers* to W. E. B. Du Bois and Martin Luther King Jr., are included. The structuralist and so-called poststructuralist theory now dominates American academic life—the work of Barthes, Derrida, Lacan, and Foucault need not be included. Some Heidegger might be read. But a few controversial thinkers whose importance is still doubted today— Hannah Arendt, for example—should be read.

8. Epic, Drama, Poetry, and Prose.

A course including the *Iliad*, the *Odyssey*, Aeschylus, *The Ramayana of Vlamiki, Sundiata: An Epic of Old Mali*, Beowulf, Shakespeare, Boccaccio, Cervantes, Dante, Molière, Swift, Goethe, Austen, George Eliot, Dickens, Whitman, Tolstoy, Dostoevsky, Gogol, Proust, Rilke, Akhmatova, Kafka, Stendhal, Joyce, Celan. There may be fluctuations in reputation; Joseph Conrad and Henry James are two possible cases.

The canon is a peculiar construct. On the one hand it is intensely conservative, as the list of authors above reveals. At the same time it is almost irrationally fickle; much like the stock market, reputations and fame have extreme peaks and valleys. There will, and should always be, a canon against which new readers match their wits. Among the novelties in a future canon may be the revival of Roman literature. In the nineteenth century, the ancient Greeks became favored, but when it comes to antiquity as seen from the year 2000, Virgil, Horace, Plautus, and Terence—great figures of Roman literature—should return to the curriculum (along with Tacitus and Cicero in history and philosophy).

Writers famous today—even Nobel laureates—need not be included, and once-famous writers now forgotten may reappear. Students might read Harriet Beecher Stowe, Rudyard Kipling, and Henry Wadsworth Longfellow again, alongside Ralph Ellison, Richard Wright, and Virginia Woolf. The "canon" of tomorrow, when it comes to twentieth-century literature, will contain both surprises and old favorites, including perhaps Italo Svevo, Robert Musil, Philip Roth, Mikhail Bulgakov, Vladimir Nabokov, and Italo Calvino, leaving out many of today's most highly prized figures.

There will even be discoveries in the future similar to the early-twentieth-century rage for Georg Büchner, the author of *Woyzeck*, which took place a century after his death. Bertolt Brecht, Jean-Paul Sartre, and Albert Camus should return from the academic periphery, as should William Faulkner, D. H. Lawrence, and Theodore Dreiser. Robinson Jeffers (who wrote *Roan Stallion*) might have a place, as might Langston Hughes and Paule Marshall, even though Sylvia Plath and Aleksandr Solzhenitsyn might not.

9. The Arts.

This course integrates the history of music, dance, and the visual arts—from sculpture and painting to film, photography, video, and computer art—with active studio experiences. Since students cannot cover everything, they will be able to choose one or another art form. In music, Palestrina, Bach, Mozart, and Brahms should be there, along with Béla Bartók, Arnold Schoenberg, Igor Stravinsky, Duke Ellington, and Aaron Copland. The history of rock music should take its place alongside the history of operetta. In art, perhaps the European narrative painters of the nineteenth century (Arnold Böcklin, for example) will be revived at the expense of Impressionists. Piet Mondrian and Jackson Pollock will still be taught, but twentieth-century figurative art may not take a backseat. And neither will the work of the great photographers, from Alfred Stieglitz to André Kertész. Classics of film and television—Charlie Chaplin films, *Citizen Kane*, obscure art films, Hollywood classics, sitcoms, and the science fiction tradition, including *The Twilight Zone* and *Star Trek*—might well appear in such a course. Each course asks students to learn about past models as well as to create their own works of art. Students may use traditional methods—canvas, paper, 35mm cameras, brushes, clay, wood, the voice, and acoustic instruments—alongside modern technological devices.

At this point, let us return to the present, for something ought to be said about the current perception of the visual and performing arts in any educational curriculum. A good way to begin to confront the popular idea that the arts are of secondary importance to education and culture in modern democracy is to cite the observation of the composer Felix Mendelssohn. As a young man, he became famous for a set of piano works entitled "Songs Without Words." Each piece had a title generally describing a scene or an emotion, such as "A Venetian Gondolier" or "Consolation." These pieces became immensely popular. Mendelssohn received a letter in response to these pieces. The writer asked what contribution music made to our understanding of things. Were these pieces simply using music to make a better picture or clearer description of something we can see or talk about? Mendelssohn answered by saying that music is precise in a way that language can never be. He argued that even though we may share common words in talking to one another, we rarely develop an effective sense of common understanding. This view was expressed a century later by the Nobel Prize–winning writer Elias Canetti, who said with biting irony that there was no crueler hoax than the idea that language is an instrument of communication among humans.

Mendelssohn was a bit gentler; for him, the issue was not that communication among humans through language was an illusion. Rather, he thought that music superseded language's limited capacity to generate a sense of agreement. Through music, diverse and often warring human beings could communicate without distortion or misinterpretation. In other words, something entirely impractical and even abstract—a work of musical art—could function spiritually and politically, and could inspire in different human beings tolerance, mutual respect, and a sense of shared understanding. Mendelssohn's view of the function of music was no doubt utopian, but his perception that the arts are forms of human expression and existence that have a powerful role to play in the way in which we live together should not be dismissed easily, particularly in a democracy. Furthermore, his sense that the arts exist in relation to language in ways that strengthen and supplement the function of language is an important clue as to why the arts need to be part of an educational system in a democracy. Language is the essential instrument of politics and the law, and the greater self-critical understanding we have of its function, the closer we will be to making a democracy work.

Painting, sculpture, so-called classical music, including opera, theater, ballet, and dance—the full range of visual and performing arts, as well as certain genres of writing, particularly poetry—have never gained the sense of prestige and importance that they deserve in our democracy. Too often they are understood as aristocratic enterprises, associated historically with nobility and royalty and distinctly European, as opposed to American, traditions. The arts are therefore considered by many as highbrow culture and placed in opposition with popular taste.

As a result, they have been relegated to a supplemental status and seen as effective primarily as a means of making someone appear cultivated and refined, rather than as being a way of improving the lot of the majority of citizens. Few Americans understand why it is necessary to subsidize arts institutions with tax dollars. The feeling is that if they fail to compete with popular entertainment, then their irrelevancy is obvious. Is it really good use of public money to support dance companies and orchestras? The truth of the matter is that, as the emerging democracies in Eastern Europe have made evident, the arts must continue to flourish if a democracy is to succeed, and for reasons much more profound than a natural sympathy for the arts.

Dissent and free speech, particularly the vigilant defense against censorship both from above and from within (that is, the circumstance when one either does not know how to think differently or restrains oneself voluntarily from speaking out), come into play only when there is something new out there that challenges the status quo. The role of the arts is analogous to that of new ideas in science. In the context of a flourishing world of research, a new idea that challenges standards of truth will inevitably occur. When it first makes its appearance, it is often ridiculed and overlooked by fellow professionals at large, and only seriously investigated by a few. But as its allure grows and its validity becomes accepted gradually, it ascends to the position of the general view, replacing the wisdom it once challenged, until the time when the idea itself will be supplanted by some new innovation.

The arts function in a similar manner. Our ideas about nature and ourselves as well as our sense of beauty and the meaning of life are influenced by poets, painters, and composers. On a more mundane level, the ways we decorate our houses, build buildings, and wear clothes derives from the work of a few innovators in the world of high art. No film score today is imaginable without the so-called elite traditions of Wagner, Strauss, and Mahler. Every serious rock musician, from the Beatles to Sting, pays homage in some way to the classical traditions. Jerome Kern, George Gershwin, and Bessie Smith were phenomena that emerged from a world of artistic production that was not initially dominated by large commercial mass taste, even though aspects of their work have been appropriated by that taste today.

The arts create and sustain new ways of keeping freedom from losing meaning. They help individuals retain their own sense of uniqueness in a world in which the pressure to conform is intense. They fill out the hollow structures of democratic rights with meaning that is profoundly personalized. They provide the imaginative world in which each individual can find a place and effectively fight the battle against deadening conformity. They are not the superfluous embellishments of life, the ornaments we can do without. Like science, the making and appreciating of art is integral to the practice of freedom. The arts challenge the monopoly of commerce in matters of fundamental values. The many generations of philosophers who have pondered the integral relationship between beauty and truth, between aesthetics and ethics, have done so with extremely good reason.

In terms of education, because of the massive misunderstanding in

America regarding the arts, they should not be segregated out of the curriculum. Rather, they should be part of mathematics and science. The study of time and space should be informed by art and music. The arts need to be part of the study of history and literature. The understanding of language is enhanced by a knowledge of how sounds and images work in relationship to both contemporary language and the evidence of history preserved in written forms. And the arts help to develop the cognitive skill we need in learning, from faculties of perception and expression to those of memory.

Citizens in a democracy need to be educated to find ways to create identities for themselves and communicate their senses of identity to others. They need to sense autonomy and choice in how they do this, so that they do not see themselves as passive mirrors of overwhelming historical and societal movements. They need to be given the means by which they can develop their own sense of self-worth without merely learning how to be consumers. They also need to come together with others in public spaces, out of the television room and away from the computer screen, to react and respond to the creative and daring challenges put forth by their contemporaries who are writing plays and music and making two- and three-dimensional art. This is why concert halls, theaters, and museums are crucial public venues in every city and region. In short, the performing and visual arts are not a luxury in a free and democratic society. They are the symptoms of its existence. And therefore, they need to be central to the educational agenda in a modern democracy.

V. COLLEGES AND SOCIETY

Given the above discussion, it might seem odd that despite all its shortcomings in our current American system of education, higher education—the end of the line for students—is in a much better state, relatively speaking, than any other sector in the American educational sequence. The trouble is that its comparative superiority cannot last. The shortcomings of elementary and secondary education will eventually erode the post–World War II achievement that the American university and college represent. We have inappropriately lent the post-secondary enterprise a differential in prestige it does not merit which has been mirrored primarily in the quality of young people who have chosen to go on to the Ph.D. level and a career of teaching and research. In contrast to the recruitment of high school teachers, there is no shortage of well-trained Ph.D.'s, except among African Americans. The systematic failure, beginning in the 1980s, to sustain a public policy that supported the recruitment and training of minorities in graduate school has left the American university with a shocking disparity between supply and demand for Ph.D.'s from underrepresented minorities.

As we have seen, the most visible source of controversy regarding American colleges in the past twenty years has been the college curriculum. In this arena, as in other sectors of education, since the late 1960s the perception is widespread that standards have declined. Initially, this was an issue of so-called grade inflation. But the debate turned to substance, to what is being taught. Critics continue to allege that once-sensible courses have been replaced by trivial fads. It is further argued that intellectual fashions, particularly in methods of interpretation in the humanities, have overwhelmed common sense. Jargon has taken the place of comprehensible analysis. Conservative critics point the blame at what is viewed to be a domination by so-called liberal intellectuals in the university classroom. The feeling is widespread that students are not learning about history, literature, and culture and instead are being fed a diet of "politically correct" ideology.

Again, affirmative action has been central to this debate. For nearly twenty years affirmative action with respect to women and minorities of color has been a primary objective of most colleges and universities. The criticism of this initiative in the 1990s is based on the assumption that standards were lowered to allow for populations once underrepresented. Furthermore, many observers of the American scene argue that, unlike the past, we find ourselves in an America dominated by discrete ethnic and religious groups, each one demanding a sort of proportional representation. Gone is any shared sensibility about being an American. This perception seems vindicated by reports of the way college student bodies are organized: into subgroups defined by ethnicity and religion. The public has been led to believe that the curriculum now mirrors this fragmentation. Multiculturalism has become the object of derision, along with the effort to broaden the range of materials used in the classroom beyond those produced by European and American white men.

This brief rehearsal of the debate in its crudest and most popular terms represents the extent to which journalism has done a disservice to higher education. No doubt there is a grain of truth in every allegation. Yes, there are ideologues in college faculties. True, there are gut courses and harebrained notions that make a regular appearance in college courses. There are even newfangled theories that are honestly put forward and later disavowed. If one takes a good look at any college graduate's bookshelf (assuming he or she has not sold the books), one will be shocked to see how easily it is to date the individual. Much of what we read is no longer read. Erik Erikson was once ubiquitous but is no longer. The historians we once read—William Langer, Crane Brinton, Joseph Strayer—have been superseded. The texts in organic chemistry are entirely new. Even tastes in modern literature shift, well beyond the realm of so-called fads and political agendas. T. S. Eliot no longer occupies the place he once did. In music history, the type of work being done has shifted, along with the changing aesthetic and cultural climate. And in many fields, entirely new and novel issues are in the forefront as a result of the progress of knowledge.

Such shifts in issues and materials have always been the case. In modern times, each discrete historical era has had its own passions as well as questionable fads and ephemeral vogues. Oddly enough, dissent in the university, whether by students or by faculty, has been much less commonplace than it ought to have been. There is as much conformity on the American campus as was the case fifty years ago.

The best argument that there was never a great curriculum many years ago that has recently been dismantled is the behavior of the alumni of our colleges and universities. Over a quarter of a century of dealing with alumni/ae from many institutions has convinced me that there is no long-term evidence that the college curriculum of the past was superior in leaving residues of cultural curiosity, civic idealism, civility, and intellectual self-discipline. Much of what we complain about in today's world is the work of the graduates of the so-called great curricula of the past, the college graduates of yesteryear. Once again, misplaced nostalgia makes for bad public policy.

What has changed, however, is that because more people go to college, higher education has become a huge industry. It is a major employer and it serves an increasingly wide range of the American economy. That makes it peculiarly newsworthy. There is much more journalism, relatively speaking, about what goes on in colleges and universities than there ever was before. Insofar as America is obsessed by youth and the lives of the young, we enjoy stories about college life. Particularly naughty behavior satisfies the voyeuristic interests of the American public.

This being said, however, journalists are not the problem. Undergraduate and graduate education in the American university could be much better than it is today. Higher education needs criticism, but that criticism must be constructive. It is nearly suicidal for state legislatures and private donors to exert short-term budgetary pressure on the institutions for which they are responsible because of motivations drawn from the short-term political controversies of the moment. In the end, the concerned conservative alumni/ae at Dartmouth have not helped their alma mater by waging a political campaign on the campus. What troubles higher education is not politics, because politics has always been at the root of what colleges have chosen to put in their curricula. If the eighteenth century was dominated by concerns about religious belief and doctrine, the late nineteenth century was obsessed with industrial progress and economic development. Beginning with America's entrance in World War I in 1917, American educators have sought to use the college years to help train the future leaders of America to deal not only with American democracy at home but with America's role as a world power. The great schemes of general education—those of Alexander Mikeljohn at Amherst, Nicholas Murray Butler at Columbia, and Robert Hutchins at the University of Chicago—were motivated by a vision of the interplay between American democracy and education. This tradition began with Thomas Jefferson, who founded the University of Virginia and urged his friends not to send their children to Europe to school but rather to keep them in the United States, where a sophisticated education for a young adult might assume a distinctively American stamp and where the life of the college student would not be infected by the aristocratic traditions of England or the European continent.

The quandary, therefore, is not whether a college curriculum has some roots in a set of political aspirations and beliefs but rather what those beliefs are and whether they can continue to exist or be replaced in a context that values the free pursuit of knowledge and basic research and scholarship. The enduring virtues of the university will survive all short-term difficulties if its basic enterprise of teaching and of research are intact, on both the graduate and the undergraduate levels. The difficulty now facing American colleges and their faculties is that there seems to be little agreement about the underlying politics. The result is that what remains intact are the traditions of academic professionalism represented in the form of disciplines. On the graduate level, these, too, will inevitably undergo transformations as fields of inquiry evolve.

As a result of a short-term (one hopes) politically grounded collapse in our ability to talk about the purposes of undergraduate education, in the college years there will still be fewer and fewer shared requirements. When so-called distribution requirements are set forth, students will continue to fulfill them by choosing among several courses. The notion of common courses or a "core" remains anachronistic because there is so little agreement, not because it might not be worthwhile. But now this must change.

In fact, core courses—shared syllabi and curricula—help vindicate the model of the residential college. If indeed one of the problems

facing undergraduate education today is the absence of a common conversation and an adequate link between the traditions of learning and
the conduct of everyday life beyond work, then a common course system would help. Students enroll in colleges without knowing one another. As relative strangers, bound together only by the voluntary act of
enrolling in a particular institution, sharing some aspect of their education with others would prepare them for communicating with neighbors, coworkers, and fellow citizens. Common readings and areas of
study would give all students a base of shared knowledge that might
change the range and quality of how members of a college community
interact with one another. Much in the same vein, at the end of college
it would be advisable to have all students experience having to explain
their specialized interests to nonspecialists, if only to encourage them
to ruminate on the larger purpose and significance of their interests.

This, in turn, leads to an important role colleges and universities
need to play in contemporary life. If we expect college graduates to
function as leaders in the civic arena, then colleges must expand the
extent to which their campuses are used as important public spaces.
Ours is an age of extremes. We are surrounded by crowds, but each
individual finds him- or herself on a somewhat isolated and autonomous outing. We have embraced the mall as the ideal shopping venue.
Although the mall has many virtues, it isn't quite like a town square. At
the same time, we spend a good deal of time isolated by ourselves,
looking at a television screen or a computer. We may be making contact
with others over the Internet, but that, too, is hardly comparable to a
public gathering.

Colleges and universities possess a unique opportunity. They have
the physical spaces and the traditions that can encourage individuals on
campus and from surrounding communities to come together around
common interests. Public discussions, exhibits, lectures, and concerts
are indispensable in our communities. The university is uniquely able
to sponsor programs in which open debate and free inquiry are sustained. They offer a neutral ground where the rules of discourse inspire
seriousness and assure civility. And institutions of higher education

must lend a direct hand to the improvement of secondary and elementary education. If we use the public space of our campuses on behalf of the cultural and political life of our communities, we also do a favor to our students. They will see that the institution they attend makes its own contribution to the outside community, particularly to the quality of cultural life and political discourse. They, in turn, may develop the expectation that they, as students (through community service programs on campus) and alumni/ae, should help sustain this sort of activity in their own communities. The university can be a center and a model of cultural creation, debate, service, and political exchange among citizens for the future, one that is not dominated by commerce and a narrow definition of utility.

AFTERWORD

A reasonable concluding question to ask might be how to begin to move our schools, colleges, and universities in new directions. Furthermore, one might legitimately ask how a serious and thoroughgoing educational reform can begin. How might a debate on the reform of secondary schooling and higher education take hold? The starting point may lie in the college and university community, where there is a critical mass of individuals, including those working in the field of education itself, who might be prepared to jettison narrow self-interests. There should be enough trustees of private and public institutions willing to take courageous educational stands and not merely dabble in institutional politics and budget review. There are certainly faculty who are idealistic enough to try something new and to forge alliances with colleagues on issues of curriculum and institutional mission without insisting that their ideas win the day or even be equally represented. Last, there ought to be administrators who look on their tasks as more than managerial: office holders who are genuinely motivated by ideas and by a sense of obligation with respect to the state of education in the country as a whole.

The impetus for reform may not be global or national. National reform may indeed be cumulative because it will depend on experi-

ments and innovations in individual institutions and districts, in particular regions, in leading states. The proper starting point, as well as the
person on whom all change will depend in the end, is the classroom
teacher. Our best hope rests with individuals and with single initiatives
which can lead the way. Beyond the realm of educators, each of us as a
citizen is in a position to influence the future of education. The opportunity stands before us now because there is such an extensive but ill-
defined dissatisfaction with present circumstances. Citizens are already
speaking out and taking action. Therefore, educators at all levels possess not only the means but the occasion to participate and lead a
genuine transformation in the quality of American education. There is
no valid reason for inaction, and no excuse for failure.